Since studying journalism at RMIT in Melbourne, Kathryn Bonella has worked as a journalist in television and print. She moved to London eighteen months after graduating and spent several years freelancing for *60 Minutes* as well as numerous English and American television programs, magazines and newspapers. She returned to Australia in 2000 to work as a full-time producer for *60 Minutes.* She moved to Bali in 2005 to research and write Schapelle Corby's autobiography, *My Story*, then *Hotel Kerobokan* and *Snowing in Bali.* Her most recent book, *Operation Playboy*, was published in 2017.

www.kathrynbonella.com

Also by Kathryn Bonella

Schapelle Corby – My Story
Snowing in Bali
Operation Playboy

HOTEL KEROBOKAN

KATHRYN BONELLA

PAN
Pan Macmillan Australia

First published 2009 in Macmillan by Pan Macmillan Australia Pty Limited
This Pan edition published in 2012 by Pan Macmillan Australia Pty Limited
1 Market Street, Sydney

Reprinted 2013 (five times), 2014 (three times), 2015, 2016 (twice), 2017, 2018

CIP details for this book are available from the
National Library of Australia

Typeset in 12.5/16 pt Janson by Midland Typesetters, Australia
Printed by IVE

MIX
Paper | Supporting responsible forestry
FSC® C018183
www.fsc.org

This book is dedicated to anyone travelling to the tropical paradise Bali.

Be careful. It could be a holiday you never forget. Even one ecstasy pill could cost you tens of thousands of dollars and a stint in the hellhole Hotel Kerobokan.

CONTENTS

AUTHOR'S NOTE

Because of the nature of the revelations contained in this book, some names had to be changed in order to protect former and current inmates from further prosecution or retribution.

FOREWORD

The first time I went inside Kerobokan Jail was in December 2005 with Schapelle Corby's sister, Mercedes. We were starting work on Schapelle's book – *My Story*. As we walked past intimidating-looking guards and prisoners, I felt slightly uneasy. Out of the blue a prisoner sprinted past chasing another with a chair held above his head. Standing against a wall a few metres in front of me, wearing oversized pink sunglasses, was a girl who I thought was a visitor. I did a double take. It was Schapelle – immaculately groomed and looking like a fish out of water in a maximum-security jail. That morning we started our months of twice-daily interview sessions.

It didn't take long for Kerobokan and its cast of characters to become very familiar. The guards were always keen for a packet of cigarettes, or asking me to bring in a copy of *Penthouse*; the prisoners, including a couple of murderers, asking for my phone number so they could get permission to get out of jail on a Saturday night by me ensuring their return. Things that at first seemed unbelievable fast became ordinary; like inmates acting as doormen and freely walking in and out of the jail.

Prisoners were usually loitering around during visits, drunk and stoned, and would come and sit with us. Like Schapelle, I quickly learned not to judge anyone by their crimes. One Indonesian inmate regularly came over to chat. I asked him what his crime was – 'Killer'. He seemed nice. Not in the least bit threatening, although we later saw him poised with his hand in the air ready to bash another inmate, only stopping when he saw us watching. But he was chivalrous and became an ally. If he was returning to jail from a workout at the local gym as I was leaving, he'd hail me a cab or call for one on his mobile phone, then stand outside chatting with me until it arrived. One afternoon an Australian journalist was hanging about just outside the front door for hours, after a story had broken on the Bali Nine. I didn't want to walk out and expose myself since the book was still a secret at that stage. Visiting time was finished, but the killer took me back inside to an office. We sat and talked, and every twenty minutes or so he'd go and take a look outside to see if the journalist had left. When the coast was clear, he rang a taxi and walked me out. Strangely, the killers were often the inmates with the most freedom.

Courteous killer doormen were only one of the reasons that Schapelle and I dubbed the jail Hotel Kerobokan in her book. With its tennis court, its manicured gardens, trimmed grass, Hindu temples and green sports area, the jail resembled a low-budget hotel – on first impression. Prisoners came around like hosts during visiting times, selling drinks and home-baked cakes, and handing out straw mats to sit on for 5000 rupiah (70 cents). The jail also sat on four hectares of prime real estate in Bali's tourist precinct of Kuta, surrounded by exclusive hotels and villas. You could also buy services like in any hotel: you could pay guards to deliver pizza to your cell, to deliver drugs, to bring in alcohol, to arrange a hooker, and even to let you out for a day at the beach – although most of the high-profile prisoners, such as Schapelle, never got that luxury.

Like any hotel you could also pay for a room upgrade at check-in. After police scared Schapelle with stories of sexual attacks, she paid $100 to be put into a room that wasn't too crowded or full of predatory lesbians. A guy from California gave the guards $950 for a room upgrade, overpaying and pushing up prices for subsequent male prisoners. But he'd been desperate to avoid time in the men's initiation cells where up to twenty-five prisoners were jammed into a single cell. So it became 'Hotel Kerobokan' – where westerners from across the globe continually check-in and out, most desperately trying to pay the judges and prosecutors to deal their way to a shorter stay.

As a visitor, I got used to going into Hotel K, but still felt in need of a shower every time I left. I was fascinated with this crazy world of drugs, sex and gambling – where paedophiles, serial killers and rapists sleep alongside card sharks, petty thieves and unlucky tourists caught at a club with one or two ecstasy pills in their pocket. I was intrigued by what time in Hotel K did to people; how they coped with being locked in tiny, crowded cells for up to fifteen hours a day and what they did to fill the interminable hours. My interest in and access to prisoners sparked the idea to write *Hotel Kerobokan.* I wanted to tell the story of this jail.

I flew to Indonesia in January 2008 and spent the next eighteen months talking to prisoners inside Hotel K, to former prisoners who are now in other jails across Indonesia and also to people who were free – although several of those are now back inside. It was an incredible adventure. I spoke to around one hundred people about life inside Hotel K, including murderers, drug bosses, petty thieves, gang members, international drug traffickers and prison guards.

To ensure the stories were as accurate as possible, I often asked several prisoners to tell me their version of the same story. Almost always, the versions tallied. The inmates didn't need to embellish. The truth is graphic and shocking enough. There are specific tales that several westerners told unprompted; ones that resonated deeply and often painfully with them all; usually of westerners getting badly bashed, trying to escape or overdosing. They all knew that it could have so easily been them.

To establish the authenticity of the stories, I also spent weeks at the *Bali Post* newspaper office in its filthy archives rooms in Denpasar, going through hundreds of local *Denpost* and *Bali Post* newspapers. In the dusty newspaper offices, my Balinese researcher and I struck gold; stories about the stories I'd been told, confirming the confidence I had in my prisoner sources.

Most of the people I approached were happy to talk and tell their tales. For those still locked up, it broke the monotony and gave them a fresh face to talk to. Often an interview with one prisoner led me to another. It took a while to track down some prisoners, who'd been transferred out of Hotel K to prisons in other parts of Indonesia. I then travelled for weeks at a time to jails in far-flung parts of Muslim-dominated Java, and to Jakarta, meeting up with former Hotel K prisoners, almost always taking in a digital recorder to record our chats. I talked to the main characters in this book at length over days, often returning for second and third series of interviews.

One of the jails I went to was on Nusakambangan Island, off the west coast of Java, where the Bali bombing terrorists were being held. The first time I went there was just before they were killed. The little harbour in Cilacap was filled with journalists watching for any sign of family members taking the wooden boat across to the island to say goodbye. I avoided the journalists and climbed into an old motor boat filled with jail visitors, motorbikes and prison wardens on the way to work. It took us about ten minutes to cross the water.

I hired a local guy, Agung, to come with me. Agung didn't speak any English but had a motorbike and knew where I wanted to go. After getting off the boat I had to show my passport and papers at the first police checkpoint. Then I climbed on the back of Agung's bike, and we rode up the bitumen along the edge of the water to the second police check point where I showed my passport and papers again to a bunch of police. Most were jovial and rifled through the bags of shopping I'd brought, holding up bars of chocolate or packets of cigarettes and pointing to themselves, illustrating they wanted them. I gave them a couple of packets of cigarettes. Then Agung and I tore off on the bike. We were usually alone on the road apart from the odd cow or a local walking his herd across the road. There is nothing on this island, accept a few local homes for workers and seven maximum-security jails stretched along its coastal road. Agung pointed as we passed Amrozi's prison, then we passed several more, until we finally came to the jail that incarcerated the prisoners I was going to interview.

Once inside the men's jail, one of the prisoners I interviewed gave me a tour; to the small shop, the gym, the Hindu temple where a priest was holding a service, and then the small Christian church. Standing at the back was a young good-looking Brazilian guy; charming and softly spoken. He asked where I came from in Australia. He had an aura of deep sadness about him and huge black circles under his eyes. He'd been crying all morning. He usually did. He was on death row. A few months earlier he'd set himself alight to end the slow, drawn-out torture.

Like most of those around him, his life was just a waiting game for the twelve-man firing squad to squeeze its triggers.

Further north in Jakarta's Cipinang jail I visited a prisoner many times. Austrian inmate Thomas Borsitzki was happy to talk about life in Kerobokan jail, making lists of more than fifty possible topics. Like many prisoners, he also wrote pages and pages for me about his experiences. Getting inside Cipinang was expensive for all visitors – by far the most costly of all the jails I visited. The guards charged Thomas 200,000 rupiah ($27) to bring him out, me 50,000 rupiah ($7) to sit with him in a room face to face, rather than through a glass and metal screen, and I paid a further 10,000 rupiah ($1.30) to other prisoners to collect Thomas. I also had to pay an additional 50,000 rupiah ($7) to another inmate who walked around with a ledger book, but did nothing else. So my twice-daily visits cost me close to $85 per day.

None of the prisoners asked for money to tell their stories. I took them food, toiletries and books, or some baby clothes for Thomas's newborn – conceived while he and his wife were sharing a prison cell when they were both on remand for drug trafficking. I also took Thomas bottles of Dettol and bars of antiseptic soap for his gaping sores. After a few days, I'd notice his sores clearing up, but when I returned after a stint away, his body would be riddled with them again. Most of the prisoners were just happy to have a visit. One of the prisoners in Nusakambangan told me that hearing a genuine laugh was 'better than sex', as it was so rare – the death row inmates surrounding him didn't have much to be joyful about.

Now I realise how precious pure laughter is, it's amazing. Even a smile is very rare here. A laugh is priceless.

– Inmate

Another prisoner I met in an East Javanese jail had only had one other visit in two years. With nothing but time on her hands, she wrote pages and pages of notes for me about her life in Hotel K.

Several times I met up with a man who had just been released from jail after being incarcerated for hacking off a man's head with a machete. I met his daughters and he came to my Bali apartment for lunch. Saidin was an intriguing person. He'd done several years in Hotel K and was keen to talk; enjoying telling his stories and explaining how he was feared in Hotel K by many prisoners and guards. When I asked the source of his power over them, he slashed a finger across his throat and laughed. He had been one of the most powerful prisoners in Hotel K, promoted to the top job of *Pemuka* – in charge of all prisoners.

Guards were also a source of information. Several times I went out for drinks or dinner with a high-ranking guard. He relished telling me jail stories; laughing as he talked about a group of guards fawning over and kissing one particularly pretty new transvestite inmate, even showing me photos of him on his phone, as well as photos of piles of drugs confiscated from the cells. On one of the nights I was out with the guard, he phoned a couple of prisoners on their mobile phones and handed his phone to me for a chat. This was indicative of how casually the guards colluded with prisoners.

Since starting *My Story* in 2005, I've spent hundreds of hours inside Hotel K. I've personally witnessed violence, drug deals and rampant sex. In a visit one day, I sat in a narrow passage opposite a couple and their newborn – undoubtedly conceived in Hotel K. He was holding the baby over his groin as a camouflage while his girlfriend masturbated him. The straw mats we sat on were often covered in semen stains. I've seen western men, often off their faces on drugs, sloppily kissing female visitors; one of the Bali Nine regularly entwined with his Indonesian fiancée, often obscenely, while his mum sat alongside them. And it wasn't unusual to see girls straddling the laps of guys on the floor, thrusting back and forth. It looked like sex and it was.

Just as Hotel K holds a fascination to me, it clearly does for many others too. The jail is now a pit stop on Bali's tourist trail. Taxi drivers are regularly asked to drive by the jail – just a little detour on the way to the beach or to a massage perhaps. Some tourists stand out the front taking photos. Others venture inside. Everyone from girls in micro minis to families with toddlers is among the endless stream of tourists who pay the 5000 rupiah (70 cent) fee – or more if they're gullible – to go inside and meet one or two of the Bali Nine or Schapelle or just take a look around for a bit of holiday fun.

Hotel K might seem like a safe place to visit, because it's Bali, and because it does regular PR stunts – pushing an image of a humane facility by flinging open its doors to cameras and journalists to show the likes of a tennis tournament, or prisoners doing choreographed exercise routines for Independence Day, or Schapelle Corby talking, in a slightly dazed state, about her hopes of opening a beauty salon in jail, giving a girl-next-door face to the jail. To the outside, it might not seem so dark, but the daily world of Hotel K is nothing like these flashes. It is a maximum-security jail, overcrowded with some of Indonesia's worst psychopaths and sadistic criminals roaming freely. It's a place that can numb a prisoner to their core and strip away their sanity by the things they continually see and endure. Three years ago in *My Story,* Schapelle described it as a soul-sucking dump and wrote this:

Right now, I'm empty, lost and numb. I used to have a clear fresh sparkle radiating within, showing through my laugh and my eyes, I never had a problem looking in the mirror, I knew who I was, I didn't question myself. Lately now, two years on from that fatal date, and after repeated blows, I'm finding a confusing, distant reflection in the mirror; it's dull, my eyes don't seem to speak any more, they're lifeless, as though my soul is drying up. Where have I gone, where am I going? I can feel I'm gradually losing the essence that makes me me. It's strange and it hurts, indescribably, to become aware of your own fading soul reflected through your eyes each time you look in the mirror.

– Schapelle Corby, *My Story*

Five years on, Schapelle's soul has faded further. And her fragile grip on sanity regularly slips. Often she wanders around lost in a daze, heavily dosed up on medications for depression and psychosis. Her family is terrified she will die in Hotel K. She's seen so many horrific things that she's shut down. Finding a dead prisoner hanging by a noose one morning barely caused her to react. I saw her shortly afterwards, and she was totally calm. Her detachment was chilling. Life inside Hotel K has changed her indescribably. Almost all the westerners I have spoken to say the same thing; it's a living nightmare that slowly eats away at you until the person you once were simply vanishes.

Hotel Kerobokan gives a graphic insight into the daily life and shows why this prison is 'a gradual killing-you process' – as one prisoner described it. The walls of Hotel K talk through the prisoners' stories of murders, suicides, escapes, bashings, vicious gangs, rampant sex and the prolific drugs. *Hotel Kerobokan* exposes the dark heart of the jail that breaks people down and slowly destroys their will to live.

It's like the end of the world. It's crazy. You feel dead when you're breathing. You just want to get drunk to take your mind out of this place.

– Mick, Australian inmate

So many times I drive past those walls; I could never have imagined what happens inside. What happens inside goes far beyond my imagination before.

– Ruggiero, Brazilian inmate

CHAPTER 1

WELCOME TO HOTEL KEROBOKAN

It was late but Hotel Kerobokan was crawling with activity; guards skulking along pathways, unlocking cells and releasing prisoners who were walking fast across the jail. Tonight was sex night and Hotel K was busier than a Bangkok brothel. Any inmate who'd paid up that afternoon could get out for some action. Pouring in through the front door were hookers, girlfriends, wives and mistresses.

Austrian inmate Thomas Borsitzki was feeling frisky as he walked down the path towards the newly built and still empty Block K. He had gone two and a half years without sex, and tonight he was treating himself to a young Balinese woman. As he approached Room 1 in the cellblock, its small barred windows blazed with light, spotlighting the crude scene taking place inside. There was nothing but a thin, dirty mattress on the concrete floor. And a prisoner banging away at a hooker.

Already eight men were hanging around under the stars outside the block, waiting for their turn on the mattress.

The men, mostly westerners, would go into the cell one after the other; some spending five minutes in there, some a little longer. But if anyone took more than thirty minutes, the waiting prisoners would get angry and impatient, and urge the next in line to walk in and interrupt. In between clients, the hooker would put on a purple sarong. It was her one nod to decorum.

The Hotel K brothel was no more than a bare concrete cell. Inside, mosquitoes swarmed in clouds, attracted to the bright fluorescent light. It was hot. It stank of sex. Used condoms were discarded on the floor. The mattress was old, and the light made it possible to see the sticky wet spots left by those before. But it was jail. A comfortable bed, clean sheets and privacy were out-of-reach luxuries from a different life, a parallel universe. Here, it was a war of survival and different rules applied. Most of the men were either too high on drugs or too smashed on the local brew, *arak*, to notice much anyway. They were horny. This was sex. Nothing else mattered.

But sex night wasn't only for hookers. The grassy sports area near the small Christian church was also alive with the shifting shadows of couples having sex. Mosquito coils burned across the area like spot fires. Some prisoners would drag their mattresses out for comfort. One Italian inmate enjoyed sex with his fiancée on his mattress, and then left it out to rent to other inmates for a few thousand rupiah a turn.

Bringing in your own woman was cheaper than using a hooker. Prices fluctuated depending on how much an inmate could afford, but most paid the guards approximately 80,000 rupiah ($11) to be let out for sex under the stars with a woman they knew. A hooker, on the other hand, could cost an inmate up to 800,000 rupiah ($105).

Inmates would usually greet their lovers holding an unromantic sex package of two mosquito coils and a packet of cigarettes, which they would have just bought from a room in Cellblock B, where one prisoner ran a little shop from his cell. He put together the mosquito coils and cigarette packages for a set price so he could quickly slip them out the window on sex nights without completely waking up. Until sunrise, customers would continue to bang on the bars of his window to get their hands on one of the packages.

Thomas was a smack addict who usually spent all his money on drugs, but earlier this particular day, when a guard had come around with photos of a pretty young Balinese girl, he decided to splurge on a hooker. Now he stood waiting in line in the humid night air with the other men, chain-smoking Marlboro cigarettes and sometimes watching the sex show through the window.

Finally it was his turn. Once he was inside the cell, the hooker slipped off her purple sarong and let it fall in a crumpled heap on the floor in the corner. Thomas tore off his shorts and got down on the mattress. She lay back, only asking him not to do anal sex because she was sore from being forced to do it earlier. Thomas spent thirty minutes with the girl, despite being promised a few hours. But it was enough.

It was only a quick serve. I was promised all night, but it was not like I was promised. It was maybe thirty minutes before another guy came in. Anyway, if you don't sleep with a woman in maybe two and a half years, half an hour is no problem.

– Thomas

As Thomas walked back to his cell, several guards were still wandering around, calling out, 'Like a lady? Like a lady?', trying to drum up some last-minute business. Every customer was cash in their pockets. The guards' cut from a busy night could easily match their monthly wages. And tonight, the sex action would go on until sunrise.

Welcome to Hotel Kerobokan.

CHAPTER 2
THOMAS

People couldn't imagine what is behind those walls at Kerobokan.
– Ruggiero, Brazilian inmate

It's a mental camp. In this place, you get worse, not better.
– Mick, Australian inmate

Austrian drug dealer Thomas slammed down the phone in his Balinese bungalow. It was bad news. His friend had just heard a news flash on his car radio that a Bangladeshi man had been busted at Bali's Denpasar Airport with two kilograms of smack in his bag. Thomas snatched up the phone again, dialled his supplier in Bangkok, and got straight to the point.

'Aptu Galang, is that our boy's name?'

'Yes.'

'Bangladeshi?' he asked, hoping like hell he wasn't.

'Yes.'

'Shit,' he cursed. 'They've busted him at the airport.'

Time was now the enemy. The man in Bangkok had to move fast. He quickly, but calmly, walked out the front door of the Bangkok hotel and vanished, leaving behind only his fake ID.

In Bali, Thomas was safe… for now. He was still invisible. They'd played it by the book, everything done strictly on a need-to-know basis, keeping the links to the network unexposed, ensuring the Bangladeshi courier knew little. If the courier talked to police, which was likely, he could reveal nothing. He had no names. He only knew anonymous shadowy figures and a single contact point, the abandoned Bangkok hotel room, where several hours earlier he'd picked up the bags of smack and his plane ticket to Bali.

The boy's ignorance was their insurance – the rules designed to protect the players. If he had successfully slipped through Bali customs, he would have checked into a cheap, random hotel in Kuta, phoned his Bangkok contact to give him the name of the hotel, and waited. The man in Bangkok would then phone Thomas, give him the details, and Thomas would collect the drugs and give the boy his $400 carrier fee.

It was a narrow escape. Thomas lost two kilograms of smack, but he'd been lucky. Even with the slick system, it was only his friend's chance hearing of the news report that had saved him from a police sting. No doubt, police would have told Aptu to call his contact in Bangkok with the name of a hotel, setting a trap for the person collecting the drugs in Bali. Thomas would have been caught. But this time, Thomas's call to abort the operation came first and ensured the boy's call went unanswered, echoing around an empty Bangkok hotel room.

But as with any gambler, the close call didn't stop Thomas. He accepted the risks. He gambled with his life and freedom every day, and knew it. Drugs were his business. Thomas felt the odds were on his side if the relay team running the drugs each took their turn with skill. But in this case, the Bangladeshi boy had lacked it. He was a 20-year-old kid who lost his nerve. He panicked. He red-flagged himself by walking through the diplomatic channel to try to avert a baggage search. It was a rookie mistake, as the skilfully packed bags of smack would have sailed easily through a routine baggage search. But the suspicion the boy aroused by taking the alternate route meant that his bags were torn apart.

This was 1991 – before the death sentence was used in drug cases in Indonesia. But the boy went down hard. Aptu Galang was sentenced to twenty years in jail, the justice system only going easy on those who could afford to pay cash to the authorities. The boy had no money. And his anonymous boss, Thomas, was unable to sling any cash to the courts without losing his invisibility and risk joining his boy in Hotel K.

Did I feel bad for him? Yeah, of course. This happened but I cannot do anything. I cannot go to the police station and help him. He also didn't have money. If he had money, maybe he get ten years. But I cannot go to police station, I cannot go to court.

– Thomas

The drug world was dog eat dog, as Thomas was about to find out. He would soon be busted himself and was destined to meet his courier, Aptu, in Hotel Kerobokan.

After three or four months, they catch me in Bali. So I meet the boy in jail. Actually, he didn't know who I am and this was the first time I saw him also. I didn't know who he is, but after people say the name 'Aptu', I realised – okay, he's my boy. He realised I was the boss. It was no problem but sometimes he liked to drink and he would yell, 'Thomas boss', like that. I say, 'Shut up, you don't need to talk too much. Stupid'. He was not angry. He was nice with me.

– Thomas

Thomas was busted one hot afternoon while lying on his couch watching television in his beach bungalow. It started with loud banging on his front door. As he stood up to get it, more than a dozen police kicked the door in and exploded through it. They were angrily yelling and pointing machine guns, swarming in and spreading throughout his bungalow. They tore it apart, opening cupboards, hurling stuff to the floor, flipping his bed and rifling through his drawers. Pinned against the wall by two officers, Thomas stood watching, acutely aware that he'd been lucky yet again.

If the police had turned up an hour earlier, he would have been sitting on the floor repackaging a delivery of one and a half kilograms of smack. But he'd finished and had taken his usual precaution of stashing it in a nearby locker, returning to his bungalow just minutes before the bust.

Having been tipped off by one of Thomas's drug dealer competitors, the police were expecting to find kilograms of drugs. Grassing on him had been a dirty tactic to try to eradicate Thomas from the Bali smack market. But the police only found thirteen grams of heroin in the bungalow, tucked in the bottom of a bedroom cupboard. Thomas knew it was a small enough find for him to cut a deal and get off lightly.

He paid thirty million rupiah ($21,500) to the prosecutors via his lawyer and was sentenced to only eight months in jail. But during his stint in the police cells, Thomas was caught with a gram of heroin that his girlfriend had slipped to him during a visit to smoke later. So, the 25-year-old Austrian went down for a further eight months.

When Thomas checked into Hotel K in the early 1990s, it was a reptile and rat-infested swamp. He was escorted by a guard through the jail, past local prisoners slashing the grass with sickles, and was put inside a concrete cell, which he would share with a local prisoner. It was a basic cell with four concrete walls, a tiled floor, a single shit-covered squat toilet in the corner and a small barred window. Thomas noticed his cellmate had spread newspapers in the corner to create a make-shift bed, so unrolled his small camping mattress along the opposite wall. After two months of sleeping on a bare concrete floor in the police cells, that night's conditions were relatively luxurious.

Hotel Kerobokan, Bali's largest prison, was built quickly and cheaply in 1976, in the name of progress. It replaced a jail in Denpasar that had been torn down to make way for a large shopping mall. Shoddy workmanship meant that over the years, some perimeter walls in Hotel K would randomly crumble, giving inmates of the maximum-security prison an easy escape route. Although designed as a men's jail, a small walled-off section was built inside to incarcerate up to thirty-nine women and children in ten small concrete cages. This would eventually be used only for women and transvestites.

The jail was filled to its three hundred and twenty inmate capacity when Thomas checked in, but within a few short years, after the drug boom in Bali in the late 1990s, it would become massively overcrowded. By then, with almost 1000 inmates consistently squeezed into the jail, both the women's and men's sections would come to house almost three times their official capacity.

But during Thomas's first stretch, space was not so precious and he often even had a cell to himself. He spent his days sitting on his thin mattress and doing drug deals on his mobile phone.

Despite his competitor's tactic to get rid of him, Thomas easily kept dealing from inside. He'd call his supplier in Bangkok and organise smack deliveries to random cheap hotel rooms, then instruct his girlfriend to pick them up. She also regularly brought smack into Hotel K for Thomas to use and to sell to inmates, smuggling it in by inserting it inside her vagina. She and Thomas had a choreographed routine. During a visit she'd go to the toilet, extract the plastic-wrapped smack, and put it in the handle of a plastic saucepan used to flush the squat toilet. Thomas would then go in and retrieve the smack, sticking it up his arse to take it back to his cell without detection.

In later years, guards would be more pliable and complicit in the drug business, but they hadn't yet worked out how lucrative drug running in and out of Hotel K could be for them.

One afternoon, Thomas's toilet tag routine was spotted by Pak Belu, who was one of the more cruel guards, known for walking around the jail and randomly shocking prisoners with his electric stick, smirking as they jumped from the shock. He stopped Thomas on his way back to his cell, and asked for the drugs. 'I don't have, I don't have,' Thomas replied, leaping back after an electrical jab. Pak Belu put down his stick and started patting Thomas down. Thomas was wearing only a T-shirt, shorts and thongs, so Pak Belu quickly finished the search and was perplexed to find nothing.

But it wouldn't be long before Thomas was caught and suffered his first Hotel K punishment.

It happened when he agreed to do a small favour for a local prisoner, Wayan. Smack was scarce and Wayan asked Thomas to buy some for him from Nigerian inmate Hurani, who hated the locals and refused to sell to them. Thomas did so. That would have been the end of it, but a huge Javanese inmate, Joko, doing time for a string of violent robberies, wanted revenge when he saw Wayan with the smack. He assumed Wayan had bought the smack from Balinese dealer Vassak – who had told Joko that morning he did not have any smack left to sell. Joko believed Vassak had lied to him and that he'd chosen to sell to Wayan and not to him. Upset and angry, Joko snatched the smack from Wayan's hands, took it to the security boss and grassed on him.

Joko is angry and goes to the front office and says, 'Okay, I got this stuff from Wayan'. But he didn't know that I actually gave it to him. They call this guy [Wayan] to the boss's office and they beat him, and after, they say, 'Who did you get it from?' He says, 'I got it from Thomas'.

– Thomas

Thomas was called to the office, instructed to remove his T-shirt, and viciously beaten. The second-in-charge of Hotel K, the security boss, hit Thomas's legs and back over and over with a rattan stick, as several guards stood around the room watching. Thomas yelled out in agony, but knew fighting back would only prolong the beating. He was also outnumbered. Guards circled him, threw punches and kicked him. Pak Belu prodded him numerous times with his electric stick. Ignoring his screams, the guards persisted, using iron bars to hit him, until he was a broken heap on the floor.

The bashing of prisoners was common, with some particularly vicious guards relishing the job. The two guards Thomas most disliked were 'Fisheyes', so nicknamed by Thomas because of a deformity that caused protruding eyeballs – and Pak Belu.

Only for fun this Pak Belu would walk around with the electric stick, and put it into people, not strongly but a little bit. Maybe on the leg or something. He enjoyed doing that. It was a long stick, with a handle and some buttons, and in the front a blue light. He [could] turn it up and down.

When they catch someone doing something and bring him to the boss's office, they beat him with rattan, they give him electric shock, until sometimes people are pissing in their trousers and saying, 'Please stop, please stop'. The visiting room was next to the office, and when people came to visit they could hear yelling, 'Stop, stop', and people got headache hearing that.

– Thomas

After the beating, a badly bruised Thomas was locked in one of the four dark solitary confinement cells, dubbed 'cell *tikus*' or 'rat cell', used for punishing prisoners. For eleven days Thomas remained in cell *tikus*, sleeping in only his underpants with his fresh wounds exposed to the bare concrete. It was dark and grim. There was barely enough room to stretch out his legs and he had to excrete into a plastic bag. Only once in the eleven days did he get out, when a guard unlocked the door one night during a jail-wide cell search for anything contraband, like knives and sickles. It wasn't to be Thomas's last stint in cell *tikus*.

You adapt. You only sit, you smoke, you drink coffee, maybe you talk (through the vent) and after some time, the time is quickly passing. You only are hanging around. You cannot do much. You cannot wear clothes – only underwear. It was not allowed in cell tikus *to wear long trousers; maybe they're afraid you hang yourself or something like that. Anyway, you cannot use clothes. Not even a T-shirt.*

In the beginning, you get a little bit of skin coming off [from sleeping bare-skinned on the concrete floor] because you move around, but after some time you get strong. In the beginning, all the bones hurt. My skin started to go black where the bones are on the concrete.

Did they tell you'd be there for eleven days?

No, you don't know. That's part of the torture. The first few days, the time is not passing. You have headache, thinking too much, but after some time you find a way. You could climb up to the small ventilation, not a window but a small vent, and talk to a friend outside. Maybe you want coffee or something. They can bring coffee for you.

And also, at this time, I use still. So, everyday my friend comes and gives me heroin from behind, through the vent.

How could you pay for it?

At this time, I still had money. Also, my girlfriend came every day and she brought food for me, and money. I was in cell tikus *but she gave it to the guards, food, anything, the guards would bring it in.*

So, every day you had food and water?

Yeah.

And you would shoot up every day?

Yeah.

– Thomas

Thomas had been addicted to smack for a couple of years before entering Hotel K, and chain-smoked Marlboro cigarettes laced with heroin. But inside, he had to be more economical, so he started shooting up to use less for the same effect. Sometimes, if he was desperate for a hit, he shared needles with other inmates. Once, in sheer desperation he used a pen, fashioned as a syringe, to plunge smack into his veins.

One afternoon, after running out of heroin the night before, Thomas was craving a hit. His girlfriend arrived and, immediately after their toilet routine, he sprinted to his cell to inject the smack. But when he got to the cell door, it was locked – something he did to protect his things – and he couldn't find the key. As he stood there rifling through his pockets, Javanese Joko turned up, gripped the padlock with one hand and snapped it open. Once inside the cell, Thomas wasted no time injecting himself. Joko stood watching, and then told Thomas, who he regularly bought smack from, that he needed some too. But Thomas only had enough for himself and told Joko, 'I don't have. Finished'. Joko grabbed the tall, thin Austrian, and stuck the sharp tip of a pair of scissors he had had in his pocket into Thomas's throat. 'Okay, take it,' Thomas said, handing him a gram. The Austrian knew not to rile the many psychopaths and killers he now lived together with in Hotel K.

CHAPTER 3
THE HEADLESS CORPSE

Seminyak, Kuta community was shocked yesterday. A headless male body was found slumped in a ditch on the side of the road . . .

The headless body is now being kept in a freezer at Sanglah Hospital's morgue.

– *Nusa News*, 3 March 1998

It was early. The sun was glistening across the watery paddy fields and the morning air was already warm. It was calm and quiet – the stillness belying the brutality of the night before. But the dark night's secret was quickly revealed in the dawn light. Three small children were playfully running across the fields, laughing and leaping over watery channels, when they stumbled across a pair of legs sticking out of a ditch. Full of childish curiosity, they went in for a closer look and got the shock of their young lives.

The early morning stillness quickly broke into chaos. Police, journalists and spectators fast descended on the scene, surrounding the headless corpse, still face down in the ditch. Photographers and cameramen got in close, snapping shots of the stocky, middle-aged body, the torn striped green shorts, the sleeveless batik shirt. They zoomed in on the mutilated, jagged neck, the bloated feet in green thongs, broken bits of teeth. It was gruesome, but graphic shots sold newspapers in Bali. Spectators gawped as police busily searched for clues; a murder weapon, a blade, an axe, anything that would give them a lead. Fishing in the corpse's pockets, they discovered a driver's licence, its photo ID instantly providing the headless man with a face.

Meanwhile, sitting at home with his wife and three young daughters, listening to the news, was the killer, Saidin. He felt no remorse and no fear. He was a hired assassin; it had been a job. And although his quickly hatched murder plot hadn't gone perfectly, he'd executed it well. He already knew what he'd tell the judge if he got caught, though he doubted he ever would.

But leaving the man's ID had been a mistake. Police were piecing the case together quickly. The dead man had lived in Java, south of Jakarta, and after police had broken the tragic news to his son, he'd told them his father had flown to Bali the day before the murder to collect an overdue debt. He gave the police a name and address. The trail was now red hot.

Police raided a residence in the Bali coastal area of Klungkung and arrested the named man on the spot. They threw him into their van and took him to the local station. He refused to talk. They hurled him against walls, punched him, kicked him and jabbed him with an electric cattle prod until he was begging for mercy. But they didn't stop. They turned up the prod to its maximum 220 volts and shocked him in the chest, the legs, the groin. His body was shaking violently. But he still refused to cooperate. They jabbed him again, and this time the shock slammed him back into the cement wall. He cried out in pain. Blood dripped from a gash in his head as he collapsed to the floor, his legs too weak and too shaky for him to stand any longer. Finally, the man broke. He named the assassin.

The killer, Saidin, was immediately arrested. The family man and former solider went without a struggle. He was not contrite. He'd killed a man for money, but the man had had it coming. He did not deny his crime. He would tell the judge why he did it. On the day of the murder, Saidin had been called to a meeting at his friend's house and was told that a Javanese man was threatening to kill his friend's family because of an unpaid debt. 'I want you to finish him off,' Saidin's friend told him. 'When?' 'Tonight if you can do it.' He offered a fee of three million rupiah ($670). Saidin felt it would be honourable to protect his friend's family. He took the job.

In the dark of night, Saidin and his younger brother Tony drove their victim to Denpasar, luring him with the promise of cash. Saidin told him that a shopkeeper in Denpasar owed his Klungkung friend millions of rupiah, which would easily repay the debt to him. But it didn't go to plan. When they stopped at a random shop, the Javanese man refused to bang on the back door, which was integral to Saidin's plan. He'd expected a fight to erupt when a random shopkeeper was woken in the middle of the night by an aggressive stranger demanding money. Saidin had planned to use the fight as a cover for when he would jump in and break the Javanese man's neck.

But he was forced to switch to an impromptu plan B. He grabbed an iron bar from under the car seat, then turned and slammed it into his victim's chest. It was a shock; the man was winded, stunned, momentarily stumbling around in pain. Saidin hit him again, in the face this time, knocking teeth out.

The man collapsed to his knees, covering his bloody face with shaky hands, giving Saidin time to get his machete from the car boot. If the man glimpsed the end coming, he could do nothing. Saidin swung the machete hard into the side of his head. It made a loud crack. The man hit the ground hard. He was dead. But Saidin wasn't finished. Guided only by the light from the stars, he lifted the machete high above his head and slammed it down through the dead man's neck. Saidin was cold and emotionless. Bits of neck and head were still attached, so he knelt down, pulled the man's long dark hair taut for leverage, and finished cutting the head off as if he were splitting kindling.

Tony had watched. He would have assisted if Saidin had needed it. But he didn't. Completely unflustered, Saidin walked over to the car and took eight black and white-striped plastic bags out of the boot. After Saidin stuffed the bloody head in bag after bag to ensure it didn't drip blood into the car, he and Tony dragged the headless corpse across the road, and rolled it into a ditch in a rice field behind Kerobokan Jail. They didn't for a moment think the location was a bad omen.

While his brother drove the forty-five minutes back to Klungkung, Saidin sat in the front passenger seat, casually holding the warm head in the plastic bags as if it were a bag of goldfish. He'd promised to show it to his friend as proof of death. Just after sunrise they arrived at his friend's house. Saidin pulled the head from the plastic bags by its dark matted hair, his hands quickly turning blood red. As he proudly held it up like a trophy, the dead man's eyes were staring with a look of terror, the whites large.

After the men finished gloating, Saidin shoved the head back into the plastic bags, drove to a nearby pond used for breeding fish, and dropped it into the water. Saidin stood watching as large fish darted towards it for a nibble. It wouldn't be long before the dead man's head was yesterday's fish food. It had turned out to be a perfect murder, or so they thought.

The police are investigating the case intensively because Balinese people think this sadistic murder could create problems for the society, especially given that the site is not far from Kuta, the centre of tourism. Most likely, the news of this murder by head chopping has already reached Bali's tourists.

– *Nusa News*, 3 March 1998

Saidin confessed to the crime but argued that he was protecting the lives of his friend's family, truly believing the court would accept his defence. It didn't. The judges wanted to cut a deal. They'd give Saidin fewer than eight years, in exchange for twenty million rupiah ($4500). It was made clear that cash would be his only effective defence in the Bali courtroom. But Saidin was broke. He'd killed for money, but hadn't yet been paid. Without any cash, he knew that he'd go down hard, but there was nothing he could do about it.

At the time, I didn't have any money, so what do I use to pay the judges? They asked for twenty million rupiah and said to me, 'You know you'll be lucky if you can get away from the death penalty'. I said 'I'm sorry. I don't have any money, if you want to give me the death sentence, go ahead, if you want to sentence me to life, go ahead, if you can. But I believe in God, if God is with you then, yes, you can kill me or you can put me away for life. But if God is with me, you can't do that.'

– Saidin

When they checked into Hotel K, Saidin and Tony were big news. Their story had been on newspaper front pages for months throughout the investigation and their trials. They were instant VIPs. They bypassed the mandatory head shaving and the check-in stint in the cramped, rat-infested initiation block, and within weeks they were *tampings*, with more control than most guards.

The *tamping* system was used in jails throughout Indonesia. The jail boss elected prisoners to assist the guards in locking and unlocking prisoners, walking them to visits and calling for help. For their roles, these prisoners would have additional time taken off their sentences in the routine biannual remissions handed out by the Indonesian Government. In Hotel K, where the guards preferred playing cards to working, *tampings* held great power. They had the keys to the blocks, they escorted new prisoners to their cells, and they looked after VIPs. Saidin would later become a *Pemuka* (leader) – the most powerful position for an inmate, in charge of all the *tampings*. In Hotel K there were usually only two *Pemukas* at any time.

Saidin's army background and his ability to kill in cold blood gave him status. The machete that he kept under the bed in his cell as a souvenir of his crime only added to his mystique. Though the brothers were of average height and build, they were the most feared men in the jail at the time.

But Saidin wouldn't be inside for long. Despite being sentenced to seventeen years, he walked free within months. He got out on a legal glitch. He wasn't the first; he wouldn't be the last. He didn't pay a single rupiah. He'd appealed his sentence, but the Bali courts failed to hear it within the legally required time frame. The permissible detention period expired and the guards at Hotel K had no choice but to open the front door and let Saidin walk free.

But within two years Saidin would be back inside; this time with more power than ever. Tony would not be there to greet him though, despite having been sentenced to fifteen years – he would be on the run after masterminding the most embarrassing gaffe in Hotel K's history.

CHAPTER 4

THE GREAT ESCAPE

As Filipino prisoner Nita Ramos walked back to the women's block, she had no idea she had just seen her boyfriend Tony, Saidin's brother, for the last time. They had met in Hotel K a year earlier and regularly spent time together, walking around holding hands or enjoying visits with his family. She was a drug dealer, he was a murderer. Together, they were a power couple. On this Sunday afternoon, when she'd stopped to talk to him briefly in front of the mosque, she had wondered why he was wearing a small black backpack, but didn't bother asking him about it.

Neither Nita nor any of the other fifty-three women in Hotel K had any clue of the storm brewing outside the walls of their block. That afternoon, as usual, they were locked up for the night at 4.30 pm, about an hour earlier than the men. Sitting in their small cages, for them it was just another day coming to a close. The initial charge of energy after lockup had not yet subsided. In Nita's cell, it was hot and noisy. Thirteen foreigners, including six Italian girls caught using ecstasy at a dance party, were crammed inside. Nita sat on her mattress, talking to a young Spanish prisoner, Gina, about her court appearance the next day for stealing her boyfriend's camera. The other women were all busy doing their own thing; writing letters home, reading books or rinsing out their clothes. They didn't immediately notice that light plumes of smoke were wafting over the walls of the cellblock.

But within ten minutes of lockup, a thick haze of smoke began to roll into their cells, causing the inmates to start coughing. Within minutes the whole cellblock was in uproar. Trapped in their cages, the women were terrified they'd burn to death. They stood at the bars, bashing them hard, and screaming for help between coughing fits. The toxic black clouds were now rolling in and it was difficult to see beyond an arm's length. After lockup, the women's block, Block W, was not guarded. Yelling out to those over the wall was their only hope. But their efforts were futile – this afternoon, no guards would be coming to their rescue, as they had insurmountable problems of their own.

Tony's escape plan was working to perfection. Outside Block W, it was chaos. Fires raged across the jail, some flames blazing so fiercely that parts of buildings were disintegrating. Red-hot ash flew through the air and burning particles rained down. Hundreds of prisoners ran freely, covering their faces as they tried to dodge the firestorm. Guards, too, were running around scared, as cellblocks kept bursting into flames. The yard was charged with energy.

Only fifteen minutes earlier, the guards had been ambling across the jail to the various cellblocks for the 5.30 pm lockup, totally unaware of the tension about to break. Piles of kerosene-soaked mattresses had been set up in every cellblock, ready to explode into infernos as a match was tossed onto each in staggered succession. These were the flashpoints. When Tony had flicked the first match into his pile of mattresses, the kerosene instantly burst into flames.

Tony's explosion was the signal the other prisoners were waiting for. As two guards ran towards his blazing cellblock, a designated prisoner at the other end of the jail flicked a match into the second pile of mattresses. Another two guards ran in that direction. Seemingly ad hoc fires lit up across the jail. But it was planned with military precision, strategically choreographed to confuse the guards, to stretch them to their limit, from one end of the jail to the other. It was designed to isolate them and minimise their force. Prisoners were ready to capture the guard teams as they reached each block, then drag them to an office to lock them up together. With only fourteen guards on duty and more than three hundred prisoners running loose, it didn't take long to catch all the guards, even the ones who were running like hell from crazed prisoners relishing the turnaround in power.

Every male prisoner knew about the great escape plan. They had all lived for weeks under threat of death if they leaked it. No one did. No one dared to disobey Tony. His reputation as a cold-blooded killer was a powerful deterrent. For months, Tony and the leaders of each of the other eight male cellblocks had been meeting to plan every detail of the escape. Every prisoner had to cooperate. All were instructed to save their daily ration of kerosene. They had been warned the death threat would still apply when the escape started. Any prisoner who failed to run would be killed. So everyone was running, even those with only days or weeks left to serve. Tony unlocked the front door with a set of stolen keys. The rest of the block leaders had iron bars to smash open locks. They didn't have time to waste. They had to get out fast.

Still, there were a couple of jobs to be done. A designated team of inmates ran to the registration office with kerosene-doused rags. They lit them, then threw the flaming rags like firebombs into the offices to burn any paperwork, thereby eradicating prisoners' records and wiping their criminal histories. Many also ran around vandalising, smashing the office doors and windows, enjoying their new sense of freedom. The yelling and banging by guards locked in the nearby office just added to the thrill. Another group of prisoners was in the kitchen, watching explosive fireworks as they set alight huge drums of kerosene to add to the mayhem.

One prisoner had been asked by Tony to do a special job: to get his girlfriend, Nita Ramos, out. He ran across to the women's block, now completely engulfed in black smoke from the nearby kitchen and office fires, and opened it with the master key Tony had given him. He went inside, shouting, 'Nita Ramos, Nita Ramos, which cell is Nita Ramos in?' 'She's in Room 2,' several women called back between hacking coughs, desperately hoping he'd been sent to save them. The prisoner found Nita's cell, unlocked the door and then ran for his life out of there, ignoring the hysterical cries for help echoing behind him.

Nita was terrified. She flew into the bathroom in a panic, painfully bashing her nose on the edge of the door as she went. She crouched on the floor, curling her arms around her knees. She'd recognised the prisoner's voice as someone's who worked in the kitchen and who she sometimes chatted with. But she had no clue what he wanted or why he'd singled her out. 'It was only me they were looking for, that's why I was so scared.'

Within moments, sirens were blaring across the jail. Time was up. Any men still in the jail were now running for their lives. Prisoners were pouring out of the large side door used for delivery trucks and out of the main front door. The streets were frenetic. A long line of taxis, booked by prisoners on their mobile phones, stretched along the roadside. Prisoners were piling into them. Others were using their criminal instincts, hijacking passing cars and motorbikes, bashing people if necessary. Others simply ran away on foot. Fleeing inmates were everywhere – running for their freedom along the roads, leaping across open sewers, darting through traffic, jumping over fruit stands and dodging stray dogs.

It wasn't long before police and journalists turned up. One policeman yelled out, 'Freeze or I'll shoot,' to a group of five prisoners running barefoot across a paddy field behind Hotel K. The officer didn't have a gun, but his threat still worked. The escapees instantly froze, and turned around with their hands up, aware how trigger-happy Bali police could be. The officer waved them over and the group obediently walked towards him, surrendering themselves.

I think it's the funniest prison escape in the whole world. We saw people scramble. I was just watching the commotion. It was quite exciting.

–Journalist Wayan Juniartha of the *Jakarta Post*

With shields up and guns drawn, teams of police entered Hotel K, unsure what dangers would be lurking within. Small fires were still burning in many of the offices. Frantic screaming and banging was coming from inside one room. The police kicked in the door and discovered the fourteen angry guards. Further inside, they found twelve prisoners hiding in the garbage area; one covered in blood from a passing beating for not fleeing; the others still cowering in fear of being bashed or killed for not running with the pack. As the police went deeper into the jail, they saw it had been evacuated en masse. It looked like an abandoned village. Spot fires were burning across the jail and black smoke was billowing out through the cell windows.

The door to the women's block was ajar. With their guns drawn, two dozen armed police stormed inside, struggling to see through the thick smoke. They rapidly did a check of the cells and found only Nita's unlocked. Several police stood on high alert outside the cell door and window with their guns held ready to fire. Three officers entered with pistols. They encountered twelve quivering women huddling under blankets and pillows. No one had run. They were too scared to move. Nita's cellmate, Gina, stayed crouched under her blanket, wailing, 'What's going on? What's happening?' as she caught a glimpse of the black leather boots walking past.

The three police walked between the women, calling 'Nita Ramos, come out. Nita Ramos, come out!' She was still hiding in the bathroom. They burst in, pointed their guns at her and screamed, 'Get up, Ramos!' They were local police, therefore knew who she was. Two of them grabbed Nita under the arms, jerking her to her feet, before dragging her outside the cell. In the smoky yard, they pointed their guns at Nita and shouted at her. 'Your boyfriend run away. Your boyfriend escape.' 'I don't know, he never told me,' she sobbed. Being a *tamping*, they suspected she knew something. 'Tomorrow is investigation, so prepare, Ramos. Security police will come to investigate you tomorrow!' they warned. 'Why me?', she asked. 'Because your room was open.'

The police then did a roll call to ensure all thirteen women were still in the cell, before fastening the padlock on their smoky cage. None of Block W's fifty-three women had escaped. None had even known of the great escape. But all would soon be suffering its consequences.

Outside the jail, large numbers of police were setting up roadblocks, securing bus stations, and increasing surveillance at local harbours. The chief of police issued a 'shoot on sight' order if any inmates resisted arrest. Smarter escapees, such as Tony, were already safely miles away. But others who weren't so bright were caught loitering in the local areas around the jail, hiding in backyard toilets or wandering around the streets. Several inmates were even caught sitting at local cafés, eating plates of nasi goreng.

If living near a maximum-security prison had always caused the locals a little dread, this outbreak was a terrifying ordeal for them. They were immediately warned by police and in radio alerts to lock their doors, be vigilant, and particularly wary of strangers who were 'sweaty, barefoot and possessed no identity card'. But some still got hurt. One woman was bashed at home by a prisoner who was stealing her car. Several were pushed off their motorbikes as prisoners hijacked them. An expatriate living up the road from Hotel K discovered her dog drowned in her swimming pool. Presumably, it had been barking while a prisoner stole clothes from her washing line.

Police were doing door-to-door searches and raiding any houses where sightings of suspicious people had been reported. They caught four prisoners hiding in backyard toilets and another sitting on Kuta beach. By sunset, one hundred and four of the two hundred and eighty-nine escapees were back in custody. Fifty-nine of these had surrendered, claiming they'd run away only under threat of death. One Balinese prisoner had run straight home to his family compound, but asked his brother to phone the police to explain he'd be back in the morning after a shower and a meal. He kept his word.

Nita awoke the next morning with a dark bruise down the right side of her face from her clash with the bathroom door. Her world had darkened too. She was under a cloud of suspicion. She was bewildered and knew nothing. But she seemed overnight to have morphed into a dangerous criminal, guilty of harbouring a deadly secret. Armed police burst into her cell, snapped on handcuffs and marched her across the prison. They were taking no chances. Nita looked around Hotel K, and was shocked by the complete devastation, and by the smell of kerosene and smouldering mattresses still hanging heavily in the air.

The great escape was a major embarrassment. The police needed answers and were sure Nita held them. Returned prisoners had been freely blabbing that Tony was the leader, the mastermind, much braver now that he was gone. And with little chance of catching Tony, the police pressured his girlfriend for information. 'Your boyfriend escaped, we know he's your boyfriend.' 'I don't know anything,' she kept repeating. They didn't swallow it. Her cell had been opened and they believed she'd been given something by the man who'd unlocked it. She was interrogated for five hours by six specialist police on a crisis mission from Jakarta. Her cell was also searched several times. They found nothing. But still they were unconvinced.

Every morning Nita went through the same humiliating procedure – being handcuffed and marched to the office to spend another five or six gruelling hours with yet another team of specialist officers from Jakarta hurling the same questions and insults at her. 'I don't know anything, I don't know anything,' she wailed for six days straight, until they finally gave up on her. The rest of the women were also suffering, cooped up in their cells, banned from visits, unable even to walk around the women's block to stretch their legs.

During the next few weeks about two dozen more prisoners were recaptured, but only one hundred and thirty of the two hundred and eighty-nine were ever caught. Many of the recaptured prisoners were temporarily held at police stations and another local jail while the destroyed cellblocks were repaired. The anger and embarrassment had escalated, and returning escapees were now being beaten with rattan whips until they bled. Their open wounds were doused in water mixed with fresh chilli to exacerbate the pain, before they were put into isolation cells without food or water. Their remissions, or days cut from their sentence for good behaviour, were automatically cancelled. Hotel K tightened its security, building wire fences around every block, so that prisoners could no longer wander freely around the jail. It was a move to prevent another prisoner coup, after an investigation found the lack of fencing had been a major factor in the great escape's success.

Nita would never see Tony again, though when his brother, Saidin, returned to jail about a year later, he organised a phone call between the former lovers. Tony was living as a fugitive in Malaysia. Relationships in jail were fickle, and Nita had swiftly moved on to a new lover; conveniently, another power player who she had a lot in common with. They would work together selling drugs.

289 inmates break out of Bali jail

Jakarta – A total 289 prisoners escaped from a jail in Indonesia's resort island of Bali following a mass breakout, a report said here [on] Monday. The prisoners escaped from the Kerobokan Jail in southern Bali at about

5:00 pm Sunday after breaking the main gate. Fourteen jail wardens on guard at the time were outnumbered and unable to stop the prisoners, the Jakarta Post Daily *said.*

– *Agence France-Presse*, 6 December 1999

CHAPTER 5
LET'S PLAY

For many months after the great escape, Hotel K's security was tight. All inmates were kept in their cellblocks, only allowed out for visits or for an occasional ten minutes of sun if they slipped the right guard about 70,000 rupiah ($10). New fences had been built around each cellblock, the usually unmanned watchtowers were active and two additional inmates were designated as *tampings* in every block. Despite her former love affair with notorious great escape mastermind Tony, Nita was given the job as *tamping* in Block W. It gave her more freedom in Hotel K, freedom she'd soon use to deal drugs, utilise outside contacts and network within the jail.

Before being in Hotel K, Nita had been a drug trafficker, working Asia for three European bosses. She spent years jetting around, making good money, until the day her luck turned. That morning she kissed her four-year-old daughter goodbye in their apartment in the Philippines, unaware they would be separated for years, and drove to the airport with only a small travel bag. She breezed through immigration, completely free of any sense of dread, and boarded the plane as innocently as any other traveller, looking forward to having a drink. Her first stop was Singapore. That's where the risks began.

But Nita was smart. She always took the standard precautions and was never blasé or arrogant. She was acutely aware that a wrong move could end with a noose around her neck or a bullet through her heart. But the risks were minimal on this trip, as she wasn't carrying any drugs on the flight. The potentially deadly packages had been couriered ahead to a fake name. Nita held the matching fake ID. This system had worked perfectly on dozens of trips, with Nita simply alternating the fake IDs.

After her day's work in Singapore, collecting and dropping off packages of drugs, Nita boarded another plane to Bali via Brunei and Jakarta, following the usual practice of travelling zigzagging routes to stay under the radar. At Bali's Ngurah Rai Airport, she grabbed a cab and went straight to the cargo office in Denpasar to pick up her package.

Using her fake ID, she then checked into a cheap Kuta hotel, chosen by her Belgian boss, and started repackaging the ten kilograms of drugs into two packets, wrapping them securely in black plastic, for two collections. At the arranged time there was a knock at the door. Nita walked across the room and called out 'ice-cream'. A reply came back fast in a heavy French accent: 'cone'. It was a password system Nita used to ensure she only opened the door to the right person. She undid the flimsy security chain and partly opened the door. A tall black man with a beard and moustache and a white man were waiting. Nita simply nodded before bending down to pick up the six-kilogram package of drugs she'd placed behind the door.

The transaction was quick. Within a minute, the two men had vanished down the hallway with the drugs, their money already wired to Nita's boss. Now it was time for Nita to get out fast; a life-preserving rule.

She checked out, paying for the room in cash, and then checked into another hotel nearby. Her work was almost done. She had a second client in the morning and would then fly home to her daughter. But as Nita stood in the shower shampooing her hair, police were gathering outside her door. Life as she knew it was about to change forever. As she casually stepped out of the shower, police kicked in the door and exploded into the room. Nita flew behind the bathroom door, gasping for breath. Her heart was slamming against her chest and her wet, naked body trembling as she hid behind the door. A male voice yelled: 'Come out, Ramos.' She didn't move. She was terrified. He knew her name. He called again, 'Come out, Ramos. Come out with your hands up'.

Nita was visibly shaking as she edged out from behind the door, her hands held above her head. A wall of pistols was pointing at her as she moved into the doorway, exposing her dripping wet body, too scared to reach for a towel in case she got shot. More than ten police were surrounding the bed. Nita continued to stand naked with her hands in the air and her wet hair splashing down her back. One of the police officers tore a sheet off the bed and tossed it over to her. Nita quickly wrapped it around herself.

Police started demolishing the room, rifling through her bags and flinging her clothes onto the floor. They ripped the linen off the bed and flipped the mattress. In under five minutes, they discovered the drugs hidden in the bottom of a bamboo cabinet. Nita claimed they weren't hers, as she watched the police laughing and talking on their mobile phones. It was a good night for them. Usually they found only grams. But tonight they'd discovered two kilograms of hashish and two kilograms of ice. Nita kept lamely protesting her innocence as she stood wrapped in the sheet, hoping the Bali legal system might go soft on her, as she had plenty of cash.

They demanded twelve years for me, but I talked to the prosecutor and the prosecutor asked me if I had money so I could deal with my case. So I paid over one hundred million rupiah [$25,000] through my lawyer and the court gave me punishment of six years.

– Nita

Nita later discovered how she was caught. She'd been set up by a dealer who owed her cash. He was due to be her next customer, but had called the police instead, with the aim of effectively wiping his debt by putting Nita away. But a loss didn't stop Nita for long. She was soon back playing inside Hotel K. The trade that stole her life would become the centre of it.

***

Hotel K was fast becoming the United Nations of traffickers as Bali became a lucrative drug market, turning from a transit point into a destination throughout the late 1990s. Wealthy expatriates and tourists had created a demand, and smugglers from across the globe were flying into Denpasar, posing as tourists, with their surfboard bags, dive tanks, sports bags and even their stomachs and anuses filled with drugs. Over the next few years Hotel K's guests would come from all over the world, including Holland, Italy, England, Scotland, Sweden, Russia, Mexico,

Nigeria, Brazil, Argentina, the US and Australia. Drug offences were also attracting harsher penalties, with a dark new era of death for traffickers dawning in Bali. The first person in Bali to face death by firing squad for drug trafficking offences was 27-year-old French cook Michael Blanc in 2000.

A French national is facing the death penalty for allegedly smuggling 3.8 kilograms of hashish hidden in scuba tanks into the Indonesian resort island of Bali. The Jakarta Post *said state prosecutors at the Denpasar District Court on Friday demanded that Michael Blanc, 27, be handed the death sentence for bringing the hashish into Bali on December 26, 1999.*

– *Agence France-Presse*, 4 November 2000

On Boxing Day 1999 Michael flew into Bali with two diving tanks in one of his bags. They were set to devastate his young life. As he walked across to pick up his dive bag, it was already being closely watched after a routine X-ray scan showed something suspicious in the tanks. Customs officers had sent the bag onto the baggage carousel with all the other holiday luggage to see who would pick it up. The moment Michael wrapped his fingers around its strap, his life as a free man was over.

Michael and the police tell conflicting stories about what happened next. Police say they took the French man and his diving tanks into an airport office and tested the tanks for oxygen while he stood watching. After the test proved the steel tubes were devoid of oxygen, they drilled into them and found almost four kilograms of hashish divided into hundreds of small packages. According to police, Michael confessed in his first interview with them, that he'd flown to Bali via Bangkok, where he'd bought the drugs in transit, and that he was planning to sell them in Bali.

Michael denied confessing or having any knowledge of the hashish. He said the tanks belonged to a friend, Phillip, who lived in Bombay and that he'd used them on several dives during a 15-day trip to India. Unfortunately, he could no longer contact his friend. He also claimed the police broke protocol by opening the tanks when he was not in the room.

Michael was living in Hotel K under the shadow of death by firing squad. His parents flew over from France desperate to help their son, sure of his innocence and outraged by the lack of a chance to prove it. Their pleas to fingerprint the bags containing the hashish were rejected. Michael had confessed and no further investigation was needed.

His only possibility of an effective defence had nothing to do guilt or innocence. Michael's mother, Helene, was told a payment of between $330,000 and $420,000 could buy a fifteen-year sentence. But she refused to consider a bribe, believing her son was innocent, and threw away the only strategy that had a chance of working. The judge sentenced Michael to life in prison, rejecting the prosecutors' request for the death sentence. But he would die in jail. Michael sat in court, slumped in a plastic chair, looking shattered. With only darkness stretching interminably ahead, Michael found a perilous way to deal with the crushing pain of losing his life in Hotel K. He became a heroin addict. Hotel K, after all, was the ideal place to score.

***

Michael was the first to face the prospect of the death penalty, and it wasn't long before the prosecutors requested the same fate for more drug traffickers in Bali. A 29-year-old Mexican scuba diving instructor named Vincente Garcia flew into Bali several months after Michael's conviction. He passed through immigration, then walked to the luggage carousel to pick up his boogie board bag and another black bag. He showed no sign of fear, despite the fact that his bag was carrying fifteen kilograms of cocaine. Vincente was travelling with a Mexican former model, Clara Gautrin, 32, who was acting as his girlfriend to help create the impression they were holidaying lovers. They made a sexy couple as they confidently walked through the airport, seemingly without a care in the world. They appeared like all the other couples starting a romantic holiday in paradise. Neither knew they had been set up and were walking straight into a trap.

Vincente had tangled with his former Mexican drug boss by cutting him out of the loop. On previous drug runs, Vincente had been a well-paid mule, but he was ambitious and wanted a bigger cut – after all, he was the one taking all the risks and few drug traffickers were brazen enough to carry fifteen kilograms in one trip. It didn't take long for one of Bali's biggest drug bosses, a Chinese man, to snap up Vincente's services. But it also took little time for his former drug boss in Mexico to find out and exact revenge. He had one of his men follow Vincente to find out his flight details to Bali. Like most smart drug traffickers, Vincente always ensured no one knew his itinerary, only ever giving clients a ballpark arrival date. But his ex-boss's man was able to find out the details, and passed them onto the Mexican drug lord, who then faxed them through to the Bali police. The moment Vincente checked in his bags, the authorities in Bali were closing in, waiting to pounce as soon as his plane landed at Ngurah Rai Airport.

The suspects, Vincente Manuel Navarro Garcia and Clara Elena Umana Gautrin, were arrested at the airport on Tuesday on the tourist island of Bali following a flight from the Thai capital, Bangkok. Police said *they found the drugs hidden in the couple's suitcases. Indonesian police said the drugs found on the Mexicans had a street value of $470,000 in Bali.*

– *EFE News Service*, 12 April 2001

Vincente and Clara did a deal with the prosecutors and judges that he would be sentenced to fifteen years instead of death and that she would walk free. But the judges reneged on the deal and sentenced Clara to seven years and Vincente to life. Sparing Vincente the firing squad was the best the judges could do without causing suspicion. It would have been awkward to explain why, in the same Bali courtroom, Vincente got fifteen years for fifteen kilograms of cocaine, when Michael got life for less than four kilograms of hashish. Yet, it was clear to anyone watching closely that a deal had been done. Vincente received the same sentence as Michael, despite being charged with trafficking more than four times the amount of drugs.

Another trafficker checking into Hotel K under the shadow of death was 24-year-old Italian jeweller Juri Angione. He was caught at Ngurah Rai Airport with five kilograms of cocaine in his surfboard bag. Juri had been living in Bali on and off for two years when he told his girlfriend he was going to Thailand for a few days' break. Instead, he flew to Brazil and picked up a surfboard bag pre-packed with five kilograms of cocaine. He zigzagged his way back to Bali, trying to avoid scrutinised routes. He stayed away from Jakarta Airport, as a Brazilian courier, Marco, had been busted there several months earlier with thirteen kilograms of cocaine in a hang-glider frame. Juri was now working for the same wealthy Italian drug boss who had employed Marco. The boss was a man who lived in Bali, indulging in the good life – watching sunsets and sipping cocktails at the most exclusive beach bars and restaurants while his couriers flew the skies. The drug boss had told Juri he needed him for an emergency run to get bribe money to save Marco from a firing squad. Juri flew from Brazil to Amsterdam to Bangkok, where he changed airlines from KLM Royal Dutch Airlines to Thai Airways. It was here he got a stark warning.

A Thai customs officer saw something suspicious in his surfboard bag as it went through the X-ray machine. 'What's this?' he asked, touching the top of the bag. 'It's plastic,' Juri said. The officer moved his hands towards the zip. Juri had to act fast to convince him not to open it. 'It's just plastic, it protects my board.' He stood watching as the officer's hand smoothed across the top of the bag. His hand stopped at the zip . . . hovering. 'It's just plastic,' Juri urged, trying to sound blasé despite his heart slamming into his chest. 'Okay,' the officer said, waving him on and casually shifting his attention to the next passenger's bag. Juri grabbed the bag and walked away before letting out a huge breath. It had been an unbelievably close call. But his sense of relief was fleeting. He knew that the bag was not well-packed when he left Brazil, but he'd taken it anyway. Now that a routine X-ray scan had picked up something suspicious, his fears were confirmed. And he still had to get through Bali customs.

Throughout the Thai Airways flight to Bali, he debated whether or not he should just leave the bag at the airport. He'd lose the cocaine but keep his life. He'd smuggled drugs at least twenty times, but this was different. He was exposed by the badly packed bag. By the time the plane hit the Bali tarmac, he'd resolved to go through with it. 'At the end I say, okay, I will try, I will keep playing. I wanted to play.' Even the 'Death to drug traffickers' signs around him as he queued to buy a tourist visa failed to change his mind.

As he walked down the long corridors from the plane's exit to immigration at Ngurah Rai Airport, customs officials were already circling. After another routine X-ray in Bali had raised suspicions, a sniffer dog confirmed the bag was piled with drugs. Customs then sent it as bait out onto the carousel to see who would pick it up. Like Michael and Vincente before him, Juri was a walking target as he entered the baggage hall and walked across to collect his bags. The surfboard bag was sitting inconspicuously on the floor among dozens of other bags. He scooped it up and walked towards the green line; nothing to declare. But this time he wasn't so lucky.

A thorough search of the bag produced three surfboards, two swim suits, two pairs of surfing shoes, a snorkel and 29 plastic packages hidden in the inner lining of the bag. Wrapped in black carbon paper, the packages contained suspicious white powder, which a simple test confirmed as high-quality cocaine. [Juri] Angione admitted that the bag, clothes, shoes and surfboards were his, but denied any knowledge of the cocaine.

Airport authorities on the resort island of Bali arrested a 24-year-old Italian national on Wednesday afternoon for attempting to smuggle some 5.26 kilograms of cocaine with a street value of about Rp 4.5 billion [$600,000] into Indonesia.

– *Jakarta Post*, 4 December 2003

The prosecutors asked for the death penalty for Juri, as they'd done with Vincente and Michael. But the Bali court sentenced him to life in jail. Juri's fellow drug trafficker, the Brazilian, Marco, lost his appeal against the death sentence and was sent to a maximum-security prison on Nusakambangan Island to await his execution.

Why didn't you listen to the warning in Bangkok?

Juri: *On plane from Bangkok to Bali I was thinking do I get the bag or I leave the bag in airport? I was thinking that. I was expecting I might get caught. But I was thinking no, I don't want to lose that stuff, what a waste all this stuff. At the end I say okay, I will try, I will keep playing. I wanted to play. So I go to get the bag and when I went outside they stopped me. They touch, they ask me what is this. I say plastic. They say open it.*

Did you try to stop them opening it?

Juri: *I say the same thing as in Bangkok. I say it's plastic, it's plastic. But they don't listen to me, they open, they cut open the bag, take out a little bit of stuff.*

How were you feeling?

Juri: *Fucked up. Yeah. Fucked up. Way bad.*

Did you offer police at the airport any money?

Juri: *No. I was thinking about that but there were too many policemen.*

How many policemen?

Juri: *A lot.*

Fellow inmate: *Want to see his eyes shine! Was the cocaine good, Juri?*

Juri: *Yeah. It was the same stuff as Marco had.*

Fellow inmate: *From Peru. The best stuff in the world, about 85 per cent pure. The most you can get is 95 per cent. If you make a big line, it can explode your heart, it's extremely pure. Juri had very good quality stuff because I know the source.*

Was it going to be sold in Bali?

Juri: *No, in New Zealand and Australia.*

Were you going to take it there?

Juri: *No, not me. Somebody else take it by boat.*
Fellow inmate: *By catamaran.*

That was your job finished?

Juri: *Yeah.*

What did the police do with the cocaine?

Juri: *The police in Bali sell it for sure. They cut it and mix it. They make fifteen kilograms with my stuff.*

How many times had you smuggled cocaine into Bali?

Juri: *In Bali, it was the first time I bring cocaine. I do other drugs – hashish, ecstasy, like that. But first time ever cocaine and it was first time I bring something for somebody else. I always bring my own stuff. I always pack my own bags. I'm a user. But I do it this time because there was an emergency for Marco. They had to find someone to bring more stuff to make more money to help Marco. I didn't know Marco that time. But to help my boss, I say, 'Yeah, okay, I go'.*

Had you trafficked drugs to other countries?

Juri: *Yeah. In Italy, in Holland, in India.*

Cocaine?

Juri: *Cocaine, everything.*

Heroin?

Juri: *No never. Ecstasy, hashish. Heroin never. I don't play that.*

And always in a surfboard?

Juri: *No, in a bag sometimes, in my stomach. I swallow balls. I swallow one kilogram of hash balls.*

How do you swallow?

Juri: *You make balls with the plastic. I roll the hash in cellophane paper for the food and make small, small balls.*

And you're stomach was okay … because you're so skinny?

Juri: *Yeah, my stomach's okay because I take a long time to swallow, like one whole day. I needed ten hours to swallow that stuff.*

And do you eat any food that day?

Juri: *No, no, cannot.*

And then you get on the plane?

Juri: *Yeah.*

How did you get involved with drugs?

Juri: *It's life, yeah. What happened like you meet someone, and then you meet someone else. Slowly, slowly. But since I'm a kid in Italy I already play, like sell hashish in Italy.*

You sold it when you were in Italy?

Juri: *Yeah, since I was 14 years old, I sell it. In the school I sell hashish many times. I sell it through the guy who sells pizza for breakfast at school. If somebody wants a special pizza, he sells it with my hashish on top.*

Did you move to Bali because it was a good base for selling drugs?

Juri: *I move to Bali because I have a friend there – he has a house. So I moved in with him and we started going to India and travelling around a little bit.*

To get drugs?

Juri: *Yeah. But India is a beautiful place as well. I like travelling a lot.*

How many times would you have gone through an international airport with drugs … ten times?

Juri: *More. Twenty, thirty times.*

And you've never got caught before?

Juri: *Never.*

Why did you get caught this time, do you think?

Juri: *It was my time.*

– Juri and fellow inmate

CHAPTER 6

NO STAR TO FIVE STAR

You cannot describe what feeling you have when you walk into Kerobokan. It's not like a normal place. Walking down into a dirty room, it's not your language, not your people, another planet. All the time you think you're dreaming; it's not really happening; you're not really there. You don't know what to do or think. It's extreme. You go up and down. It's like you've been kidnapped.

– Mick, Australian inmate

Checking into a third-world jail is a frightening ordeal for most westerners, but at Hotel K after a mug shot, a haircut and paperwork in the offices, inmates are taken on a surprisingly pleasant walk through nicely groomed gardens to their new cell. On that walk, Hotel K resembles a cheap Balinese resort. Prisoners stretch out like cats under shady palm trees, reading or sleeping. Some play tennis or pray in the small Hindu temple. The path turns at a small canteen, where a group of prisoners might stand about chatting. A laughing child runs across the lawns, flying a kite. Under a palm tree, a couple is kissing. This initial snapshot lulls a new inmate into a false sense of calm.

It doesn't last long.

When the door of their new cell slams shut, the pleasant scenes cease. In the initiation or pre-sentencing blocks J and C2, there is no sunlight, only bright fluorescent lights. A thick blue haze colours the air, from the clove cigarettes dangling from people's lips. They're hot concrete boxes, each crammed so tightly, with up to twenty-five men, that the prisoners are constantly touching elbows or knees. There's not enough room for everyone to sit down at the same time; they sit and sleep in shifts. No one can stretch out unless they nab a spot near the door where they can scissor their legs through the bars. Everyone else sleeps with their legs and arms weaving in and out of the sticky limbs of others.

In the corner is a single hole-in-the-ground toilet, which is usually blocked with old, hardened faeces. The stench attracts a cloud of mosquitoes. Rats run in and out of the cells. New western inmates watch in disbelief when a local corners a rat, breaks its neck and then eats it raw.

The initiation cellblocks are filled with heroin addicts, including some with AIDS and hepatitis, who will later be put in a cellblock specifically for drug addicts, known as 'the junkie block'. Often they're covered in sores, obsessively picking at them. The addicts shoot up, wrapping their arms tightly to find a vein before plunging in a blunt needle, taking a hit and passing the dirty syringe on. The tight squeeze ensures all prisoners are exposed to their diseases, skin rashes, sores and infections.

Three times a day in the initiation cellblocks, inmates are fed like they're monkeys. Usually they just stretch their arms through the bars to those prisoners who wheel the food carts around the jail, holding out a hand or a piece of plastic to get a spoonful of undercooked hard white rice with a ladle of watery cabbage stew slopped on top. The inmates' only respite is a walk across to the visiting room, although many have no one to visit them, so are deprived even of that.

When I first came from the police station, they put me in C2. When anyone comes from the police station, they put you there first, in one small room with twenty-five people. Not enough room for twenty-five people. Some people sit down to sleep. I was there for two months. That time there was no toilet. You have to shit in plastic. Piss in plastic. I went two weeks and five days with no shit.

Did you get out once in two months?

No. You cannot go out in the day time. That time I have no choice but to stay there. If you have money you can pay to move to another block. Some people make arrangement so that immediately they are moved from that block. American Gabriel started to make everything expensive. He paid seven million rupiah [$950] to move, because he didn't want to stay even for one hour. So they start to charge everyone more. The guy from Africa, he paid seven million also to move.

– Emmanuel, Nigerian inmate

Although the guards always let westerners, with money, fast-track themselves out of the initiation cellblocks or skip them altogether, some are unaware of the upgrade system. Millionaire Australian yachtsman Chris Packer, jailed for having unregistered guns on his yacht, was not clued up and suffered a few days crammed inside an initiation cell, sleeping with his legs skewed through the bars, before cutting a deal to move into a cell with a soft bed and furniture.

Paying for a cell upgrade could put an inmate in up-market real estate offering private rooms with grassy views, a plasma television and DVD player, a soft mattress and the internet. The best rooms were given to VIP prisoners, such as the Balinese king or the governor of Bali, or inmates with cash and influence. Mexican drug dealers Vincente and Clara both had cell upgrades, courtesy of their rich Bali-based drug-dealer client. He ensured they were looked after; in return, they would not turn him in or name him. He could also still use Vincente to organise his cocaine deliveries. Being inside Hotel K didn't stop Vincente from working, calling contacts in Mexico and organising couriers from his cell. Vincente had installed a 26-inch LCD television on the wall, a water pump for hot and cold water and a small bath; things that were luxuries even in local homes.

Clara had exclusive real estate in the women's block. Her cell was at the end of the path, and was shielded from passers-by by a Japanese bamboo screen that provided the most precious commodity in jail: privacy. Outside, she'd planted a small garden. Inside, she'd had the floor tiled blue and a western toilet installed, and she had the rare privilege of deciding who shared with her. Usually, she had only two cellmates, despite the other nine cells in Block W being crammed with up to fifteen women.

Powerful Balinese drug dealer Iwan Thalib's luxuriously comfortable cell could rival a five-star hotel room. Iwan had designed the interior, decorating it tastefully and with a state-of-the-art Bose sound system. He had his workers hand-craft wooden furniture to fit the space perfectly. They laid a sumptuous Bordeaux red carpet and painted the walls a light coffee colour. His home theatre comprised eight speakers mounted on the walls for surround sound, a plasma screen at the foot of his bed, a DVD player and a PlayStation. In the corner he had a small fridge for beers, a freezer and a microwave. His builders had expanded the cell by knocking down a wall to an adjoining communal toilet and turning it into an en-suite bathroom. He also paid a gay inmate, Dedi, a small wage to be his servant, cleaning his cell and washing his clothes. If Iwan had to be in jail, he was going to do it in style. In reality, though, he rarely slept there as he had VIP privileges and was free to walk in and out of Hotel K as he pleased. But he let other prisoners use his cell to watch his plasma television or use his PlayStation. Life behind bars was not too bad for Iwan. He had money, influence and more power than the guards.

From the beginning, Iwan was Number One VIP. He is the one who can openly use a laptop or hand phone because he's the one who is the Number One sponsor for the jail. Whatever is needed, he's the one who takes out the money.

So he ran the jail?

Yeah of course, he was the Number One sponsor. Whatever is needed, he's the one who gets it. Want to make garden or want to renovate cell. He pays. Pay everything. Even if the chief of jail wanted to go somewhere, wanted to go to Jakarta, he was the one who paid the money. He's the one who takes care of it, plane fare, hotel, everything. With money, whatever you want, you can do inside. Whoever wants to sell the drugs inside the jail, no problem. Every week you have to pay the money to the chief of the jail.

– Den, Nepalese inmate

This was Iwan's second stint in Hotel K. His first was in 1996 when he and his Dutch wife were caught at Bali's Ngurah Rai Airport with 20,781 ecstasy tablets worth one and a half billion rupiah ($200,000) hidden in a loudspeaker box.

The suspects, Iwan Thalib and a woman he says is his wife, Jolita, were arrested upon arriving at Ngurah Rai Airport from Amsterdam on Friday. A police source said that the authorities have long suspected the two. It is believed that Iwan opened a furniture and silver souvenir shop as a cover. The police said they believe Iwan is one of the island's major ecstasy dealers. The police source also said that a police officer, who was suspected of cooperating with Iwan and seen waiting for him at the airport, disappeared as soon as he saw Iwan was in trouble.

– *Jakarta Post*, 12 June 1996

Iwan was sentenced to only fourteen months in jail the first time, barely interrupting his drug business. After his release, the charismatic, pony-tailed drug dealer, who had once acted in a couple of movies, started pressing ecstasy tablets in his two-room apartment above his high-end electrical shop in Bali's Seminyak – an exclusive beach area populated with five-star hotels, villas and rich expatriates. Iwan lived upstairs in the drug den, drove around in the latest BMW and supplied all the clubs with ecstasy pills.

He was well known to the Bali police, who for a back-hander mostly let him fly under the radar to get on with business, although a few always had him in their sights for an extra stripe on their uniform. He had evaded arrest a couple of times. Police had stopped two drug couriers with a kilogram of *shabu* (ice) hidden in the BMW they were driving. It turned out to be Iwan's car and, they claimed, Iwan's drugs, but he went untouched. Police also tried to arrest him in a Kuta nightclub after getting a tip-off that he had illegal drugs on him. But he was empty-handed when they nabbed him. Iwan's elusiveness and the police's inability to make a case against him resulted in several Bali police being suspected of taking gifts from him (even a house and a car), being guests at his parties and colluding with him. He'd been on the police's most wanted list for years. Late one night, they finally got him.

Police patiently waited outside Iwan's Seminyak shop, hiding in bushes or inside and behind parked cars, avoiding the security camera perched above the shop's front door. They were armed and ready to strike. As Iwan walked down his stairs at about 2 am, he suspected nothing. He was on his way to see a friend in hospital after late-night surgery. He casually stepped out of his front door and *boom*. His world lit up. Bright lights hit him in the face as police turned on their car headlights. Blinded momentarily, he didn't see police jumping out from the shadows and surrounding him with guns. But he heard their shouts. 'It's him, it's him', before they called out to him, 'We want to go upstairs and search your premises'. Iwan simply nodded and put his hands in the air. He knew one day this would happen. He also knew that upstairs he had enough stuff to put him in front of a firing squad. He kept his cool. Without evidence, police weren't allowed inside.

But when a police officer walked across and searched him, he hit pay dirt. Iwan had eight grams of *shabu* in the pocket of his shirt. It was the green light that police needed to go inside. It was crazy for Iwan to carry drugs outside his drug den, but he had become blasé after years of police tip-offs and immunity. Twenty police officers followed him up the stairs to his den, two or three pointing guns at his lower spine. Iwan stayed cool. Once upstairs, he walked across to his fridge and pulled out a few beers to offer to the police. They declined. He snapped one open for himself anyway and sat down on the floor. Several of the officers joined him on the ground, amicably talking about the latest football scores. In the next room, officers ransacked his den.

He's a very cool guy, very Al Pacino. I arrived a couple of minutes after they took him upstairs. They were already chatting with each other, sitting in a circle on the floor. I was there with three other journalists. They had already taken several drugs from the next room and put [them] in the centre of this circle. There were several piles of ecstasy tablets. Iwan just kept sitting there on the floor smiling.

–Journalist Wayan Juniartha of the *Jakarta Post*

Despite his casual attitude, Iwan had a lot to be stressed about. Police searched for three hours, regularly flashing smug smiles at each other as they uncovered a small-scale ecstasy factory. By the end of the night they had found 80,000 ecstasy tablets, six hundred grams of cocaine, several kilograms of powders, one kilogram of heroin, and five pill-pressing and stamping machines. They also discovered fourteen .22 calibre bullets, a pistol and an active hand grenade; basic protection for a drug dealer.

'The arrest was really good news for us because he had been the most wanted criminal for years in Bali,' a high ranking narcotics detective said. 'We have been trying to capture him for years, but he was too smart and too elusive. We believe that he is one of the four biggest drug dealers in Bali, the ones with extensive networks and important connections,' he said.

– *Jakarta Post*, March 2002

At 5 am police finished the raid. They handcuffed Iwan and drove him to the Denpasar police cells, where he was put under tight security. Now he had to start a costly fight for his life. Ironically, Iwan's long-standing tacit immunity had been wiped at a time when he'd been considering turning legit and moving into the booming Bali villa-building business. But his illegally made wealth would now be needed to pay the courts to let him live.

Cash flew around wildly. The payments were funnelled through his lawyer to grease the many outstretched palms in the system that needed to be paid. One payment slipped to police was to slash the number of ecstasy pills they would report they'd found. Another was to botch a court demonstration of Iwan's pill presser, so the pills pressed in front of the judges looked nothing like the 80,000 confiscated pills. This exonerated Iwan from a serious drugs-manufacturing charge, making it easier for the judges to lighten his sentence without showing overt favouritism and so red-flagging their deals.

'Yes! Yes!' Iwan cried out, leaping off the plastic chair when the judges read out his sentence of thirteen years for drug possession. Death had been a real possibility; the deals had saved him. But his lawyer quickly yanked him back down in his seat, telling him to be quiet. Indiscretion was dangerous. Everyone was watching their back. They all had dirty hands and it was unwise to draw attention to the sentence. If there was suspicion that the judiciary had been compromised, the prosecutors could still appeal for death.

In his verdict [the judge] stressed that the 48-year-old defendant was not guilty of drug distribution or manufacturing, which were more serious offences that carried heavier sentences.

– *Jakarta Post,* March 2001

In a separate case, Iwan – dubbed 'Godfather' by the press – was sentenced to a further three years for the weapons.

With his cases finally over, Iwan threw himself into new legitimate and old illicit businesses inside Hotel K. He converted a building near the tennis court, previously used by an inmate as a printing factory, into a furniture workshop. He invested $US50,000 of his own money in buying machinery and he paid forty-two prisoners small weekly salaries to work in the factory. It was a win-win situation. Even those with little skill could put their long and boring jail hours to use by endlessly polishing a table leg, ensuring that Iwan's workshop was soon turning out the finest legs in furniture and attracting clients from as far as Spain and the United States.

Iwan's wealthy and smartly dressed clients were welcomed through Hotel K's front doors like official jail guests. They were escorted down the paths past the many staring faces of the curious prisoners who were usually loitering in the yard or sitting around drinking beers and smoking dope. Anyone new entering Hotel K, especially dapper-looking business-people, provoked interest and broke the monotony. But not all Iwan's clients were so well-heeled. Some tended to look as scruffy as the inmates in jeans and T-shirts and appeared more suited to sitting on a concrete floor than on Iwan's expensive designer chairs. When these clients walked into Iwan's workshop, furniture shopping was the last thing on their minds.

Behind the front lines of noisy machines and flying sawdust, prisoners were quietly pressing and packing ecstasy pills. It was the ideal set-up. Iwan's drug clients could breeze in and out without fear of being searched. Police were not allowed inside Hotel K unless they got a warrant, which meant Iwan would get ample warning from the guards on his payroll to hide the drugs. Furniture-moving trucks freely drove in and out of the jail's service gate; superficial random searches always failed to uncover the tens of thousands of ecstasy pills neatly packed inside his high-end speakers.

On the street outside, Iwan had also set up a furniture showroom among a row of shanty-style shops that mostly sold cheap mobile phones and cans of Coke. Iwan did deals with his high and low-end clients at the showroom, using an intercom system to talk through the jail walls. Under the guise of going to his showroom, the business magnate easily slipped in and out of Hotel K, with the guards or *tamping* prisoners working as doormen – standing ready to swing open the wooden doors whenever Iwan walked out and disappeared for the day or night. As part of his deal to run the furniture business, Iwan was issued with an official piece of paper giving him a licence to roam freely. He carried it in his pocket in case he was stopped by the police.

Several people, including several police officers, suspected his workshop is just a front for his drug business inside the prison.

–Journalist Wayan Juniartha of the *Jakarta Post*

Being the jail's furniture tycoon had many perks. Twice a year he got generous chunks of time slashed off his sixteen-year sentence, as the prison system recognised his enterprising efforts to set up a vocational program in Hotel K. His illicit business was given a simple nod and a sly wink by the jail boss, who took fifty per cent of the cash earnings from the furniture business and had his pockets regularly filled with wads of drug money.

Iwan's largesse ensured the jail doors swung open freely to his family. His Dutch wife, Jolita, who shared a house behind the jail with their kids, two maids, a gardener and a driver, wandered through Hotel K daily, wearing her trademark slash of bright red lipstick. She knew the jail well after doing her own short stint for a drug possession charge. During her court case she was released from Hotel K on two hundred million rupiah ($40,000) bail and put under 'city arrest' before being acquitted four months later. But Hotel K had now virtually become an extension of her own backyard. Life as a jail wife wasn't easy.

She couldn't have failed to realise her husband fooled around; his pony-tailed good looks, charisma, power and money were a heady aphrodisiac for lonely, lusty female prisoners – who were always keen to fill the long boring and empty hours of jail life, in any way they could.

CHAPTER 7

TOUCHING PARADISE

My heart is crying baby. If I was in jail in fucking New York . . . but I'm in jail in Bali. I know that five minutes outside the front door I had the ocean . . .

For a surfer, it makes it worse that you are in Bali and the waves are very good right outside your front door. And you're in jail. I'm two minutes from my own restaurant, from my little swimming pool. From my friends, five minutes from Ku De Ta restaurant and I'm locked inside. I feel like I'm buried alive.

The crazy thing is that here in Bali we party every day, surf, eat, take a pill, go dancing. Outside the Kerobokan walls, it's Bali. If you go through that wall, it's hell; locked in a small room everyday from seven at night until eight in the morning, thirteen hours, tiny fucking room. Not a hot shower. You struggle to eat every day ... the most difficult thing in jail in this country is that you have to struggle every day for food. You don't eat the food they give you. I wouldn't feed my dog with it. Every day is a struggle.

– Ruggiero, Brazilian inmate

Brazilian inmate Ruggiero's soul was drying up. He had to get out of Hotel K and for weeks now he'd been working on a crafty escape plan. Each night in his cell he'd been loudly strumming his guitar and singing at the top of his lungs 'I know it's only rock'n'roll but I like it', over and over, like a maniac. He sang for hours every night; prisoners in other cells thought he was just a crazy Brazilian. But his raucous singing was deliberate. It was to mask the noise of his Italian cellmate, Ferrari, sawing through the eight steel bars on their cell window.

Since the moment of his arrest, the Brazilian civil engineer and surfer had only one focus – to get his life back. First he'd tried to pay his way to freedom. But when that failed, escape became his new obsession. He wasn't rash about it; he didn't want to fail. He was working it step by step, like an engineering job, which, in a way, it was. Getting to the point of sawing the bars took weeks of preparation. Step one had been to empty his cell of six local prisoners who couldn't be trusted to keep the plan quiet. It wasn't hard for the hot-blooded Latino to scare the hell out of them by acting like a crazed lunatic, screaming, bashing the walls and threatening to kill them all. He kept this up every night until all six asked to move cells.

I pretended to be a madman. I eventually got all six so shit scared of me that they left.

– Ruggiero

Next, he had to get the blade inside. Not too difficult, though the first attempt failed. Ruggiero had paid a friend to bring it to the jail, but he was busted when he rode up on his motorbike and handed it in a plastic bag to a Balinese inmate sweeping out the front. Drug transactions were routinely done in this way. But this day, a guard dozing on a wooden bench out the front saw it. He knew if he nabbed something illegal, it would mean a cash sling. So when he found out the blade was for a wealthy westerner, he confiscated it and went to talk to the Brazilian. For two million rupiah ($270) he agreed not to report it, but he still refused to let it inside. It was only a small setback for Ruggiero, as a few days later the local inmate simply used a more covert tactic, smuggling it in inside a papaya.

You know how Kerobokan is, it's a joke. You can bring an elephant inside if you want!

– Ruggiero

Ruggiero realised he needed an accomplice to help him cut the bars. When Italian Ferrari checked in, it was a lucky break. By chance, he cut metal bars as part of his job at home as a mechanic. Ferrari had been on his honeymoon in Bali when he bought a little straw of smack from a Balinese kid at the hotel pool. It was a police set-up. As soon as the kid left, officers pounced. It turned into an expensive honeymoon. Ferrari paid $70,000 and got just four months in Hotel K – enough time to help Ruggiero, and get out. So, for a daily fee of a couple of straws of smack, Ferrari began to saw his way through the bars. Night after night, Ruggiero and Ferrari would sing and saw in a rhythm. Before morning, they would glue the bars back into place and wait for lockup to continue the job.

Ruggiero spent about $18,000 on setting up his escape, investing in a false French passport, green contact lenses and a long-haired wig – 'I looked like a fucking freak but it was the only one my girlfriend could find'. He thought of everything. He'd even procured a syringe with snakebite anti-venom, in case he was bitten by a cobra in the grassy passage between the inner and outer jail walls. He had a long rope with large knots tied into it for footholds. He had a little hammer to smash the jagged glass stuck on the top of the wall, and a bent metal tray to throw over it like a saddle so he didn't get cut.

Ruggiero knew that once he got onto the wall and jumped into the real world again, his next move would be crucial. Many prisoners had been dragged back inside after their feet had hit free soil. Neglecting to plan the getaway was the flaw in countless failed escapes. Ruggiero had no intention of failing. Two friends would be outside on standby to phone him when the coast was clear. Parked just outside would be a tiger motorbike he'd already hired; the key hanging like a lucky charm around his neck. He planned to leap onto the seat of the motorbike and roar off down the potholed Kerobokan streets, riding for thirty minutes to a waiting boat at Turtle Island, which would whisk him across to Java. He'd already organised for an immigration official there to stamp his passport with an entry stamp and tourist visa, so he could leave Jakarta Airport without suspicion. It was the perfect plan.

Ruggiero had worked hard at this chance for freedom. He needed it. He was suffocating. His impulsive nature hadn't served him well inside Hotel K. He'd been badly beaten many times. Now, he believed, this was it. He felt sure he'd soon be inhaling the fresh air of real life and was convinced he'd be free for Christmas. Mentally, he already had one foot outside the jail. He felt the Bali gods were finally smiling down on him.

He had only one move left to make before he climbed out of his cell window in his wig, saddled up the wall with his metal tray and threw himself over it like a drunken cowboy. He needed a clip to hook over the wall, to which he'd attach his rope and haul himself up. So, very early one morning, after his cellblock had been unlocked but most inmates were still asleep, he slunk behind the medical clinic and started cutting a metal bar off the roof, which he could bend into a clip. He sawed almost right through and then snapped it off. This was a fatal mistake. The bar made a loud clunk. A local prisoner heard it and started screaming, '*Maling, Maling* [Satan, Devil]'.

One Balinese guy snitched on me. He was the biggest motorcycle thief there. The Balinese hate foreigners, they are so jealous. He was just a piece of shit. The guards came running. I got back to my cell and threw the bar outside the window and hid my hand phone. But they found the bar. They asked, 'What are you doing with this?' 'Oh, people are threatening me, it's for self-protection,' I told them. They didn't even know yet the window was cut because I made a beautiful work of gluing it, so they didn't know. But they said, 'You can kill someone with that bar'. That was enough. They put me in solitary.

– Ruggiero

An anguished and desperate Ruggiero was dragged to cell *tikus* after being bashed by the guards. He spent the first 48 hours without food or water, lying on the concrete floor of the small concrete box. It was hot, and he was hungry and hurting. They'd stripped him down to his underpants. The cell was dark, with only a small barred window high up on one side. The Brazilian surfer who loved life, wine, women and poetry wondered for the millionth time how his life had come to this.

I fell down from heaven to hell in a blink of an eye. I was so confused. I didn't even know if I was in jail. When I woke up I was like, 'Am I in jail?'.

– Ruggiero

Ruggiero had been living the good life for many years, following his dreams of surfing the best waves at the best beaches around the globe. The fast-talking dark-haired Latino was always a player; he quickly made friends, had many lovers, got married to and then divorced an Australian woman, and surfed endlessly. In Bali, he worked hard and played hard. He started to build a lucrative business renting and selling luxury villas, mostly in the expensive areas around Hotel K. Business was doing well, but, as part of the surfing culture, he dabbled in drugs. For years he'd subsidised his surfing by selling drugs on a small scale, usually by being a middleman and taking a cut. He'd done a week in jail in Brazil once, but paid his way out. Another time he'd been taken off a plane at Heathrow Airport and X-rayed when officials suspected him of carrying drugs, but they found nothing. He was no angel, but he'd just started to throw all his energy into his legitimate business when his world exploded.

I could never have dreamed what the gods of Bali had in store for me. I was driving my bike home after another amazingly beautiful sunset, wondering what to cook, when all of a sudden I was blocked by two bikes with four men, while a car with five more stopped me. Screaming, 'Police, police', they pushed me against the car and tried to start a body search. I was shocked, powerless, and they searched me, finding a small plastic container with 3.8 grams of hashish in my shorts pocket. I couldn't believe my eyes. They got euphoric, and started hugging each other, saying to me: 'You see? What is this? You're going to jail.'

– Ruggiero

Police raided his girlfriend's hotel room in Kuta, and allegedly found one hundred and forty-six grams of hashish, forty-three grams of cocaine and one green ecstasy pill. In court, Ruggiero disputed the amounts, claiming they were a lot smaller.

But he knew it wasn't about the evidence, but about getting the right lawyer. He knew his way around the system a little and called the best negotiator in town, a lawyer whose clients got sentences other prisoners only dreamed of. He told Ruggiero that for three hundred million rupiah ($43,000), he could have the ecstasy taken out and the other amounts made almost insignificant. But it wasn't to be. During their first meeting, the lawyer got a phone call. He had to leave, but would be back.

The lawyer didn't return for eighteen days, a period that felt like a lifetime to Ruggiero. As Ruggiero hadn't signed him up and his court date was getting closer, he made the rash decision to switch lawyers. He met with the new guy, was showered with promises of being free in six months, and signed him up on the spot for the same fee. The first lawyer, coincidentally, returned the next day, but it was too late.

Biggest mistake I ever did. I cancelled the good one, I kept the shit one. He kept coming to see me always saying, 'So far, so good'. He kept saying six months, six months. It might be a year if you're not lucky. Then he came to see me right before I got my sentence and he says, 'Listen, there's a problem.' I said, you promised me six months. He says, 'They don't want the money anymore and they're even considering asking for a life sentence'. I said, 'What? Sorry, can you repeat that?' He said, 'Life'. I felt the earth shake. 'So far, so good a couple of days ago, now life. Why you even talking to me, man? If I get a life sentence, you will get a death sentence because I'm going to kill you.' He still had the guts to say, 'You know what, if you pay two hundred million rupiah to one guy I know, we can get it down to five but it has to be by Tuesday'. He was a thief.

And the day finally came. Eleven years and $43,000 fine. It seemed to be an endless nightmare. What to do? Well, I decided: I have to escape.

– Ruggiero

Ruggiero had spent weeks imagining himself back in his old life; eating delicious food at fine restaurants with a bunch of friends, drinking a perfectly chilled bottle of wine, beautiful women, blazing sunsets. He imagined catching the perfect wave, slicing his board through the crystal-clear ocean waters, feeling as free as a bird and gazing into the horizon. This was his old life. He ached to get it back. But now it was just an unattainable fantasy in a parallel universe that was devastatingly close, just the other side of the Hotel K walls. Ruggiero knew all too well that the beauty was intangibly near, but all he could see was blackness.

His world was now the dark, claustrophobic concrete box of cell *tikus*; hot and airless with a sickening stench of stale piss. The only amenities were at one end of the cell: a filthy hole-in-the-ground toilet caked with dried shit, and a concrete trough full of slimy, putrid water with a cloud of mosquitoes hovering above it.

Cell tikus *was disgusting, disgusting. The toilet was filled up with dry shit. I found out why it's called cell* tikus *[rat cell] because the first time I went in I had to take a pee and I took it on the hole. The dry shit became soft and the rats came out of there, so in the dark I listened to them.*

– Ruggiero

This was Ruggiero's third time in cell *tikus*; his hot temper had landed him there twice before. Experience made it easier only in that he knew what to expect. The first time he was incarcerated in cell *tikus*, he went ballistic, gripping the barred door and smashing it hard back and forth, back and forth, back and forth until he ripped it off its hinges. He was angry and hurting. He punched the concrete walls over and over, screaming abuse at the top of his lungs: 'Motherfuckers, let me out! Fucking motherfuckers!'

The first night they put me there I broke the door, it was rusted, you know when iron gets rusty – eaten by the moisture of the ocean. I bend it back and forth hard. I was so furious. I broke the whole door. They beat me a bit more, they beat me a lot. I was screaming anything … any bad word you know in your life was part of it. Fuck, motherfucker, shit people, Muslim fanatic. I don't know how many times I punched the wall, but I hurt my hand, I was a madman, I was totally possessed. I was scary.

The first 48 hours, I didn't eat. I didn't drink water. I refused to eat the stuff they gave me. And then, on the third day, I see Benoit … bad guy Benoit … a huge black guy from Cameroon. He was my best friend … I hear the voice of that gorilla, 'I'm going to kill everyone; you have to give him food'. And then he managed to get there, he pushed the guards and then he opened the door and gave me some water, apples, a plastic bag because I refused to go to the toilet in the hole. I used the plastic bag. But the thing is: where am I going to get rid of it? I go like this with my foot against the wall for leverage and throw it out the small window up high. The funny thing was, the plastic bag I threw landed right on the edge of the mosque and the shit was flying into the mosque.

– Ruggiero

Hurling a bag of shit out the window each day gave him fleeting sense of rebellion, but mostly it saved him from the stench of his own waste as he languished in the cell. Days and nights passed in such a blur that Ruggiero lost track of the time he'd spent in there. There was virtually nothing to do, though some days he'd do a marathon burst of one thousand sit-ups. Finally, after being in there for a long stretch of time, a guard opened the door to release him back into the jail. He was like a man taking his first steps after being in a deep coma, walking out dazed and confused, squinting hard as the blinding rays of light pierced his eyes. It was Christmas Eve.

The next morning started off cheerfully enough when he was called to his first visit in weeks, to enjoy a heavily spiked fruit salad with a couple of friends. But he was still edgy and angry; he desperately needed the whisky to numb his frayed nerves. He was still being punished; the only difference was that he was now in an ordinary cell twenty-four hours a day and was allowed out to visits again. Unfortunately, they hadn't returned him to his former cell, where the cut bars remained tantalisingly undiscovered. Instead, he'd been thrown in a cell with two local prisoners; one of whom was notorious for his grizzly crimes of digging up graves and stealing from the dead.

After the visit, Ruggiero returned to his cell a bit drunk from the fruit salad. It was good. Being drunk helped to blot out the world. He was ready to plummet further into the familiar comfort of an alcoholic stupor after buying a crate of cold beer from another prisoner. But, already fractious, pissed and bitterly unhappy, his hot temper flared when he discovered his mobile phone, which he'd managed to retrieve and slip under his mattress, had been stolen while he was out. His knew the grave robber had swiped it. He was outraged by his own situation, and the fact that this pathetic little piece of shit was walking around with his phone made his blood boil further. The grave robber was standing outside the window, and Ruggiero turned and screamed abuse, 'I'm going to kill you, give me back my fucking phone!' The grave robber threw back a taunting response, simply telling the foreigner to pass him a cold beer. Ruggiero went nuts. 'I'm going to kill you. You come in here, you will be locked in here later and I will kill you,' he screamed, grabbing a stick and stabbing it through the bars, trying to gauge out his eye. He missed. But the scene had been set; they were both ready to fight.

Just before the 5.30 pm lockup, the grave digger entered the cell accompanied by a back-up crew. He was not going to let the aggressive Brazilian attack first. At least ten men armed with pieces of wood and a solid wooden bench circled Ruggiero, then tore into him, kicking and slamming the wooden bench into his head and knocking him off his feet. His attempts to defend himself were futile. He was bloody and bruised on the floor, but the beating continued. They kicked him, and stomped on his face until *tamping* Ketut Dana turned up and called them off, undoubtedly saving Ruggiero's life.

That night was a massacre. They demolished me. They broke my lips and my nose; they broke my head in two places. It was so fast. They were using wood, punches, whatever. But the worst was the guy with a solid wooden bench. It broke my nose here and here. It was very bad.

– Ruggiero

A guard told a couple of prisoners to carry Ruggiero to an isolation cell in another block, where he was soon lying in a pool of his own blood. His head and body were bleeding profusely. In his semi-conscious state he knew he was badly hurt, and feebly called out that he needed a doctor. The jail boss came across to the cell but simply stood at the door and mocked him.

Asshole. He didn't give a fuck about us if we die. I was in a small cell lying on the floor, full of blood and he says, 'Doctor, yeah, I'll bring a doctor'. Then he sat in the block, smoking a cigarette and laughing.

Did a doctor come?

Course not.

– Ruggiero

A month later, the Brazilian made headlines for his audacious escape attempt. It had taken that long for the guards to discover that the bars in his former cell were being held in place by glue. Ruggiero copped another beating but this time the guards didn't have to work too hard to hurt him, as his injuries from the last round were not yet healed. As the cell *tikus* punishment cells were full, Ruggiero was put in the maximum-security tower with the terrorists Amrozi, Mukhlas and Imam Samudra, who had been sentenced to death for their part in the Bali bombings in 2002.

Ruggiero could not have been further from his old life.

You put a lion in a small cage and don't feed him well; he's going to become an angry lion. That's what happened to me.

– Ruggiero

CHAPTER 8
THE WOMEN'S BLOCK

'Nita, Nita, somebody drink insecticide,' anguished voices carried across Block W from Room 9. All one hundred women were locked up for the night, padlocked in their cells. 'Nita, help!' The desperate cries easily reached Nita's cell as she settled in for the night on her mattress, watching television. She yelled back, 'I'll call security,' as she quickly grabbed her mobile phone.

Moments earlier, in Room 9, 30-year-old inmate Dani had stumbled out of the small washroom flopping like a rag doll with vomit pouring out of her mouth. Instantly she had the attention of her nine cellmates, who looked up to see Dani's eyes rolling back and her legs collapsing as she crashed onto the concrete floor. Panic hit. Some of the women curled up sobbing. Some started praying feverishly. Others called out to Nita as they leaped from their thin mattresses, surrounding Dani, clutching her trembling hands, whispering, 'Don't die, don't die'.

One girl ran into the bathroom and saw two empty bottles of poison; one of insecticide spray and another of Vixal porcelain floor cleaner. Dani had drunk the contents of both. She needed a hospital fast, but it would be at least an hour before the guards arrived. The keys to Block W were held outside the jail after 4.30 pm lockup. The time it took for the guards to collect the keys, return to the jail and unlock the women's block varied between one to three hours.

Tension filled every cell as the women listened to the sobbing and hysteria escalating in Room 9. No-one could do a thing. They were all trapped. They just had to wait as their fellow inmate's life teetered on the brink. A bleak hour passed before a sound outside the steel door finally signalled the guards had arrived. Two men strode in and walked directly across to Nita's cell and unlocked it. Nita burst out and ran like the wind down the path between the cells, ignoring the dozens of distraught faces pressing against the bars. As a *tamping* prisoner, Nita had dealt with several overdoses and was the most qualified to save Dani.

Once inside Room 9, Nita knelt down on the concrete floor beside her, snatching a nearby T-shirt to wipe the vomit off her face. She was unconscious, but still retching and gurgling a stream of frothy vomit from the corners of her mouth. Nita knew it was vital to get coconut milk into the woman's stomach. But it would be difficult as Dani's mouth was almost shut. Nita stuck two fingers between Dani's teeth and turned them sideways to prise her mouth open. But it was hopeless – her jaw was too stiff and Nita merely got a nasty bite as Dani involuntarily bit down hard. Her body was now shaking and convulsing uncontrollably. Several cellmates were crouching around, trying to pin the thrashing limbs to the floor. Nita tried to pour the coconut milk into the slit of her mouth. It was useless. The milk just spilled across her face. Dani needed a doctor fast.

The guards stood around idly watching as a male *tamping*

ran in with a stretcher. Nita and a few of the inmates lifted Dani onto it. With the help of the male prisoners who'd turned up, Nita carried the stretcher out of the cell, down the path past the locked cages of women now clinging to the bars, yelling, 'What's happened? What's happened?'. Nita kept walking. The guards trailed alongside saying nothing. They hurried across the jail lawns to deliver the stretcher to an ambulance waiting out the front of the jail. It was the last time they'd see Dani. She was pronounced dead on arrival at Bali's Sanglah Hospital.

An affair of the heart had caused Dani to drink poison. She'd felt betrayed and abandoned by a cheating husband. His visits had ceased and he refused even to bring in their two young sons after confessing to being with another woman who he planned to marry. It had only been a few months since Dani was arrested for stealing forty-two million rupiah ($5600) from a bank where she worked. But her case was still being heard in court and she had no idea when she'd be free.

She had started to spiral into a deep depression. Her life outside had vaporised. She'd lost her husband, and was facing years behind bars, and day and night there was nothing to do but dwell on her problems. Hurt, fury and frustration tore her apart. When Dani's husband turned up the day after her death to collect her personal items, he asked Nita what she'd drunk and what time it happened. Nita told him and asked if he planned to re-marry. He admitted he did.

The loss of Dani created a sombre mood in Block W. They were all shocked, but also knew it could easily have been any one of them – collapsing into a lonely, dark hole was something they all understood. In jail, hurt and loss were amplified. Snatched from life, friends, family and other support networks, the women were very fragile, their emotions more volatile than ever. Living among so many could be terrifyingly lonely. Suicide attempts were common.

Drug runner Schapelle Corby is on suicide watch in hospital. The 30-year-old lost 12 kilograms in four weeks and suffered hallucinations and paranoia following the failure of her final appeal, doctors and her mother revealed yesterday. Corby had to be taken from Bali's Kerobokan Jail on Friday to the international wing of Sanglah Hospital in Denpasar suffering depression.

– *Sun Herald,* 22 June 2008

'The patient Corby has suffered a total mental disturbance,' Dr Leli Setyawati said. 'Corby must be treated for one or two weeks. If there is no development, then the treatment can be extended further. But if it reaches a critical level, we must consider moving her to a mental institution.'

– *Sunday Herald Sun,* 22 June 2008

Australian inmate Schapelle had been fighting off depression since she'd entered Hotel K five years earlier. She'd desperately tried to stay positive, forcing herself to wear make-up, dress neatly and continually replace negative thoughts with positive ones. But it was exhausting and lonely. The long, dark stretch of twenty years in jail was terrifying. She'd been caught at Ngurah Rai Airport with over four kilograms of marijuana in her boogie board bag. She swore she did not put it in there. She swore she was innocent. But she lost her final appeal. In quick succession, she also lost her beloved father and stepfather to cancer. She didn't get to say goodbye. It broke her heart. The loss of hope threatened her fragile grip on sanity.

After spending two weeks at Sanglah Hospital, she was returned to Hotel K on heavy medication. But with only fifty cents a year spent on each prisoner's healthcare, she got little medical help once back inside. Her family did what they could from the outside, but they could not ensure she took the medication. Other inmates, such as Australian Renae Lawrence, dispensed her pills, but they all had problems of their own and were unreliable. Schapelle quickly slipped back into the same poorly state she'd been in before she went to Sanglah. She grew disorientated and deeply paranoid, hearing voices and seeing things. Regularly at night she'd imagine someone spying on her through a hole in the ceiling, and would try to climb up to look. Subtitles on TV or writing on a magazine cover, she believed, were secret and cryptic messages sent especially for her to decode. She would spend hours manically trying to work them out. She swung from this hyper manic state to being almost catatonic, barely able to speak or look after herself.

On her worst days, the jail boss let her sister, Mercedes, go into Block W to wash and feed her sibling. She'd spoon food into Schapelle's mouth like she was a baby, even physically moving her jaw until Schapelle remembered she was meant to be eating and started to chew.

On the brink again, Schapelle soon returned to Sanglah Hospital for her second stint within a year. She spent those days like a child, clutching a doll and resting her head on her mum's lap. She was improving. But after twelve days, authorities unexpectedly arrived late at night to take her back. Schapelle and her mother, Ros, were asleep. Schapelle woke up and became hysterical. She flew into the toilet and locked it. Crying and desperate not to go back to her pitiful concrete cell, she slashed her wrists and arms with a compact mirror. Ros was distraught.

There was nothing she could do to help her baby girl. When TV cameras started pushing into the room to film, Ros lashed out screaming, aware she was being filmed, but unable to control her frustration and anger over her total lack of power to care for her daughter. A short time later, Schapelle walked out to a car, wearing her pyjamas and clutching a pillow.

Without proper monitoring, Schapelle slipped back to her psychotic state almost as soon as she returned to jail. It was a vicious cycle. She couldn't get better in Hotel K. She was back to hearing voices and was found trying to climb the water tower. She spent her days dosed up on psychiatrist prescribed anti-psychotic pills, often walking around in a daze, confused about where she was, thinking she could walk out and go home. But freedom was still a long way off. Her first five years inside Hotel K had already changed her indescribably. The vibrant girl she once was had vanished and she was losing her will to live. She twice sliced up her arms in suicide attempts or cries for help. She didn't care who had to clean up the blood. Her desperate family live in fear she will die in Hotel K. They will keep fighting to get her clemency, and to get her out of Hotel K before they lose her altogether.

Life in Hotel K was very hard. It was not unusual for women inmates to become mentally unstable from the sheer hell of living in Block W; the ceaseless noise, the fighting, the lack of sleep and filthy conditions.

Ketut Suparmini, 20, really felt the pain of living behind Kerobokan Prison bars. Not because she was badly treated by the guards but because she was fed up with her cellmates. 'I'm fed up. There are good people and bad people in there. When I had a meal, my rice was snatched by another woman convict,' she revealed yesterday.

Ketut who has spent the past two months in prison for stealing gold jewellery now has to lie in a Sanglah hospital bed. Last week she took

16 paracetamol tablets at once before she became weak and vomited. The married woman was rushed to hospital and arrived at Sanglah at 6.27 pm.

She was caught stealing a gold necklace belonging to her husband's friend and was reported to the police. She was then arrested, and after an interrogation, Suparmini was put in the cell. She said that her husband had never visited since. Plus, she had to face other prisoners' behaviour which often gave her headaches and stressed her. She was placed in a cell with 7 other women inside. Four of them were inside in connection with drugs cases, two were involved in a murder case and another was [inside] for killing a baby. 'I couldn't cope and it made me stressed,' said the young, rather beautiful woman.

– *Denpost*, 11 November 2003

When female inmates checked into Hotel K, they walked down the concrete paths, through the gardens and past the palm trees, the temple and the tower, to a large steel door twenty-five metres across from the tennis court. Behind it was their new world: Block W. It comprised ten small concrete cells, usually home to approximately one hundred women, despite being designed for only thirty-nine. Four of the cells were for inmates whose cases were still being heard in court. These had fluorescent lights that stayed on all night, and high ceilings to prevent suicides. They were always stinking hot, particularly as the ventilation was poor, with no windows at the back of the cells and so no air moving through. The other six cells each had a switch to turn off the lights, and a small window at the back. This created a bit of a breeze, but had a downside, as the open sewers directly at the back of the cells created a sickening stench, especially when they stewed in the hot afternoon sun.

For westerners, the lack of hygiene was always a nasty shock. The hole-in-the-ground toilets regularly blocked and overflowed, spilling sewage onto the floor. Some locals would just squelch around in the faeces with bare feet. Several were peasants from tiny villages, serving a few months for crimes as trivial as stealing one sachet of coffee or one apple. They'd lived primitive lives and knew nothing about cleanliness or hygiene, often horrifying their cellmates with a gross lack of decorum: urinating and defecating on the bathroom floor; bleeding menstrual blood directly onto the cell floor, refusing to use pads or wear underpants. Some almost never washed their clothes or bodies, causing disturbing body odour in the cells.

After developing calluses from weeks of sleeping on a concrete floor in the police cells, one improvement for new prisoners was having a thin mattress. Poor inmates unable to afford a mattress still slept on bare concrete or threw down a sarong. Hotel K provided nothing but the four walls of the cell. Everything, from essentials like soap, detergent and drinking water, to emptying out the septic tanks, was paid for out of prisoners' pockets. The poor simply went without or depended on the charity of others, or earned cash by massaging wealthier prisoners or washing clothes for them.

Those with money brightened their lives with contraband luxuries in their cells, like televisions, DVD players, mobile phones, and single gas burners to boil water, cook simple meals or heat heroin, although the guards often swept it all up in random cell searches. But aside from the drugs, which could potentially involve a new case in court, the guards would simply sell this all back to the prisoners within a couple of weeks.

Primarily functioning as a men's jail meant the women in Hotel K were treated as second-class citizens, rarely allowed out of their block and banned from the privileges of playing tennis and walking freely around the jail. Their sexuality was an issue. The authorities didn't want the women inciting the men sexually. Doing a weekly aerobics class or yoga session in the hall, walking across the jail to a visit, collecting mail or walking to the little canteen or church were their only permitted outings.

As in the men's block, there was no segregation between cold-blooded killers, card sharks and callgirls; no lines were drawn between a woman who stole an apple to feed her hungry baby and a woman who pre-meditated the stabbing death of her husband's mistress. The huge divide between petty crimes, like stealing a bag of prawn crackers or playing cards at the kitchen table, and dark crimes, such as assisting in illegal abortions on eight-month-old foetuses, was invisible. They all slept side by side, so tightly squeezed in that they often woke with their limbs entwined.

In Block W there were many callgirls who'd been swept up in police stings at karaoke bars in Kuta and Denpasar. Many of the girls had deep resentment towards the police who'd used their services, asked them to procure a couple of ecstasy tablets, then turned around and snapped on handcuffs. Others were angry at being harassed by police for sex in exchange for a lighter sentence. While some refused, others acquiesced but were left bitterly disappointed when their sentences were read out in court.

Police at Poltabes *said, 'Do you want to have sex with me, we can drop the charges?' She agreed and was taken out of* Poltabes *and had sex with the policeman . . . But her sentence was not cut. She got the maximum of five years.*

– Elsa, inmate, talking about her friend

One policeman asked me for sex in a flirty way. He asked in a very nice way. He wasn't scary.

Was he serious?

Yes. He asked many, many times during the two months I was in police cells. He told me sex would reduce my sentence. I said no and finally he stopped asking me.

– Wanda, Indonesian inmate

Block W was a highly charged environment, tempers fraying and snapping at the smallest things. Within a split second, a slow afternoon could turn; two girls suddenly slashing each other with broken glass bottles or attacking with a pair of scissors over the theft of 10,000 rupiah ($1.30), a bowl of rice or a bucket of water. Or even just over one of them coughing.

Often in the centre of the storm was fiery Timorese prisoner Sonia Gonzales Miranda, nicknamed Black Monster. She was notorious in Hotel K for her fighting, her psychotic behaviour and for regularly being locked up for months in cell *tikus*. She tore around the jail, pulsing with energy, instigating spats and catfights wherever she went. If someone refused to give her a cigarette, she'd pinch their breasts. But usually she didn't need a motive. Her fuse just blew anyway. She always managed to break the daily monotony.

When one afternoon a new prisoner gingerly walked into her cell for the first time, Sonia sprang like a cat off the floor and started strangling her. Other girls jumped up to unclasp Black Monster's fingers from the woman's neck. As they pulled her off she went nuts, flailing her fists around and yelling like a lunatic. A male guard walked in and started slapping her around the head, before dragging her out by the hair and down to the guard's table. It was like a game to Sonia. The second he let go, she sprinted off, laughing maniacally. He angrily tore after her, snatching her by the shoulders within a couple of strides.

He whacked her a few times and led her back. She enjoyed creating a show like this. All the women stopped to watch. The guards sat discussing what to do with Black Monster. The punishment cells were all booked up. They decided to isolate her in her own cell for a few weeks, expelling her cellmates and dispersing them into the eight other cramped cells, excluding Mexican model Clara's paid-for ninth cell.

Sonia craved attention and didn't mind disrupting everyone's life to get it. During the night she'd suddenly let out a long, piercing scream and thrash the cell door back and forth, just to wake up as many women as possible. Angry screams telling her to shut up would tear back until the entire block was awake, and abusive yelling was coming from every cell along the path, often accompanied by the loud din of saucepans being banged against the bars. It could last all night, until the fury exploded into a fight in the morning.

One such fight broke out on the eve of a court hearing. Sonia started screaming abuse at a girl, Dewi, a few cells down. The pair fought often and had a joint date in court the next day. Dewi stood at her barred door, yelling, 'I'll get you in the morning, Black Monster!' Black Monster yelled back, 'I'll get you, Dewi!' Their inane slanging match continued for hours.

In the morning, when a guard opened Black Monster's cell, the fight blew up. The guard grabbed Sonia by the arm to take her straight out of the block before a fight started. But Dewi was already crouched near the door. As Sonia walked past, they both spat abuse. Sonia snapped. She broke the guard's grip, snatched a broken glass bottle from the ground nearby and threw it at Dewi. She missed, but the fight was on. They were both dancing around each other with jagged shards of broken glass. A crowd gathered to watch the action – it was better than breakfast television. Black

Monster didn't let her audience down. She dumped the glass and charged at Dewi, knocking her to the ground. They rolled around, tearing out clumps of each other's hair. The guards pulled them apart. Sonia broke their grip again, and hurled Dewi to the ground for the grand finale. Dewi crashed hard, twisting her wrist and crying out in agony. As the guards yanked Sonia away, she turned back to smirk at the crowd. She didn't go to court that day. She was locked back into her isolation cell.

If Hotel K issued membership cards, Sonia's would be platinum. For years she'd been checking in and out. When she wasn't a guest, she'd return as a visitor to see a friend, usually dressed up in her latest clubbing outfit. She couldn't stay away. One afternoon she was even arrested during a visit. She sat talking to a friend on the floor of the busy visiting room. She was working as a dancer at a nightclub, and was casually flicking through photos of herself dancing and of her new Spanish boyfriend. The relaxed scene turned when three uniformed police officers briskly walked across and snapped handcuffs on Sonia. She went psychotic. Everyone in the visiting area turned to watch. She was thrashing her body about as the police dragged her out with her high heels scraping along the ground. The police had been looking for the Black Monster since the day before, when a New Zealand tourist had reported she'd stolen his money and mobile phone from his hotel room.

Sonia was unrepentant. The time she was arrested in Hotel K's visiting room would lead to her sixteenth incarceration in the jail. She'd do stints of three or four months here and there, and then a longer stay. But she clearly wanted to get caught. She never bothered trying to conceal her identity or cover her tracks, despite her intelligence – which revealed itself in her skill and ingenuity at luring men and in her fluent English.

But her arrests were always a spectacle. She fought ferociously, once even stabbing a policeman.

The arrest went well, although at the beginning Sonia refused to be taken to the station. She tried to run away several times when the police put her in the car. They had to call the station for backup. When the policeman Nyendra entered the car Sonia suddenly attacked and stabbed him in the neck with a knife. He was caught off guard and pulled away. Luckily other officers turned up at the scene and rushed him to hospital. Nyendra was treated and had to have several stitches. They didn't know where the knife came from. During questioning Sonia who is known at Kerobokan as Black Monster, admitted to stabbing the policeman.

– *Denpost,* July 2003

Sonia's crimes were as audacious as she was. She started her career stealing tourists' bags from the beach, and slowly graduated to poisoning men's drinks in bars, until they were so bleary eyed she could slip her hand into their pockets and steal their wallets. She went from that to meeting western men in bars around Kuta, going back to their hotel – ensuring the receptionists saw her – and sleeping with them. Then she'd either drug them and steal their stuff or return the next day, ask the receptionist for *her* room key and then empty the room of jewellery, watches, mobile phones, cameras, cash and credit cards. While her victim was still out enjoying the Bali beaches, she'd be splurging online with their credit cards. A drunken night of holiday sex with Sonia Gonzales could be very costly.

The accused, Sonia Miranda Gonzales, 22, really is daring and doesn't repent. The very dark skinned, East Timorese woman, nicknamed Black Monster, is also very cunning. She's at least been in and out of prison four times for stealing tourist's belongings in hotels. Black Monster is willing to sleep with those tourists before stealing their stuff ... It was revealed during the trial that the big lipped woman's victim was a foreigner called Jorge Salasar. The accused carried out the act on May 8th around 10 pm in room 3027 at Wina Hotel. She came to the front desk asking for the key to room 3027. The front desk staff gave her the key without suspicion because she was often seen with Jorge Salasar who stayed in that room. It was also revealed that the accused had spent the night before in his room.

– *Denpost*, August 2002

According to the public prosecutor, other than becoming a 'frequent prisoner' the act of the accused has disturbed the circle of hotel owners as she often stole at hotels with the target of in-house guests. Her last operation was carried out on August 20 at Panorama Cottage II, Kuta. The accused smartly posed as a tour guide. She came to the hotel and borrowed the room key of Joel Tarming, a Swedish tourist. Strangely, the front office staff believed her due to her sweet lips. With the key in hand, the accused Sonia Gonzales freely took the belongings of Joel Tarming in the form of electronic devices and 17 million rupiah cash. The accused delivered the key back to the hotel receptionist and casually left the hotel.

– *Denpost*, December 2001

Sonia was a curious dichotomy; charming and charismatic one minute, but like a deranged lunatic the next. She dressed in trendy outfits, styling herself with flair; she was rarely seen in the same clothes twice, thanks to the sizeable wardrobe she'd bring into Hotel K, most of it bought online with stolen credit cards. She'd also check in with a full makeup kit, turning part of her cell into a theatrical dressing room. If Sonia had been a movie star, she would have been paparazzi manna, biting into every banal day with a new edgy story. But she was a star only on the Kerobokan stage, acting out daily scenes to give everyone a bit of a show. Her antics were tireless. She'd abuse someone, then return with her guitar and sing them a song she'd written in apology. When Schapelle Corby was sentenced to twenty years, she spent months yelling out, 'Ha ha, Corby, you got twenty years'. She'd bang her head with a rock until it bled, she'd start screaming for no reason, and she often made feeble suicide attempts. But instead of flashbulbs, she got flashes of Nita's coconut milk splashing down her face.

Sonia wants to kill herself for a trick only, just to get some attention from the security. One time I had to call security for help when she drank Rinso. Another time she tried to kill herself by hanging but a girl had already grabbed her around the waist by the time she kicked over the chair she was standing on.

– Nita

The afternoon she performed her chilling trapeze act, she stepped up on a chair inside the cell toilet, put a noose around her neck, then stood as still as a statue, waiting for an inmate to glimpse her in the pose. Not until a girl frantically ran in and grabbed her around the waist, did she kick away the chair. But her well-choreographed stunt turned unexpectedly dicey. The girl wasn't strong and Sonia started slipping through her arms, the noose tightening around her neck. Screams fast drew a crowd. Girls helped to hold her as someone slashed the plastic cord. Sonia was safe but her neck was laced with deep red welts that she proudly showed off around the jail for the next few days, like designer bling.

But drinking Rinso was her more regular thing. The catalyst one morning was simply a guard refusing to let her out of Block W to go to the visiting area; standard practice if a prisoner hadn't been called to a visit. Sonia turned on a tantrum like a two year old. Used to her psychotic behaviour, the guards just sent her to clean the drains. As payback, she drank a couple of mouthfuls of Rinso and started vomiting. Yells for Nita Ramos preceded the ritual pouring of coconut milk. The guards' counterblow was to ground Sonia in Block W for three months. She upped the ante by drinking a few more mouthfuls of Rinso after lockup. There was the usual insane wait for keys before Nita patiently dispensed her antidote, yet again. Sonia was still punished. During her three months stuck in Block W, female inmates brought her food, drinks and magazines, and Nita bought her cigarettes in return for massages. Sonia had an uncanny ability to win sympathy despite antagonising every other inmate.

One morning, after a three-month stint in cell *tikus*, three guards arrived to release her back into Block W. They were ready for her inevitable angry spit. But when guard Herman opened the door, Black Monster was quiet as a mouse. When his eyes adjusted to the dark, he saw why. She had hanged herself. Three weeks earlier, a popular male inmate had also been found dead in a toilet cubicle. This looked like a copycat suicide. Black Monster was strung up in an elaborate noose, her head flopped to one side, her tongue hanging out of her mouth. She'd finally done it. Herman went in to grab her. But, just as his hand touched her, she sprang at him like a tormented ghost, screaming and clutching at him with tentacle-like arms. Herman flew back against the wall. The other two guards ran off screaming. Sonia was laughing as she casually untied the noose and pulled the cord up over her head. The guard sat on the floor, gasping for breath. The stunt had worked perfectly. Sure, she'd do a bit more time in purgatory, but it was worth it. Now she'd be the talk of the jail.

That girl is one of a kind. You ask if I've ever been afraid of anyone. Among all the men in Kerobokan, I've never been afraid of nobody, but I would be afraid to share a room with Sonia. She made me shit scared. I would be shit scared to share a room with her.

Why?

Because she might stab me. I would never be able to relax and sleep with Sonia in my room, she's a lunatic. She loves it in Kerobokan. Everyone is shit scared of her. The only woman, I think, who would face her is Australian Renae Lawrence. Renae would hit her harder but she would come and stab Renae. She is mean and she's crazy. That's the kind of person I'm afraid of.

– Ruggiero

CHAPTER 9

THE BLUE ROOM

Everyone is fucking everyone in every corner they can find.

– Mick, Australian inmate

Black Monster was unusually cooperative and solemn as the guards escorted her across the jail back to Block W after another long stint in cell *tikus.* She quietly slipped in through the steel door, almost unnoticed, with her head hanging and her eyes staring at the ground. Her subdued re-entry to Block W was because she'd got the shock of her life. She'd just been told she was seven weeks pregnant.

Inside Block W, the escorting female guard walked along the gravel path between the cells, breaking Sonia's news as she asked who would take her into their cell. Black Monster trailed forlornly behind. No-one wanted her. She was too much of a headache. Finally, one cell agreed to take her in. The cellmates knew that life would be edgier and more disruptive with Sonia, but cell leader Trisna felt sorry for her. Black Monster was soon herself again, playing up the pregnancy to get attention, relishing the jail-wide speculation about who the father was and where the conception had happened.

I would rather cut my cock off … I wouldn't do it. I would never get her pregnant.

– Ruggiero

The cellmates spent many nights stroking Sonia's belly, praying the baby would have a better life. But as her pregnancy progressed, she became more stressed. She was scared of giving birth and worried about who would take care of the baby, as she had nowhere to live and no family in Bali. Late one night, two months before she was due, she cried out in pain. Nobody thought Black Monster was faking it this time. She lay on a dirty mattress with her knees up in the birthing position, clutching at her stomach, gasping for breath between long, bloodcurdling screams. Tears poured across her temples and down the sides of her face. The cellmates screamed for help. They all thought she was going to have the baby that night. But the doctor finally arrived, gave her some medicine and settled her down.

Sonia gave birth in a local hospital two months later, two weeks after finishing her sentence and checking out. A few weeks later, she returned to visit her friends in Hotel K and to show off her tiny infant. Jaws dropped as prisoners took a look at Black Monster's baby girl. She was beautiful, with milky white skin and curly blonde hair. Sonia's stints in jail had always created talk, but this inspired frenzied gossip. Who the hell was the father? The intense intrigue was fuelled by Black Monster's own stories. As the baby was being cared for by French inmate Michael's mum, she convinced everyone that Michael was the father. Then her story changed to him being Brazilian drug trafficker Marco, the most wanted man in Indonesia. He was big news. He'd run like a crazy man out of Jakarta Airport when customs officials discovered thirteen kilograms of pure Peruvian cocaine hidden in his hang-glider frame. Sonia had never met him. But she now claimed he was the father of her child.

The true identity of the father was eventually revealed in a late-night drunken confessional between Australian inmate Mick and Scottish prisoner Robert. It transpired that Robert had simply grabbed some quick dirty sex when he'd been locked in an isolation cell in the tower next to Black Monster. A guard had come in and asked, 'You want some fun, Robert?' He was drunk. He did. The guard unlocked his cell, then stood back to watch. Black Monster was still locked up in her cell. She stripped, bent forwards and through the bars she and Robert had sex and conceived a beautiful baby girl.

Robert knew the baby was his. One night he told me, 'I rooted her'. I said 'What?' 'It's my baby.' How? I asked. 'I was drunk. Guards say, "Do you want to have fun, Robert?"' But the next morning, Robert said, 'Don't tell anybody, don't tell anybody'. He already had two kids in Scotland. The baby's mouth shape, the eyes, and the curly blonde hair were all like Robert. I gave the adoptive parents a photo of Robert and said, 'In case one day the kid asks about the father, this is him'.

– Mick

Within a couple of months, Black Monster was back inside Hotel K for biting a woman at a nightclub who was apparently trying to steal her new European boyfriend. She took her baby girl from Michael's mum and with her into Hotel K, where there was no shortage of clucky females. But she changed her mind after a few days, and sold the baby to an inmate's family for four bags of *shabu.*

As time passed, Black Monster did nothing to dispel the myths about the father. His true identity stayed an unusually well-kept secret inside Hotel K. Robert seemed to have a unique power to scare Black Monster into submissive silence, although the ongoing intrigue suited her as well. But most prisoners had accepted the little girl was Frenchman Michael's baby.

Pregnancies didn't usually provoke this much interest, as inmates often conceived, some giving birth and keeping the baby for a while, but many aborting their foetuses by self-inflicting rough daily stomach massages. Some girls, especially those who'd worked as callgirls in Denpasar and Kuta karaoke clubs, had shredded their wombs from so many brutal home abortions. One 22-year-old prisoner regularly awoke screaming in pain as her pureed insides started to slip out. Her cellmates knew the drill. Two held her arms and stroked her forehead, while another pushed a foot up between her legs to stop anything leaking out. She'd seen the jail doctor, who advised her that he could do nothing, but suggested it might help to wear a tight girdle. This seemed to do the trick temporarily but her insides were irreparably damaged.

Hotel K was a sex-crazed little world, despite a belief among inmates that the drinking water was spiked with libido-lowering drugs. A walk through the jail could be like walking onto the set of *Boogie Nights*, with prisoners giving blow jobs up against trees or fences, thrusting away behind Iwan's furniture-building workshop or in the visiting room. Nowhere was sacrosanct. Prisoners banged away in the church toilet, the temple toilets, the library toilet, the cells, the medical clinic and even in the boss's office. If the drinking water was spiked, the dose wasn't strong enough.

When the jail boss unexpectedly turned up one Sunday afternoon, he walked into his office and straight into a porn show. A male prisoner and a woman were thrashing away under his desk. 'Fuck off, get out,' the inmate yelled without looking up, angry for the intrusion because he'd paid 50,000 rupiah ($7) for privacy. The boss walked to his desk, his black lace-up boots stopping right next to the prisoner's head. The prisoner looked up, shocked. Suddenly the pair was scrambling for their clothes. The woman ran straight out the door, grabbing awkwardly at the sides of her dress as she tried to pull it down over her breasts. The prisoner was made to stay and explain. He stood uncomfortably in his underpants, clutching his shirt and shorts in a bundle against his chest.

He told the boss that the woman was his wife, who he rarely saw; they were lonely and missed each other desperately. The boss was lenient. He bellowed at the prisoner for fucking in his office, and then dismissed him with a casual wave of his arm, sending him back to his cell without punishment. But the boss soon heard he'd been conned. The woman was a hooker. The prisoner was sent to cell *tikus* for a few days until he was able to organise some cash to pay a guard to let him out.

As with drugs, mobile phones and plasma televisions, sex was officially not allowed in Hotel K. But this did nothing to stifle the prolific fucking; it simply forced prisoners to use their naturally devious instincts so they didn't get caught. Some simply waited until the more amenable guards were on duty so they could sling them some cash. Many did it at the changing of the guards at midday, when there was a ten-minute blind spot in the supervision. It was a frenetic ten minutes of lunchtime fucking. But if prisoners got caught in compromising clinches by strict guards, they could suffer a brutal bashing.

One afternoon, female inmate Komang got a pass out of Block W by telling a female guard she needed to talk to the jail security chief about her case. In truth, she'd just got a text message from her boyfriend in the men's block, saying he'd be waiting for her in the music room if she could get out. Their little rendezvous started well; they met, stripped and started having sex. But it ended badly. The female guard noticed Komang was still not back in Block W twenty minutes later and went searching for her. She quickly realised she'd been conned. No-one had seen Komang go to the offices. The guard started to panic, thinking Komang had escaped on her watch.

She instigated a jail-wide search. It didn't take long to find Komang in the music room. She was naked and alone. Her boyfriend had abandoned her. He'd dived though a window into the adjoining kitchen as soon as he heard someone tampering with the door handle. Guards grabbed the naked girl, dragged her outside and bashed her, smashing her in the face over and over. For the next week, Komang sat sobbing in Block W, with two black eyes and a bloated face. Her boyfriend had also been badly bashed after he was caught running naked through the kitchen.

The impact of making sex illegal in Hotel K was to turn it into a booming illicit business. Behind the backs of stricter guards, the sex industry in the jail thrived. The doctor rented out a room with a mattress in the clinic for sex. Guards as pliable as plasticine and hungry for cash sanctioned sex, some even partaking in it, many lining their pockets by working as pimps to book callgirls, organise sex nights and rent out offices.

The guards usually opened their offices for sex at around 3 pm, once they'd closed for the day's administration work. If a prisoner had requested it, a guard could organise a hooker for the room for around 800,000 rupiah ($110). They'd show a selection of photos of three or four girls to pick from, who were usually from a local brothel, or they'd use a Block W inmate who used to work as a callgirl at a karaoke club but now took bookings within Hotel K. Most offices had only carpet or desks to use for sex – the mattress in the clinic was a luxury. On busy nights prisoners would line up waiting for their turn in the rooms. Prisoners were in and out fast. In the mornings, guards often found condoms left on the floor. Some guards gave their keys to a trusted prisoner to do the deals and split the profits. Brazilian inmate Ruggiero had two sets of keys to offices, which he'd sell in the afternoon, sometimes during visits, or at night, at hourly or half-hourly rates varying from 50,000 rupiah ($7) to 300,000 rupiah ($40), depending on the wealth of his client. He regularly used one room himself.

An Australian drug courier, Martin Stephens, caught at Denpasar Airport with more than three kilograms of heroin strapped to him, was one of Ruggiero's friends and a good customer. He would book the office for rendezvous with his Indonesian fiancée, Christine. They'd met in the jail while she was visiting someone else. She was a slightly older woman, who had an eight-year-old daughter. He was part of a high-profile drug syndicate dubbed the 'Bali Nine', comprising nine young Australians. When the two made eye contact across the visitors' room, he amorously poked his tongue out and that was it. Despite his life sentence, she began the rigorous routine of visiting her boyfriend daily in Hotel K.

Each morning she'd stand out the front of the jail in the blazing sun among a crowd of visitors, all pushing and shoving to get in first. Then she'd pay the 5000 rupiah (70 cent) fee to get inside the front door, some days having her bags rifled and her body searched. Inside, she'd pay the guards another 5000 rupiah to bring Martin from his cell. Her daily ritual was to bring his breakfast – fried chicken and chicken paprika were his favourites. Then she'd wait. When Martin arrived, they'd sit on the tiled floor, sweating, crammed among three hundred or so others, vanishing into their own little world wearing earpieces to listen to music. Oblivious to the people around them, including his devoted mother, Michelle, who would often be sitting right beside them, they'd passionately kiss. In the late afternoon or at night, Martin would pay to allow Christine to come in for sex. The two guards at the front door usually took 50,000 rupiah each, and he also paid Ruggiero for the office. The price went up when police were stationed out the front of Hotel K in a security boost. It simply meant an extra sling to the cops. However, Ruggiero sometimes waived Martin's fee, offering him a gratis corner, so long as he didn't mind sharing an office.

The owner of the office [a guard] gave me the keys and I rented it out. The next day he comes to me and I say I made 1.2 million [$160]. I keep 200,000 [$27] and I give him a million, or something like this. I rented it sometimes during visits.

If Martin had a visit with his girlfriend, I'd say, 'You want to go in?' I unlock and they go in. Martin was lucky because the girl I used to shag always came inside with his girlfriend because they knew each other from outside. So, whenever I go to the room, I give him a corner and we use the same room.

Having sex at the same time?

Yes, you go there, I go there. I didn't look at him. We're in a jail, man, we're not in a fucking villa. What you think we're going to expect, a nice soft bed with air con, and champagne? Wake up to reality, it's a war for survival.

– Ruggiero

Despite being sentenced to life, Martin's wish to one day have children with Christine could easily be accomplished in Hotel K. They were both keen. He was desperate for some semblance of the normal life he'd thrown away; she was one of a universal club of females who fell in love with prisoners, despite little hope of ever having a normal life.

'God teaches loyalty and I will be loyal to Martin until we are old. I was attracted to Martin the first time I met him because he is a nice person,' she said.

– *The Daily Telegraph*, 26 December 2006

'I do believe miracles exist and that could happen to Martin too. I rest it in God's hands and I will keep coming to the jail until he is free.' She said when they first met in June last year, he gave her a silver friendship ring. She told of how Stephens had proposed to her. 'He just asked me. He said, "We have to get married soon and have children",' she said.

– *AAP*, 22 December 2006

Prison governor Ilham Djaya said authorities would allow a [wedding] ceremony to go ahead. 'Yes they can, there is no prohibition to it. Only one small problem – they cannot go on a honeymoon.' Nor are conjugal visits allowed, officially.

– *AAP*, 20 December 2006

Unofficial conjugal visits in the stinking hot visiting room were rife, but guards didn't make any money from them as they were tacitly allowed. Poorer prisoners, who couldn't afford to pay for sex nights or office rooms, and horny westerners took advantage of this freedom. The visiting room was about the size of three quarters of a tennis court, with large white tiles on the floor, open concrete drains running down both sides, and a plastic heat-absorbing roof that magnified the sun's rays and turned it into a sauna.

Most days, more than three hundred people sat crammed together on the hard floor, often fanning themselves with anything they could find to move the cloying air. Strangers had to almost sit on top of one another. If people sat cross-legged, their knees touched. Spines of people sitting back-to-back connected. But the sticky closeness didn't smother the sexual activity. Kissing, groping, hand jobs, blow jobs and full sex rippled through the room. In one direction, a girl's head would jerk up and down for a while, then she'd pull out a mirror and wipe her mouth, completely ignoring the people next to her and the kids running around. Across the room, girls sat straddling guys, thrusting backwards and forwards; strangely wearing their jeans done up. To the uninitiated, it appeared to be dry humping. But the illusion was simple. A female prisoner ran a business sewing trapdoors into the crotches of girls' jeans. The girls could go to a visit wearing no underpants and just flip open the flap for easy access.

Some prisoners didn't even bother trying to be discreet. One inmate, a French drug-dealer named Filo, didn't care how much he exposed himself. He would sit against the wall while his Indonesian girlfriend gave him a blow job in full view of everyone, with it sometimes turning into full sex. His graphic displays became a running joke among other western inmates. Daily, he embarrassed the people sitting on the floor around him. He didn't care. He would just pull out his erection and his girlfriend would go to work, sometimes draping herself on top of him, her summer dress covering her backside but the jerking back and forth of her long bare legs doing little to disguise what they were up to.

His girlfriend would suck his dick. He was famous for it.

– Thomas

Apart from providing a place for quick sex, the blue room was a line to the outside world; a means for prisoners to stay in touch with friends, family, lovers, spouses and children. Visiting times got shorter over the years, but prisoners could sling the guards cash to stay there for up to three hours. It was a place where new relationships started, like that of drug mule Martin and Christine, and where old ones flourished; where husbands and wives met, and where male and female prisoners spent officially sanctioned time together.

But jail relationships came in many tangled forms. Nothing was off limits. Some prisoners perilously juggled a string of lovers, hookers and spouses, often exposing their web of liaisons in the blue room. They were bored. They had opportunities. It wasn't unusual for a male inmate to meet a hooker in a morning visit, and his wife and kids in the afternoon. One inmate regularly sat with his European wife, while his jealous inmate girlfriend, who he regularly had sex with behind the furniture-making workshop, sat across the room staring at them with killer eyes. His wife was apparently oblivious. A young female prisoner met her fiancé in the blue room most mornings and her prison lover there in the afternoons.

The juggling didn't always go smoothly. One morning the blue room erupted into a volatile scene when a man turned up unexpectedly to surprise his incarcerated wife. When he handed the guard the 5000 rupiah fee to collect her from Block W, the guard pointed across to a corner of the blue room where she was already sitting. The man turned to look and got a nasty shock. His wife was on the floor, straddling and kissing a male prisoner. He stood stunned at the guard's table for a moment. At the same time a woman arrived to surprise her inmate husband. She spotted him instantly and flew across to the corner where the guard had pointed a moment earlier. Her husband was intimately entwined with another woman.

It turned out to be a set-up. Both the husband and wife had been asked to visit that morning by another prisoner, who'd been watching their cheating spouses in the blue room for weeks. The four started angrily yelling abuse. Everyone in the packed room turned to look. Several guards rushed over. They knew what was going on; as did most inmates. It was only news to the prisoners' spouses. The guards snatched the prisoners by their arms, and marched them out of the blue room and across the jail yard. For punishment they were put into two of the isolation cells behind the tower; sex in the blue room was condoned but not when it turned into a public spectacle.

The prisoner who'd set up the stunt had watched it excitedly from the sidelines. It successfully broke up two marriages. But the cheating couple carried on their sexual relationship, making the most of the week they were locked in adjoining isolation cells by paying guards to let them slip into one cell and snuggle up together each night.

Another blue room tryst broke the heart of a female prisoner and sent her spiralling into a deep depression. She had unwittingly instigated it by inviting a lonely cellmate to join her when she went to the blue room to see her husband. She hoped it would lift the woman's spirits and brighten her day. As the weeks passed, she was unaware of the spark she'd ignited. She had no clue her husband and her cellmate were conspiring to meet alone in the blue room. If her husband's dwindling visits gave her any hint something was wrong, she ignored it. By the time she discovered the betrayal, it was too late. The woman, who everyone believed was a lesbian, had checked out of Hotel K and walked into the arms of her new lover. His visits to his wife dried up completely.

Still inside Hotel K, she quickly morphed into a sad, lonely figure – similar to the woman she'd naively tried to help. They'd traded places.

But relationships in Hotel K didn't always bring heartbreak. For some, they brought joy and filled in the empty hours with romance. Girlish squeals of delight could be heard in the women's block when a boy selling crushed ice delivered a rose or a box of chocolates from a prisoner in the men's block. Women wrote love letters and gave them either to the ice boy or the rice boy to deliver to the men's blocks. Although the men and women prisoners had no hope of being together once Block W was locked for the night at 4.30 pm, many girls sat in their cells obsessively texting their boyfriends for hours or chatting on the phone, happy to know he was close by, just over the wall.

The men could sometimes pay an amenable guard to allow them to enter Block W during the day, despite it officially being off limits to male prisoners. One prisoner went in several days in a row to spend time in his wife's cell playing with their new baby. Brazilian Ruggiero was besotted with Australian Schapelle Corby. He would sometimes slip into Block W to deliver a handful of little chocolates or massage her feet after she'd had a tough day in court. He sent her flowers, boxes of chocolates and a book on Buddhism, and regularly sidled up to her in the blue room, promising more chocolates, begging her to kiss his lips and professing his love. Despite his efforts, his love went unrequited.

For some women, jail relationships simply improved life in practical ways. It was not uncommon for the women to have several lovers in the men's block without any emotional ties. Poorer women would target wealthier male prisoners, providing sex, washing their clothes and cooking them food, in exchange for drugs, like *shabu*, money, and regular call-outs to the blue room to give them a break from claustrophobic Block W. The women who were too poor to own mobile phones wrote letters and couriered them via the rice or the ice boys over to the men.

She writes: 'I love you, my darling. I miss you, I need sugar, I need coffee, I want to have shabu.*' Men who have drugs can easily find a girlfriend. If you give her a little bit of* shabu, *she loves you very much.*

– Thomas

There were also Hotel K relationships that gave prisoners status. Australian inmate Mick and his younger Balinese girlfriend, Trisna, had been casual lovers outside before they were both sentenced to fifteen years for hashish possession – a charge they both vehemently claim was a set-up. Mick would pay the guards to allow them to meet on the lawns, to eat lunch or stretch out under the trees and enjoy each other's company. Trisna's relationship with Mick was very important to her, as being with a westerner gave her status in the jail hierarchy. Poor Balinese girls were usually on the bottom rung. They earned money or food by working for the wealthier girls, doing menial tasks like washing their clothes, cooking or giving foot massages. So, Trisna fiercely protected her relationship with her Australian boyfriend.

Her days lying in the shade with him sent a clear message to other inmates that they were together. It was what she wanted. Mick was aware of the politics but didn't mind. He knew that when she begged him to let her wash his dirty clothes, which he preferred to do himself, it was to stake her claim. Washing a man's clothes was a standard method that the women used to mark their man. Ignoring these signals could be perilous, as one pretty new girl quickly learned. She started stopping to chat to Mick whenever she saw him on her way back from visits in the blue room. Trisna saw red. Her status was threatened. She stormed into the woman's cell and bashed her up. The woman didn't fight back. She was caught completely off guard. But she learned her lesson. Mick was perplexed when she scuttled past the next day without lifting her head. But nothing stayed secret for long and he quickly heard about Trisna's jealous rage. He didn't bring it up, it wasn't worth it. But the possessiveness was one way. Mick knew Trisna regularly had girlfriends in Block W, including at one point, Nita.

Like Nita and Trisna, many women had both boyfriends and girlfriends. While straight women had to make do with texting at night, bisexual women enjoyed the best of both worlds. Block W was crammed full of lesbians, and many women turned to other women for sex for the first time in Hotel K. Some tried it just days after checking in, despite having boyfriends or husbands outside or in the men's block.

One woman whose husband was just over the wall in the men's block developed a crush on a female prisoner. Too shy to approach her, she wrote a letter professing her love and then asked the rice boy to deliver it to her cell at the end of the path. It was either a misunderstanding, or for his own entertainment, that he wheeled his rice cart straight out of Block W and across to the tennis court, where the woman's husband was leaning against the fence and chatting. He was taken aback when the rice boy handed him a letter from his wife. She'd never written to him before. He tore it open and started reading, clearly surprised by its content.

The quick switch to being lesbian or bisexual was not only a convenience, it was also sometimes a comfort for vulnerable, scared women. Javanese woman Wanda had never been with a woman before checking into Hotel K, but she quickly turned. She was ripe for the picking after being badly hurt by men. She had married young to a man who regularly bashed her, until the day he left her and their two small children for another woman. Wanda moved to Bali to work as a singer in a karaoke club and make money to support the children, who were still living in Java with her mother. But she picked the wrong man again. When her new boyfriend was caught with drugs, he sacrificed her in a deal with police. To buy his freedom he gave the police some cash and gave them Wanda by planting twenty-three ecstasy tablets at her house. It was a commonly used 'changing heads' system. In the police cells, Wanda was hassled for sex by police promising to get her off. But she refused, and was sentenced to four years and ten months jail.

Wanda entered Block W a hurt and fragile woman. At night she wept for her children. During the days she often didn't eat. She spent her first Ramadan with no visits. She had no family and no friends in Bali. But the women comforted her, cheered her up with food, and gave her massages and affection. She was easily seduced into the nurturing bosom of the lesbians, the physical connection easing the pain in her heart.

Wanda was petite and beautiful. She was fought over by the lesbians. Renae Lawrence, the only woman in the Australian Bali Nine drug syndicate, who was a lesbian before checking into Hotel K, made a play for Wanda. She visited her cell, gave her food and tried to make her laugh. Renae's girlfriend, Eda, was bitterly jealous. She refused to even speak to Wanda. One day, Renae's flirting tipped Eda over the edge; she snapped after Renae offered Wanda a slice of cheesecake. Eda and Renae started laying into each other in their cell. With everyone locked in for the night, all the women were forced to listen to the screaming and the violence until it suddenly went quiet. Eda had collapsed. A doctor was called, but she was okay. Eda soon checked out of Hotel K.

The other lesbians called Renae Lawrence the playboy of the women's block. She was big, muscular and masculine, had money and was western. Women threw themselves at her. Renae could comfortably accommodate the girls, having paid guards to have a soft double bed delivered to her cell. Renae soon fell in love with a cellmate, Ira, who she believed was 'the one'. And despite still having fifteen years left to serve, and Ira now being free, Renae hoped to marry her in a Hindu wedding ceremony inside Hotel K.

Our love has given me hope. In the Hindu religion, same-sex weddings are controversial. But some believe marriage is a union of spirits – not male and female.

– Renae, *New Idea*

CHAPTER 10
PLASTICINE GUARDS

Kerobokan is the guards' little kingdom.

– Thomas

Kerobokan Prison is repeatedly being caught in humiliating situations, when the chief of security is arrested by the police over drug possession . . . when two security officers from Kerobokan Prison were caught by the police in, let's say, a red light district, let's say escorting one of the inmates . . . it keeps happening in Kerobokan.

Why?

Corruption, I guess.

How much do the guards get paid?

Those guards who actually guard the prison, not the administration or the higher ranking prison officer, the guard guarding the prisoners basically receive less than 3 million [$400] a month.

–Journalist Wayan Juniartha of the *Jakarta Post*

There are two constants in Hotel K – prison guards and prisoners. Every day they live and work together, while often despising one another.

Hotel K was a paradise for savvy guards on the lookout to make extra money, and, in much the same way, prisoners who had money could manipulate guards for their own purposes. The guards being so poorly paid opened up almost unlimited possibilities for prisoners looking for ways to make jail more liveable.

'Prison guards struggle to survive. Their salary is the bare minimum. When people give them "tips", they are usually grateful and tend to do their bidding. This is a big problem,' said Djoko Sasongko, spokesman for the Indonesian Justice Department.

– *South China Morning Post* (Hong Kong), 1 September 2006

Your main goal is to get free, but beside that, you still have a little bit of freedom if you pay the money. You can bring cans of beer, movies, girls, whatever you want, but every step you have to pay the money.

– Den

While guards were always looking for ways to make extra money, they were also happy to use their power and influence to get sexual gratification. Several male guards regularly slipped into Block W for some quick lunchtime sex. They would give the female cellmates a bit of cash to play cards out the front and keep watch while they had their way with a prisoner.

It was easier for the lesbian guards who worked in the women's block. One afternoon, a prisoner returned to her cell and found a female guard sitting on a mattress, kissing and fondling an attractive new female prisoner. The new prisoner was simply lonely, and wanted to use the guard's mobile phone to ring her boyfriend. Phones were banned in prison – unless you had money, or something else, to offer a guard. In this case, it was sex.

It didn't seem to trouble the conscience of the guard herself, who was married with three daughters. This guard was particularly slimy, often pulling prisoners onto her knee and fondling their breasts. She'd give them little treats, like letting them walk to the canteen. One day she took Australian inmate Schapelle Corby out of Block W and across to the tennis court to watch the men having a hit of the ball. The guard had seen the sadness and desperation on Schapelle's face as she stood at the slightly ajar door of Block W, looking out longingly at those male inmates lucky enough to play tennis. The guard took her by the hand and walked her to the court. One of the players gave her a racquet, and for five minutes she forgot about being cooped up in jail and played tennis. Unlike the locals, westerners such as Schapelle didn't succumb to sleazy advances, but it was worth smiling and being nice to the guard – just for the chance to be let out again one day.

For many westerners, that was the crux of the matter. As much as the guards made the inmates feel uncomfortable, or even disgusted, they knew that they could prove useful in the days, weeks and years ahead.

But, more often than not, it was money that drove the guards. Even a costly mistake, one that could result in an inmate being beaten and put in cell *tikus* for a month, could be overlooked provided the offending inmate paid up. One night after lockup, Italian inmate Fisco had just injected himself with heroin. He was spaced out, enjoying the high, singing 'la la la la' as he washed out the bloody syringe in a glass of water. No-one else was taking any notice. It was a routine night. He finished cleaning and casually tossed the filthy water out through the small barred window. Angry shouting erupted outside. Fisco froze while his cellmates leaped to the window and peered into the dark night to see who was there. It was a guard; his T-shirt splattered in bloody water. He was yelling, 'Juri! Juri! Juri! Juri!', aware that Fisco didn't speak Indonesian and that his cellmate Juri did.

I got down from the upstairs bunk. I say, 'What's happened?' The guard says, 'He is using drugs, using heroin'. I say, 'Yeah, why?' He say, 'Cannot, cannot'. So I say to the guy, Fisco, 'Give him 100,000'. So he gives 100,000 rupiah and the guard goes away.

– Juri

It wasn't only poorly paid guards who used their position for ill-gotten gains. One jail boss regularly made Balinese girls strip and pose naked for photographs at his house, near the jail. Prisoners were permitted to work as cleaners in his house, and this boss took advantage of the fact the girls would do just about anything to escape for a few hours. He kept his nude shots of them in an album. The girls all knew that volunteering to clean his rooms meant they would have to strip naked in front of the ageing pervert. Still, a few hours shopping or time outside with their boyfriends was enough reward for them to take part in the demeaning act.

While some prisoners would have sex with guards because they wanted something, others would do it out of boredom or because they had formed an attachment to them.

The inmates sleep with the guards because they like each other; they actually have a relationship, boyfriend and girlfriend, although most of the guards do have wives. The sex happens in the clinic; we pay the doctor. The sex happens in the hall, the offices, empty corners, anywhere.

– Elsa, female inmate

One Hotel K security boss had a girlfriend in the jail. The two had met when she checked in, and the boss regularly gave her leave to go to his place – a room he rented separate from the house that came with the job, which accommodated his wife and children. Hotel K really was a sexual playground for the guards, even the gay ones. In the men's blocks, there were usually gay inmates and several transvestites, known as *bencong*. They wore wigs, tight sexy shorts, and T-shirts around the jail during the day. Several guards gathered in an office one morning to fondle and kiss one particularly pretty *bencong* who was checking in. The *bencong* were usually well-liked, often making prisoners laugh with their antics and girly conversations. 'Thank God I got my period today, I thought I was pregnant,' one *bencong* giggled to another in front of several prisoners one day. In the afternoons they'd often go to their cells to do up their faces, change wigs and put on evening frocks, spraying a cloud of perfume in the air and haughtily walking into it. The *bencongs* and gays often played sex games together, and sometimes the guards joined in.

One afternoon, a few inmates were sitting around smoking joints listening to local transvestite Dedi complaining about being broke. It sparked an idea. Dutchman Aris and Australian inmate Mick suggested shooting a gay porn video and selling it on the internet. Dedi was instantly convinced it would make them rich. A gay Nigerian inmate was also keen to do it. They devised a simple scene with the Nigerian inmate acting as a guard, who would pull off the pants of the transvestite and have sex with him on the bed. Mick asked one of the guards, who was married with kids but always sleazily touching men, if he would bring in a spare uniform.

He did. The next day they were ready to shoot. The guard stood watching, with Mick directing and Aris shooting.

Dedi stepped out of the bathroom in a towel and underpants. The huge African 'guard' picked Dedi up, carried him to the bed, stripped off his own uniform and then tore off Dedi's towel. The African already had an erection. Mick and Aris looked at each other. They'd both seen enough. Aris quickly handed the camera to the real guard and left him excitedly holding the camera with one hand, and fondling the two naked men with the other.

When the guard came out, he was so excited. His face was as red as a tomato.

– Mick

They looked at the footage and it wasn't any good. So the next day they decided to shoot another scene, with the actual guard acting in this one. Dedi dressed up as Cleopatra, with a wig, a full face of makeup, false eyelashes and wrapped in towels. The guard was dressed in a sheet as Cleopatra's butler, and the African was a black bushman who would run in and rape Cleopatra. Aris started filming Cleopatra, who was sitting on a *batik* bedspread, holding a mirror while the butler brushed her hair. Then the bushman came in, stabbed the guard and raped Cleopatra. Mick and Aris filmed it this time, but walked out straight afterwards, leaving the guard and two prisoners all lying naked on the bed and smoking. Their blue movie didn't reach the internet or make them a dime. But it was fun and broke the tedium.

Aside from sex, cultivating a relationship with a guard through paying them money could make life a lot more bearable. As part of the great hypocrisy in Hotel K, the guards keeping the prisoners under lock and key were often working as drug couriers themselves, overlooking drug use inside the jail and sometimes even using drugs with the prisoners in their cells. Getting drugs like heroin or *shabu* was no problem at all. Guards would bring in drugs in their shoes or pockets, usually safe in the knowledge that they would not be searched. The majority of guards were happy to turn a blind eye to all the smuggling, so long as they got a piece of the action. Need a clean syringe? Easy, just order it in.

Guards also smuggled in bags of the local brew, *arak*, for prisoners to drink. It was banned but that didn't stop a nightly traffic of the stuff by a few of the guards. However, while the majority of guards were keen to make some extra money, there were a few who were either against drinking alcohol, or who were honest or didn't want to risk getting caught. One particular guard smuggled in huge quantities of *arak* by pulling it up into the watchtower. Each night during his rounds, he climbed into the rarely manned tower to drop down a rope. Below, someone would be ready and waiting to tie the plastic bags of *arak*. Then he'd haul it up again. To avoid carrying it past other guards, he'd dug a hole under the inner perimeter wall, so he could pull it through. It was a smart strategy, but caused havoc one year when torrential rains washed his small hole into a gaping big one. The wall above it collapsed and two prisoners escaped.

There was no such thing as the perfect drop in Hotel K. The quality of the *arak* was largely dependent on how much stuff the guards mixed it with to increase the quantity and make more cash. One sly guard was notorious for diluting *arak* with water. The prisoners knew, but there was not much they could do – a little booze was better than no booze.

Of course, some inmates were smarter than others and targeted specific guards to bring in the *arak*. One in particular was known for bringing in the quality stuff from his village in East Bali, Karangasem, where the purest *arak* in Bali was distilled.

All an inmate had to do was fork out the cash, and the next night the guard would bring a plastic bag filled with enough booze for prisoners to get very drunk. Some guards scammed extra cash by selling *arak* to an inmate, only to then punish him for having it, locking him in the tower. The inmate would stay there until he could afford to pay to get out – so the guard won twice. Another lucrative racket the guards used was walking around confiscating phones, then simply selling them back.

As in every jail, it wasn't only the crooked guards who inmates had to keep an eye out for. There were guards who were just plain sadistic and enjoyed torturing prisoners whenever they had the opportunity.

There was one guard called Fisheyes. When he was young, he was a real motherfucker.

– Thomas

Fisheyes was one of the guards who enjoyed punishing and inflicting pain on inmates with his electric stick. He would walk around jabbing people on the arms or legs and stomach to amuse himself. The inmates would reel away in pain. But it would bring a smile to Fisheyes's face. Other times, if Fisheyes or other guards caught somebody breaking the rules or causing a problem, they'd beat them with a rattan stick, throwing in a few electric shocks for good measure. Fisheyes often used *shabu* and other drugs, but if you weren't on the right side of him or paying him off, or if he was just bored, he would wander around checking prisoners for drugs and if he caught one, punishment and pain would follow.

When eight bosses of the gang Laskar Bali were sentenced to Hotel K, the power politics in the jail changed overnight. Laskar was no ordinary Indonesian gang. It was one of the toughest and most brutal, and bashings were part of their daily activities. The fear of them was such that they took over Hotel K. Not only were prisoners terrified of them, guards were too. Crossing Laskar resulted in swift and brutal retaliation – inside or outside the jail. Such was its power, the gang would often be doing something illegal in their block, like using drugs, and one of the gang members would simply lock down the block so no-one could get inside. When this happened, an unsuspecting guard was sometimes accidentally locked inside the block. But there was nothing the guard could do until someone came and let him out.

Kerobokan is the only jail where the prisoners totally control the jail. Prisoners have the key of the block. Once I see guard closed inside the block. He cannot get out and had to wait two hours. A prisoner finally comes and opens the door and he can go out. Yeah. That time Kerobokan was like that. Prisoners had full power, you know. Total control.

– Juri, Italian inmate

CHAPTER 11

TERRORISTS CHECK IN

In jail, there's not much happening any day. Sometimes you just look in the fish pond and you see fucking frog eggs, everybody is looking at these fucking frog eggs and studying these frog eggs for half an hour. Just looking and wondering … so when Amrozi is coming in with guns and everything, it's a big story, it's something to look at, for sure.

– Thomas

It was like a movie. There was a helicopter, so many cars escorting. I was inside the block when Amrozi arrived. There was too much crowd, like a football match was going to begin. Everybody was in front of the windows, watching.

– Den

Sirens whirring faintly in the distance grew louder by the second as the police convoy carrying the terrorist Amrozi sped towards Hotel K. By the time the armoured cars and motorbikes arrived in a blaze of red flashing lights and screaming sirens, almost all inmates had gathered to watch the spectacle. In the blue room, people were leaping up to look through the doors and windows. At least one couple, a good-looking Argentinean drug dealer in his early twenties, Frederico, and his long-term Israeli girlfriend, used the minutes of distraction for some quick sex on the floor.

But most were glued to the scene as Amrozi, handcuffed and surrounded by police with machine guns, climbed out of the police van and walked into the office to check in. For months his grinning face had been splashed on the front pages of newspapers. Prisoners were leaping on each others' shoulders to get a good look at Bali's most hated man. Hundreds more stood clinging to the fences near their blocks, or hung off them for a higher vantage point. Many stood around on the grass in an angry mob shouting, 'Kill him, kill him!' as police corralled them at least twenty-five metres back from the terrorist.

The 41-year-old Muslim mechanic was despised by the Balinese for his key role in two nightclub bombings in Kuta, which killed two hundred and two people, decimating tourism and wiping out hundreds of local businesses. Amrozi's flagrant glee afterwards turned him into the smiling monster of the blasts. He cheered and gave the thumbs up to the judge and the victims' families when he was sentenced to death, two days before checking into Hotel K. Now the smiling assassin would be living among the Balinese. Riots by Balinese prisoners or Amrozi-sympathising Muslims were feared.

'Kill him, kill him, kill him!' prisoners started yelling again as Amrozi came back out. His hair was cut razor short, but his Muslim beard was left unshaven. Surrounded by police, guards and head *tamping* inmate *Pemuka* Saidin, Amrozi walked across the path from the offices to the tower block that housed a new top security cell. The walls were freshly painted white and the floor tiled grey. The only furniture was a metal bed frame with a thin green carpet laid on top as a makeshift mattress. A floral-patterned pillow fluffed up on the bed was a hint of some sympathy towards him inside Hotel K. It had been donated by a Muslim inmate. But it was the only splash of colour in the stark cell. Two small barred windows let in a little light. In the corner was a squat toilet and concrete wash basin. Amrozi would be banned from mixing with all other inmates and locked up twenty-four hours a day, with only rare, court-approved visits with family. Or so it was supposed to be.

A guard followed the terrorist into the cell with four white plastic bags of his belongings, including traditional Muslim garb and a Koran. In one swift move he put them down, turned around and walked out of there, swinging shut the barred green door and locking it with two large industrial padlocks. As the police filed out, the guard locked two more padlocks: one on the front door of the tower block and another on the gate to the steel picket fence surrounding it. Outside, the inmates were still waiting to watch the police convoy leave. But then the 5.30 pm lockup bells started to ring and they began walking to their cells for the night. Today's show was over. Tomorrow they'd be back to watching fish eggs.

Within a couple of days, many Balinese and western prisoners were displaying their anger by hurling stones at the bomber's tower as they walked past on their way to the blue room, and by wearing black T-shirts, designed and cut in Hotel K's printing factory, with orange and yellow 'Fuck terrorist' slogans slashed across the front.

A second terrorist, Abdul Aziz, best known by his self-created title Imam Samudra, meaning 'preacher of the oceans', checked in a month later. Swarming police and a scrum of journalists circled him as he walked from the police van and through Hotel K's front door. Journalists yelled questions, but 'Allah is great. Allah Akbar, Allah Akbar' was his only response. It was the same chant he'd screamed over and over in court, displaying only glee for the mass killings he'd choreographed, right down to selecting the nightclubs, recruiting the suicide bombers and designating Amrozi to buy the chemicals to make the bomb. When Samudra checked in, a new era of terrorist teaching began in Hotel K, with the killer preaching his beliefs every chance he got.

He was put in a cell next to Amrozi's at the front of the tower block. It was a room with a view, giving him a platform to lecture to anyone walking past. He looked directly across at the junction of the path and the doors to the offices, where prisoners usually farewelled their visitors. If couples dared to kiss goodbye, he'd scream at them through his barred window in response to their forbidden public display. When female inmates walked past, he'd intimidate them by angrily screaming, 'Allah Akbar, Allah Akbar', because they weren't shrouded from head to toe.

By then, Hotel K housed thirty-five terrorists involved in the nightclub blasts. Thirty were there on lesser charges, such as working as drivers or sheltering the bombers. These inmates were all locked in Block J, near the mosque. The five key players were caged separately. The death row trio – Samudra, Amrozi and his brother Mukhlas – were in cells inside the water tower. Previously, these cells had been used for everything from isolating prisoners, to functioning as a small shop, a library and VIP rooms. Former Bali governor Ida Bagus Oka had spent time in a VIP tower cell during his embezzlement case. He was notorious for giving the nod to re-zone sacred land for controversial multi-million-dollar building projects, earning him the nickname 'Mr OK' and fuelling widespread suspicion that he took lucrative backhanders. With the help of his lawyer, he was exonerated on the embezzlement charges.

He [the judge] claimed the verdict was based solely on legal considerations, and not because, as many people have speculated, the judges had been bribed or too intimidated to convict the powerful Oka.

– *Jakarta Post*, 9 April 2002

Before it was modified into maximum-security cells for the terrorists, the tower had been used for storing axes, grass slashers and other gardening equipment. The walls were rebuilt to eradicate any face-to-face contact and the terrorists had to shout out to hear each other. Outside, the metal picket fence topped with barbed wire created an outdoor pen. Behind the tower were a further four cells used for isolating inmates. Two of these were now occupied by the other two key terrorists – Mubarok, and Amrozi's younger brother, Ali Imron, both of whom were serving life sentences.

Despite being locked away in the tower, the terrorists had an overwhelming presence. Their fanatical beliefs were penetrating the jail, eagerly soaked up by bored, uneducated and easily impressed Muslim guards and inmates who were in awe of the terrorists. Guards on tower duty would sit in the hot sun for hours talking to the terrorists. The most blatantly starstruck guard was Dedi, who trailed behind them like a puppy when they walked across to the mosque each day. Amrozi and Samudra would sit like celebrities talking to fans in front of the mosque before midday prayers. For drug dealers, petty thieves and card sharks, it was something new. Mingling with some of the world's most notorious terrorists gave a boring day a bit of zing. Tommy, a 22-year-old ecstasy dealer, soaked it all up like a sponge. He was soon working for Samudra; ironing his clothes, buying food for him at the canteen, and selling scented massage oil around the jail to raise cash for further terrorist attacks. The awestruck boy, who'd been less than devout before the terrorists checked in, was now fanatical, insisting that his fiancée wear full Muslim dress and cover her face. She obeyed him for her visits, but tore off the garb as soon as she walked outside Hotel K. Their usual sex in the blue room stopped abruptly, and they no longer even kissed goodbye.

Early one morning, all five terrorists walked the fifty metres along the path from their tower cells past the canteen, to the mosque. It was the first time they were all allowed out together. They stood hugging in front of the mosque; it was the end of the Ramadan fast. Never failing to seize a chance to preach, Samudra began to call out, 'Allah Akbar, Allah Akbar, Allah Akbar'. The jail boss was shocked to see how easily Samudra incited the others – more than four hundred prisoners screamed back, 'Allah Akbar'. The boss hadn't had any sense of the insidious influence the terrorists were having in his jail until that moment. It was a nasty shock.

He took swift action to tighten security. He transferred Dedi to a jail in Java, as a stark warning to all guards not to get too close to the terrorists. He moved Samudra to a cell at the back of the tower. He restricted them to one hour of sun every second day in the tower pen and permitted mosque visits on Fridays only. Life got tough for the terrorists – the way it was supposed to have been from the outset. They were served slop prison food in tins pushed into their cells three times a day, now rarely supplemented by canteen fare. Visits with their families were also curtailed.

From then on, the death row trio spent their days in their cells praying, reading religious texts, and yelling through the walls to each other or to the endless rotation of inmates doing stints in one of the two vacant isolation cells out the back. But the isolation did nothing to impede Samudra spreading his message of hate. He spoke to fellow fanatics on his mobile phone, but, most dangerously, had wide-sweeping access to people in cyberspacc. Initially, he used fellow inmate Iwan's laptop, after the Muslim drug dealer was elected spokesman for the terrorists and officially allowed into their cells. Samudra used it to enter chat rooms, where he would recruit terrorists and raise cash. Agung Setyadi, a lecturer in economics at Semarang State University, was one cyber recruit who did his bit for terrorism. Samudra sent him $470 to buy a laptop, which the lecturer sent via motorcycle courier under his daughter's name, Annisa, to a Hotel K residence that housed unmarried guards.

At the house, Muslim guard Beni Irawan was ready to collect it. He was motivated to help the terrorists by a personal vendetta against the Balinese. He had been viciously bashed by Bali's Laskar gang members for refusing to let them out of jail one night, and the incident was simply dismissed. If nobody was going to punish the Balinese gang, Beni would avenge himself. He wrapped the laptop in newspaper and delivered it to Samudra in his cell whenever the terrorist asked for it.

While the Indonesian legal system kept granting appeals and extending his life, Samudra was using his time to direct the killing of another twenty-three people. Sitting on his bed in his tower cell, he recruited three suicide bombers for the second round of bomb blasts in Bali, in 2005. The guard, Beni Irawan, was later sentenced to five years jail for giving him the laptop, and lecturer Agung Setyadi got six years for sending it.

One of the 2002 Bali bombers used a laptop smuggled to him in jail to help organize the triple suicide blasts that rocked the resort island last year, Indonesian Police say. ... 'Imam Samudra directed the fundraising for the second Bali bombing,' cyber crime unit police chief Petrus Golose said.

– *Reuters*, 24 August 2006

The police recently revealed that Imam Samudra had recruited the perpetrators of the second Bali bombing through the Internet.

– *Jakarta Post*, 14 September 2006

Last week anti-terror officers learned that Samudra had been recruiting young people in cyberspace, chatting with them through a laptop smuggled into his prison cell in Kerobokan, Bali.

– *New Straits Times*, September 2006

In his Hotel K cell, Samudra also wrote his autobiography, *Me Against The Terrorist.* The book sold out its first print run of 4000, earning him royalties – not confiscated under any proceeds of crime legislation – to fund future terror attacks. Cash was vital to the terrorist network, and via mobile phone and the internet he successfully got sympathisers to empty their pockets. He also recommended the use of online credit card fraud as the cutting-edge way to raise cash for terror, and devoted a chapter of his book to this practice. But the terrorists weren't limited to talking to a niche market. Samudra, Mukhlas and Amrozi also kept high media profiles, doing countless sanctioned print and television interviews with journalists around the world.

Samudra and Amrozi also made smaller amounts of cash from businesses inside Hotel K: Samudra selling his scented

Kathryn Bonella

Hotel Kerobokan sits on four hectares of prime real estate. Its capacity is 320, but numbers sit at between 900 to 1000, often with more than ten prisoners squeezed into one cell.

Bali Post

Powerful inmate Iwan Thalib ran an ecstasy factory at the back of his furniture workshop inside Hotel K. A jail sentence didn't stop the drug boss being one of Bali's biggest ecstasy suppliers.

Saidin

Indonesian Saidin was a powerful inmate, appointed *Pemuka* and given a lot of freedom. Westerners like Englishman Steve enjoyed watching him play with the many snakes he kept as pets under his bed.

Ruggiero Paezzo

'Yep. And I'd do it again.' Brazilian Ruggiero (left) asked his Indonesian friend Saidin (right) one day if he'd really hacked off a man's head.

Ruggiero Paezzo

Brazilian Ruggiero (left) with one of his local girlfriends, and Australian Martin Stephens from the Bali Nine with his fianceé Christine. No champagne and soft beds in jail. Both couples would have sex in an office, sometimes at the same time; privacy was a luxury they could not afford.

Ruggiero Paezzo

From left to right: Steve Turner (English), Pascal (French), local inmate, Aris (Dutch), three locals, Peruvian inmate, Juri (Italian), Gabriel (American), Alexei (Russian) and Michael Blanc (French). 'Don't we look happily fucked up?' – Ruggiero.

Ruggiero Paezzo

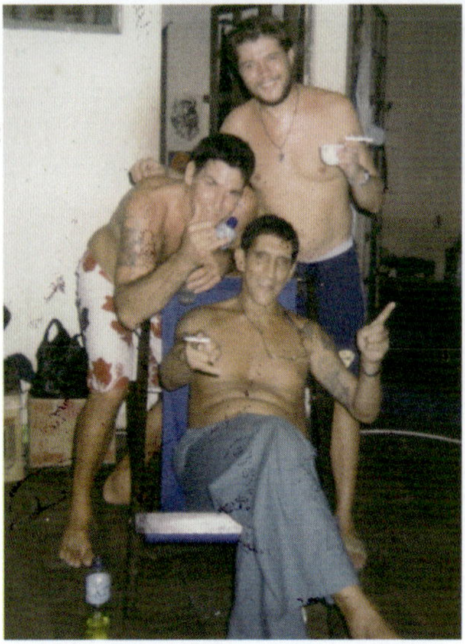

Brazilian Ruggiero in his deckchair with his booze in the bottle in front, American Gabriel in his pink hibiscus surf shorts, and Russian Alexei. Every day was a party.

Kathryn Bonella

Inmates can buy anything from noodles, soap and cigarettes to bags of *shabu* (ice) or smack at the little canteen near the tennis court.

Juri Angione

Juri and Ade have their big day in Hotel K. The wedding dress and Juri's suit were made out of Italian silk in Italy. They had 100 guests. During the ceremony, two other inmates were caught by a guard having sex in the toilet, and best man Englishman Steve Turner was barely able to stand up due to all the drugs he'd taken beforehand.

Made Nagi

Death row inmates team up to play a tennis tournament. Australians Scott Rush and Andrew Chan – heroin traffickers and part of the syndicate dubbed the Bali Nine.

Made Nagi

Australian Renae Lawrence (right), one of the Bali Nine, is the playboy of the women's block, and top dog. She got a big bed put into her cell to entertain the girls.

Made Nagi

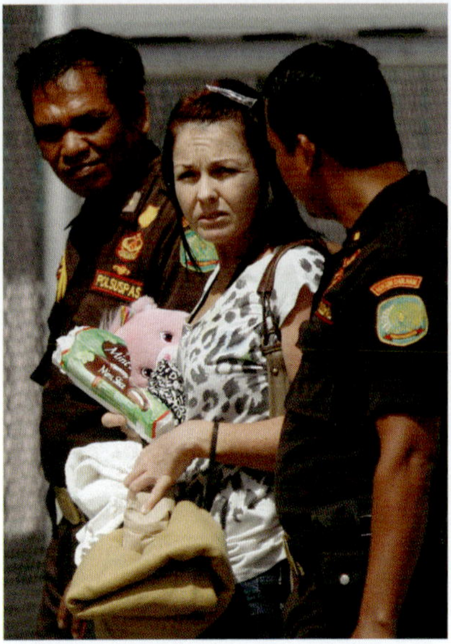

Schapelle is brought back from Sanglah Hospital, still not well. Within a year she'd be rushed back there comatose and under suicide watch.

Ardiles Rante

Scottish Robert was carried back to his cell daily, drunk. Black Monster gave birth to his child in Hotel K after they had sex through a cell door.

Ardiles Rante

One of the cells in Block W. Up to fifteen women are locked up for the night at 4.30 pm every afternoon. The cells are noisy, hot and often stinking from all the sweaty bodies. Poor locals, who know nothing about hygiene, will sometimes menstruate or urinate on the floors, wiping it up later.

Ardiles Rante

Terrorist Iman Samudra yelled out his cell window at visitors showing public affection and to female inmates who weren't covered from head to toe. Inside his cell he used a laptop to direct the second Bali bombings, and also wrote a book on terrorism.

Roberto Maldonaldo

Brazilian Ruggiero enjoys freedom for a day with the police pretending to take him to the dentist. He'd meet his friends at the beach, his girlfriend at a hotel and was the one to bring and provide the drugs from Hotel K. 'So nice outside, then back in jail. The time outside runs so fast.' – Ruggiero.

Roberto Maldonaldo

Brazilian Ruggiero enjoying a break from Hotel K on a day out at the beach.

Roberto Maldonaldo

Austrian heroin dealer (and addict) Thomas kept dealing inside Hotel K. This was his second stint in Hotel K and his third in jail in Indonesia. But he usually paid to keep his sentences short.

Roberto Maldonaldo

Big wave surfer Gabriel, from California, inside for drugs. He was bashed almost to death by guards and the Laskar gang when he jumped from the watchtower and tried to escape.

Roberto Maldonaldo

French inmate Michael Blanc smoking a joint. Michael was caught bringing almost four kilograms of hashish from India concealed in dive tanks into Bali, and was the first to face the death penalty for drugs in Bali. The final verdict was life and he became a heroin addict in Hotel K.

Roberto Maldonado

'It's only rock and roll': Brazilian Ruggiero, in for drugs, sang and strummed his guitar loudly every night to conceal the noise of his Italian cellmate cutting the bars on their cell window. Ruggiero got caught just when he was set to escape and was brutally bashed and locked in cell *tikus*.

Roberto Maldonado

The western inmates do whatever they can to make life more bearable. They renovate their cells, build little gardens. Here, Ruggiero created a little oasis for himself to meditate.

Juri Angione

Italian Juri and his wife Ade spend precious time together.

Komang Sutrisna

Prisoners usually get warning from the guards about police raids, but sometimes they aren't quick enough. This inmate was caught with drugs in his cell and is being searched outside the front door of the jail before he is taken to the police station and charged with another offence.

Made Nagi

Schapelle is cooped up in the women's section: even when the door is open, there is an imaginary line.

Kathryn Bonella

Australian death row inmate Scott Rush was caught with more than a kilogram of heroin strapped to his body at Denpasar Airport. He is sitting with Hotel K guard Wayan.

Bali Post

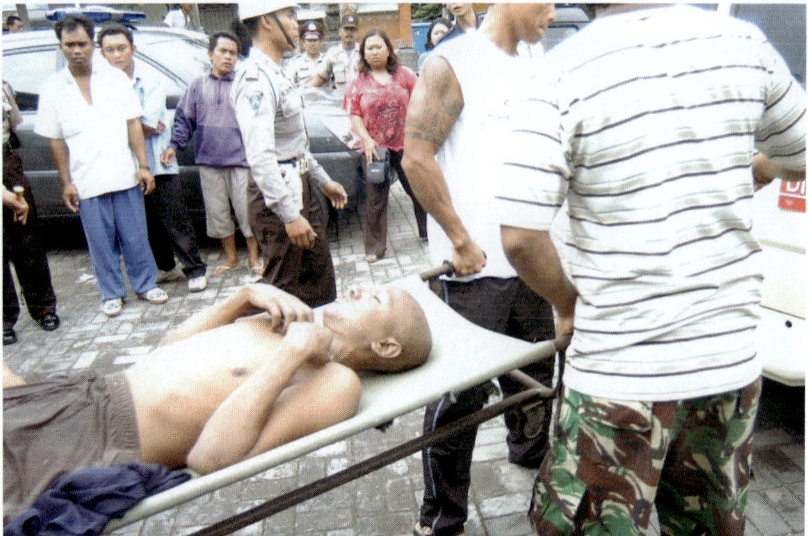

Prisoner Abdul Habib swallowed 25 ecstasy pills to hide the evidence during a police raid. He died shortly after this photo was taken, at Sanglah Hospital.

Roberto Maldonaldo

Nigerian Emmanuel is on death row for trafficking 400 grams of heroin from Pakistan to Bali. He's spent many nights smashing everything in his cell, furious at the hypocrisy of the system. 'They put me in here for drugs, but I see they are selling drugs like coffee.' He is now sharing a cell with Australian death row inmate Scott Rush.

Made Nagi

The 'death tower': home to the eight Australian men in the Bali Nine, death row inmate Emmanuel and several locals. It was previously home to the Bali bombers.

Kathryn Bonella

Death row inmate Scott Rush is told by guards to talk to journalists after his tennis match. It's all part of the PR spin, as Hotel K promotes itself as a rehabilitation facility – despite that being so far from reality.

Newspix/ Renee Nowytarger

The most hated man in Bali. Terrorist Amrosi, dubbed the smiling assassin for his glee in helping to kill 202 people in two Kuta nightclubs with his bombs. In Hotel K, he was a celebrity terrorist. Here, he is being escorted through the jail by *Pemuka* Ketut Dana.

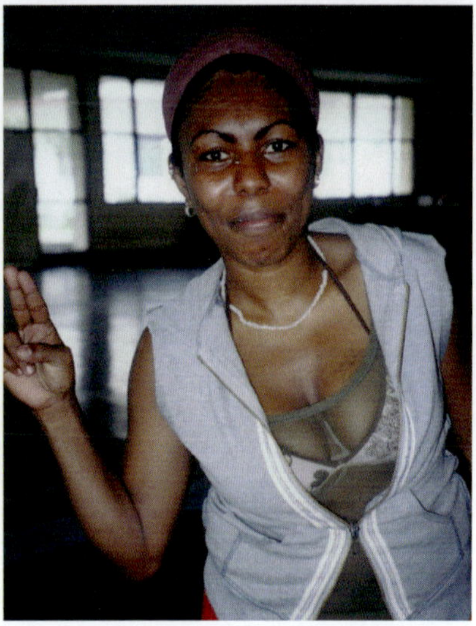

Sonia Gonzales, nicknamed Black Monster, has been in and out of Hotel K nearly twenty times. Her crime is sleeping with tourists, drugging them and stealing their valuables. She conceived a baby in Hotel K through the bars of her cell.

This is Hotel K's notorious cell *tikus.* Prisoners are sometimes stripped down to their underpants and locked in here for months as a form of punishment. Several prisoners have died from AIDS and TB while in the cell. Australian Scott Rush spent a month locked in this cell, some of that time crushed in together with fellow death row inmate Nigerian Emmanuel. 'The worst thing about cell *tikus* is that they put you in there and you feel like you are completely forgotten.' – Scott. 'You have to lie like a dead man.' – Emmanuel.

Each cell has only one hole-in-the-ground toilet for all inmates to share. They often block up and spew sewage across the floor.

This prisoner is cooking dinner in a makeshift kitchen, right beside the squat toilet.

Roberto Maldonaldo

This warning smacks you in the face as you walk through immigration at Bali's Ngurah Rai Airport. It couldn't be clearer – but so many continue to perilously ignore this sign.

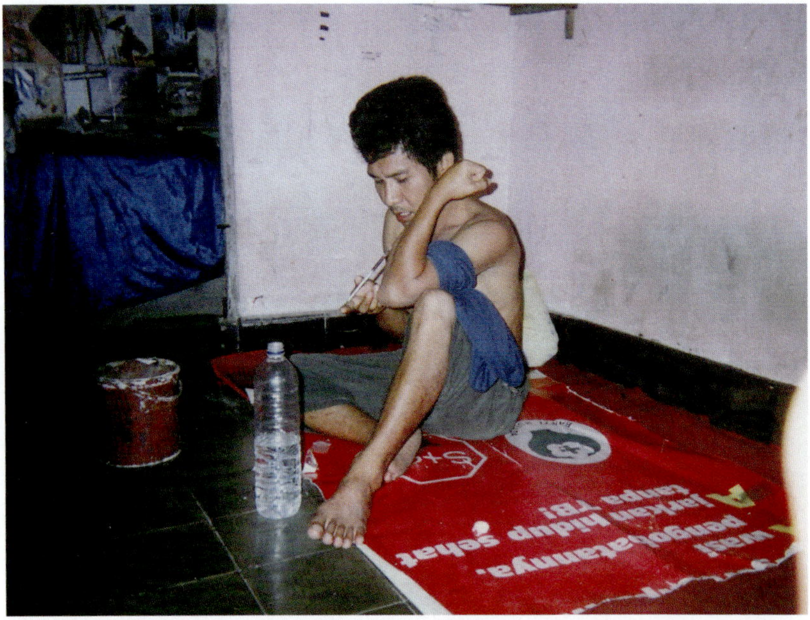

Ironically, Hotel K is the cheapest place to score smack. This inmate is one of hundreds who regularly shoot up in their cells.

oils; and Amrozi selling phone credit, using inmates as sales boys. Austrian drug dealer Thomas was a regular customer for phone credit, burning it up fast in his business. He avoided dealing directly with Amrozi until the day he got ripped off. He complained to the sales boy that he'd been sold a spent phone card and the boy took him across to the tower. The terrorist was sunning himself in the pen. Through the fence, Thomas told him about the problem. Amrozi simply turned, apologised and offered to swap it.

But while the terrorists were busy recruiting, they'd had one of their own turn his back on them. Amrozi's younger brother, Ali Imron, had turned police informant and exposed the matrix behind the blasts. He gave details of his own role – mixing more than a ton of chemicals into bombs and packing the lethal explosives into fluorescent pink, green and blue plastic filing cabinets fixed to the floor of a white Mitsubishi van. Then, on the chosen night, he drove the white van and two suicide bombers to Kuta, and parked the van five hundred metres up the road from the target clubs and the crowds of tourists out for a night of dancing. Ali Imron also confessed to training the two suicide bombers; the first got out of the van and walked along the street in his explosive vest, down to Paddy's Bar and onto the crowded dance floor, where he detonated it. Terrified survivors fled out onto the street and straight into the second bigger van bomb explosion; all timed and choreographed perfectly to maximise the carnage.

But Ali Imron was now sorry for his part in the massacre, crying in court and apologising. For his treachery, his two brothers and Samudra harassed him through the walls of the tower, yelling insults and taunting him with a mantra that his corpse wouldn't be fragrant after death if he didn't die a martyr. But the repentant killer didn't recant. He was on a good wicket.

His change of heart had saved him from a death sentence; instead he'd been given a life sentence in jails with revolving doors to the good life outside.

One day, while most people believed Amrozi's little brother was languishing in a stinking, rat-infested cell in Hotel K next to his big brother, he was actually drinking coffee at Starbucks and eating dinner at the Hard Rock Café in a new entertainment movie complex beside Plaza Indonesia, one of Jakarta's most exclusive shopping malls. He was sitting with police boss Pak Gorries and several black-clad armed police. He regularly spent hours out of jail in this way, as part of Indonesia's anti-terror strategy. The assumption was that police would get more information from him sitting in Starbucks than in a jail cell. So, while his brothers were eating slop, he was sipping lattés, eating cheeseburgers and browsing in the windows of luxury designer shops alongside Jakarta's most elite shoppers.

Pestered by the two reporters as to why he was drinking with the police chief, Ali Imron was reported as saying this was not the first time. 'I often wander around with Pak [Mr] Gorries,' Detik quoted him as saying. But one of the plain clothed policemen immediately silenced him. 'You have no right to talk,' Detik reported.

– *Courier Mail*, 3 September 2004

What, do you think that going out for a walk is forbidden? Brig-Gen Gorries said. I walk often with Pak [Brig-Gen] Gorries, Ali Imron said, his head lowered and flanked by several black-clad armed police.

– *PNG Post Courier*, 3 September 2004

Inside Hotel K, the bombers' influence persisted, visible in ways as subtle as guards growing goatee beards. The initial anger among the inmates had waned into complacency, with them all busily absorbed in their own daily headaches. But Balinese people outside the prison were fuming that the terrorists were still alive nearly three years after the massacre, and called for a stop to the unending appeals and for the guns to come out. But instead the terrorists struck again in the triple suicide blasts that Samudra directed from his Hotel K cell. It was twelve days before the third anniversary of the first blasts. Two men blew themselves up in a strip of casual fish restaurants on the beach at Jimbaran Bay, and a third in a steak house in the tourist heart of Kuta. Twenty-three people were killed, including the three suicide bombers.

Balinese anger turned to fury. The paradise island was a zone of death and destruction again. No-one felt safe. Nowhere was safe now – even beaches were a target. All hotels searched the bags of all guests. Restaurants and shops ran metal detectors over customers' bodies and bags. The island was a war zone, as far from an idyllic tropical island as it could get. Bali was braced for more attacks at the three-year memorial services for the first blasts. Security was visibly heavy. Snipers were perched on rooftops, hundreds of police lined the small lanes leading to the service, and five armoured vans were parked close by. But no bombs exploded that day. It was the Balinese anger that finally blew, outside Hotel K later that afternoon.

'Kill Amrozi, kill, kill, kill', 'Bring back our peaceful Bali', 'Kill Amrozi now'. More than 1500 people were taking out their fury on Hotel K, kicking the front fence, tearing at the gates and pelting stones onto the roof. Eight Balinese *gamelan* groups – one hundred and fifty musicians – were beating drums and xylophones, creating loud rhythmic music, invigorating the locals into a hypnotic frenzy. Protesters thrashed the front iron gates back and forth until they ripped off, stomping on them and screaming, 'Kill Amrozi!' Others attacked the low concrete fence stretching along the road, kicking it until it collapsed.

Fired by the beating of drums, the crowd surged towards the front doors but was blocked by three hundred riot police standing with shields and batons along the front wall. One protester charged forwards wielding a long iron spear above his head. He threw it at a concrete slab, screaming: 'Bali has already been destroyed. It will make no difference if we raze this prison to the ground.' In nearby streets, it was chaos. Traffic was gridlocked. Police had shut all roads leading to the jail. Local traders had also shut up shop, fearing an escalation of violence. But the insanity outside had instilled a calm within Hotel K. Prisoners sat listening to the stones crashing onto the roof and the screams of the protesters, desperately hoping they'd break down the front wall and create an easy escape route. They were ready to run. Some had even packed their bags.

But it wasn't to be. The riot fired for two hours and then fizzled out. The Balinese police boss knew the hypnotic power of music for his people and when he finally got the *gamelan* troupes to stop playing, the emotional tension instantly vanished. Protesters soon dispersed, leaving behind a demolished fence and gate, and a single banner flapping on a pole with the poignant message. 'Hello SBY [Indonesia's president Susilo Bambang Yudhoyono]. Kill the person who has hurt Bali [Amrozi].'

'It is a natural response from a wounded community that has been treated insensitively by the central government. In fact, it is a mild response compared to the anger that is seething in our hearts,' a protest leader Madra Adnyana said.

– *Jakarta Post*, 13 October 2005

But their protest had missed its mark. The death row trio had been smuggled out of Hotel K wearing black hoods and hustled into armoured cars, a day earlier. Police were aware that the protest outside Hotel K was planned and had feared a security nightmare on the anniversary. An entourage of two hundred police armed with machine guns escorted the hooded men to the tourist island's main airport in Denpasar. They were immediately put on a police charter flight to Cilacap, a Muslim-dominated coastal town. Then, from the small local harbour, they took a final ten-minute boat ride across the water to their new home, the notorious penal colony Nusakambangan. Dubbed Indonesia's Alcatraz, it was a bushy, sun-kissed tropical island with a nasty scar of seven maximum-security prisons stretching along its coastal road.

The terrorists spent another three years living on Nusakambangan while their lawyers appealed. Throughout these years, the celebrity terrorists were permitted to do many more press and television interviews, spreading their twisted ideals, including holding a press conference close to the end. Then finally, one night six years after the Kuta blasts, thirty paramilitary police masked in black balaclavas entered their death row cells, shackled the three hand and foot, and led them shuffling out of the jail to waiting trucks. Separately, they were driven three kilometres in convoy to a clearing. There they were tied to wooden posts several metres apart, with Amrozi in the middle. They were then shot dead.

The explosive bang of thirty-six simultaneous shots, fired by three teams of twelve specially trained shooters, echoed across Nusakambangan. The sound of the bullets that pierced the terrorists' hearts sent shivers down the spines of at least one hundred and sixteen prisoners in Indonesia's jails, who were threatened with the same fate. Hundreds of kilometres away in Bali, it was an icy reality check for three young Australians and a Nigerian who were living under the shadow of death in Hotel K. The execution line was moving. Australian death row inmate Scott Rush was shocked.

Honestly, I didn't think they were going to and then, just all of a sudden, bang, they've done it. Like, they talk about it, they talk about it, they move them, they're not going to do it and then one day it just comes up. You know. Like they're not going to do it when they say they are and then they just surprise them. I watched it on TV. I had to see it to believe it.

Was it a feeling of, as long as they don't shoot them, I am safe?

Yeah, kind of.

– Scott

Another death row inmate at Hotel K, Nigerian Emmanuel, was similarly shaken.

Every day for five days before they killed them, water was coming out from my eyes. I wasn't crying, it was just water coming from my eyes from morning to night. But as soon as they killed them, it stopped. On Sunday this water stopped from my eyes. I don't know exactly why. I knew something was wrong. But I didn't know what.

– Emmanuel

CHAPTER 12
THE DEALERS

Kerobokan is drugs paradise. Drugs all the time. No special time for drugs. Drugs twenty-four hours. You smoke cigarette, you smoke shabu. *The party was daily. Every single day right after lunch we'd sit outside and get pissed, those who want to smoke* shabu, *smoke* shabu, *those who want to use smack, use smack. That's on a daily basis.*

– Ruggiero

They will never stop drugs, impossible. It's a free market. Everybody is smoking shabu *in almost every room.*

– Den

Honestly, Kerobokan is full of drugs. The dealers are working with the prison guards, that's Indonesia.

– Saidin

French inmate Filo was throwing a drugs party in his cell at 4 pm. The Frenchman was as famous for his off-the-wall party antics as for his blue room blow jobs. At a party a few weeks earlier, he'd set fire to the bare skin of English inmate Steve, sending him to casualty with third-degree burns and all of the other partying inmates to cell *tikus*. Today, to make it up to Steve and his other friends, Filo had invited them to a celebration of his birthday. He had two bags of drugs to share – one bag of smack and one of coke. Several of his friends were now walking across the jail to his cellblock, Block B. It was time to party. It would end with a bang.

When Brazilian Ruggiero turned up first, Filo held up two bags of white powder, one in each hand. 'Smack or coke?' he asked. Ruggiero didn't do heroin, so opted for coke. Filo dropped one of the bags on the table, and hid the other in a small compartment he'd carved into a step in case guards showed up. He then got down to business, chopping several lines on a CD cover. Ruggiero sprang from the bed as soon as he finished and quickly inhaled a line through a straw. Instantly he felt an excruciating pain in his head and slid down the wall to the floor. Several other western inmates had turned up, but no-one noticed Ruggiero's unusual behaviour. They were too busy taking their own turns to snort.

As more westerners walked across to Block B, a couple of guards noticed the convergence and headed the same way, guessing the foreigners were up to something. The guards reached the cell at the same time as Australian inmate Mick, who was too late now to join the party. The cell door was being held shut by a German inmate, Joachim, to keep guards out, while French inmate Michael, Englishman Steve and Filo snorted lines. Ruggiero was still slumped against the wall, feeling worse. He was shaking his head and making strange noises, trying to clear the haze closing in around him. Still none of the others noticed, too preoccupied by doing lines and then dashing across to hold the door to keep the guards out, taking it in turns like it was a party game.

The guards were getting angry, yelling and shoving their weight against the door, banging it slightly ajar each time. Any second, they would knock the skinny inmates flying and burst into the cell. Filo knew he had only seconds to make the rest of the white powder vanish. He had to decide whether to throw it down the squat toilet or use it. He opted not to waste it. He inhaled three lines in three seconds. It was a bad decision – he had confused the two bags of white powder. What he was snorting was pure heroin.

A moment later, Filo collapsed on the floor near Ruggiero, breathlessly muttering pleas for help before passing out. Ruggiero was teetering on his hands and knees, unable even to lift his drooping head or focus his eyes. He was in no shape to help his friend. Filo was out cold and turning blue. He was overdosing. No oxygen was getting to his brain. His body was going into a spasm. Michael, still upright, knelt beside Filo and started yelling for someone to get salt to put on his tongue to stop him choking on it.

They'd let go of the door and the two guards were inside, shocked by the scene. Ruggiero and Joachim were crawling on the floor, and Filo was on his back with his eyes shut and his lips and face turning blue. They had to get him to hospital fast. The guards didn't want a foreigner's death on their hands – a local's death could be swept under the carpet; a foreigner's would involve a consulate and a major investigation. That was too much trouble.

Instructed by the guards, two *tamping* prisoners scraped Filo off the floor, slung his limp arms around their shoulders and rushed him across the jail to the front door, passing a throng of gaping inmates. As the guards drove Filo to hospital, Ruggiero was called to the offices. He stumbled along the jail pathways, heavily supported by two prisoners. The guards wanted to question him. But Ruggiero was incoherent and the guards told the *tampings* to take him back to his cell. Prisoners along the way all stopped to look at the lifeless Brazilian; his head dropped like a dead weight and his bare toes scraping the ground.

I was overdosing because I never use this shit before. I didn't know what was going on. They put me in my room, and I was crawling on the floor and puking. After I puke I enjoyed the high.

How were the others?

Michael and Steve were okay. Those two used to buy smack, chop some Xanax, mix and snort it together, every day. Ten Xanax, not one. That was how much they were doing. They used smack every day, so they were happy. I don't use it. I'm not used to it. Filo didn't either. He was just like me. He looked like snow when he came back from hospital after three days.

– Ruggiero

Almost as soon as he was conscious, Filo took steps to stop the incident turning into a big deal. If news of his heroin overdose leaked, he would face new charges, Hotel K would lose face, and police would get a warrant to raid the jail. Everyone would suffer, especially the big drug dealers who had to dump thousands of dollars of drugs before every police raid. So Filo splashed $7500 to the doctors to keep it quiet. It worked. Newspapers reported that a French inmate had overdosed on the legal pain killer Tramadol.

A French guy overdosing on heroin in Kerobokan Jail is big shit. He paid around $5000 to keep it quiet.

– Inmate

It was uncommon for the westerners to overdose, but local addicts were regularly overdosing, and were often not taken to hospital for hours.

Overdose happened nearly every second day. Many, many overdose – when it happens to a foreigner, they take them to hospital. Locals – bad luck. After Filo overdosed, this local guy, a tamping, *died a couple of months later. It was 4 am Ramadan and he hadn't eaten, and tried loading himself up with ecstasy and* shabu, *but used too much. He was coughing; people started to massage him, called the doctor, but couldn't take him to hospital because the boss of the jail had to come first. But if he'd been a foreigner, they would put him in a van and just take him to hospital. By 7 am he was dead. Before block open, they'd take body away. I was sad, because he was another drug person who became an addict in jail. Overdosing happens many times – all the junkies, they have this experience – they know how to bring him back. The blood stops flowing to his brain – this will either kill or they bring him back – if they bring him back, the guards would not even know.*

– Mick

First thought to be overdosing on drugs, a prisoner at Kerobokan Prison, Arifin 45, died yesterday, however there is no detailed information on the exact cause of death. The head of Kerobokan Prison Tulus Widjajanto confirmed the inmate had died, however, he denied that a drug overdose was the cause of death. 'His death was not because of a drug overdose, but because of ill health. He had been sick since 3 am. The doctor examined him, but then he had a seizure.'

– *Denpost*, November 2004

Most inmates were on drugs charges, and incarcerating them in Hotel K was like sending a gambler to Vegas. They were buying, selling and playing twenty-four hours a day. Across the jail, inmates were chasing the dragon, smoking *shabu*, shooting up, and popping ecstasy pills like tic tacs. In almost every cell and in every corner across the jail, drug deals were being done. Prisoners would sidle up to new inmates and croon, 'You want *shabu*? You want ecstasy?' Hotel K was Bali's drug hub, its biggest and busiest drug market.

'We are aware of the illegal drugs trade in big quantities in this prison. That's why we wanted to launch a crackdown yesterday by dispatching 300 personnel to give them shock therapy,' police spokesman I Gde Sugianyar said last night.

– *The Daily Telegraph*, 20 June 2009

Most dealers were small time, selling a few ecstasy pills or a bit of *shabu* or smack to pay off their own drug bills. But there were also drug bosses checking in, the high rollers. They could earn up to $10,000 a day, supplying to nightclubs in Bali and Jakarta, to other jails and to their regular customers outside. The high rollers organised shipments across the globe, moving drugs from as far as Peru to Sydney from their cells, utilising their regular suppliers in places such as Mexico, Bangkok, Pakistan and Jakarta.

Hotel K drugs were the cheapest, and often the purest, in Bali. The free market and international dealers inside jail, who could buy high quality drugs in bulk from their overseas sources, drove the prices to rock bottom. A 50,000 rupiah ($7) packet of heroin inside Hotel K would cost 200,000 rupiah ($28) outside.

Inmate and Mexican dealer Vincente was working exclusively in the Hotel K high-roller room, and didn't bother dealing on the public floor with the inmate masses. He didn't need to. He was making thousands of dollars a month, using his private cell as an office. He regularly made calls to contacts in Mexico to organise deliveries of cocaine for his high-profile multi-millionaire Chinese client on the outside. Before each delivery, his client made a payment into Vincente's falsely named bank account, which Vincente checked by phone. His courier then flew into Bali, checked into a cheap hotel designated by Vincente, hid the cocaine in a drawer or cupboard, and gave the key to the front desk, saying, 'My friend Wayan will arrive soon, please give him the key'. After Vincente had confirmed with his courier that the drop was made, he rang his client to give him the collection details. Vincente set it up so the client and the courier never met. It ensured his client's invisibility. More importantly, it secured Vincente's lucrative job as the middle man.

The system served both Vincente and his client well. The client still got his pure cocaine, which he cut and sold to a network of customers in Australia and New Zealand, sending it by boat, and keeping him rich. It also made Vincente a wealthy man from jail, and ensured he and Clara were treated like platinum guests at Hotel K. By applying a cash lubricant to just the right people, Vincente's rich client was able to look after him. The client bought the Mexicans their up-market private cells, and also conjugal time together – after their sham airport relationship had turned into a real love affair in jail. Some nights the client would come into Hotel K, and send a guard to collect Vincente and his own brother, who was also doing a stint for drugs, from their cells. They'd sit in front of the tower block with the jail boss, drinking Johnnie Walker in the warm night air.

Although Vincente didn't bother with selling drugs inside, most of the drug traffickers and dealers who continually checked into Hotel K fought for a slice of the lucrative market. For a while, female inmate Nita was working with a local man, Ketut Dana, whom she started a relationship with after Tony had run away in the great escape. Ketut was stocky, with tattoos covering almost all of his skin from his fingers, along his arms and right up around his neck. He was a member of one of Bali's biggest gangs, Armada Rucun – a rival gang to Laskar Bali who later ruled the jail – and was doing time for hacking a man's head off. Ketut shared the top inmate job of *Pemuka* with fellow head hacker Saidin – the power spots in jail always taken by the toughest. Being *Pemuka* put him in a useful position for the dealers. Ketut was also able to walk in and out of jail freely, so was often used as a drug courier.

Ketut and Nita joined together in business after their love affair started. It was a smart move. She knew the suppliers outside; he could easily collect and deliver the drugs. Nita was also in a prize position to sell. She worked as a cashier in the small canteen in the centre of Hotel K, selling everything from Nescafé, instant noodles and Sunsilk shampoo, to packets of *shabu* and hashish. She was also the main seller in Block W, where drugs were equally as popular. Whenever random groups of women were urine tested, usually eighty per cent came back positive for drug use. The women often sat smoking *shabu* in Nita's cell during the day. Because she was a *tamping*, the guards usually left her cell alone.

The most ruthlessly competitive dealer was Arman Maulidie. He'd worked as a drug boss on the outside for years, and had spent five months in a Jakarta jail before being busted again in Bali. Police had raided his home and, after shifting a heavy cabinet in his bedroom and ripping up suspicious floor tiles, they had found a bunker filled with thousands of ecstasy pills and hundreds of grams of *shabu*. There were also bank books showing deposits of A$3500 a month, and drug ledgers. Arman went down for ten years. But in Hotel K he didn't miss a beat, selling *shabu* and ecstasy to the strong domestic market, and also working as Iwan's front man. He had cut-throat ambition, striving to be Hotel K's drug lord with an exclusive and protected monopoly, like dealers in some of Indonesia's other jails.

In Jakarta's Cipinang Jail, for example, the drug world was tightly structured. One drug boss inmate paid a monthly fee of fifty million rupiah ($6700) to the jail authorities to own exclusively the hugely lucrative marketplace of 3000 inmates. Guards knew the system and enforced it, brutally bashing anyone else caught selling and locking them in tiny isolation cells, sometimes for months.

In another Jakarta jail situated right next door, the drug business was also strictly controlled but worked differently. Several dealers paid for immunity. Only these five or six inmates could sell, but it was still fiercely competitive. Each dealer would sit at a small table in his cell selling heroin to a long line of addicts. Out the front of each of these cells, a prisoner who'd paid to own a syringe business would sit at a card table, renting out needles and syringes for ten cents a turn while spruiking for business, 'Come my place, come my place, buy something nice'.

You pay one thousand rupiah, you take the syringe, you go inside, you give money to one guy, syringe to the other guy and he fills it in for you. If you have your own syringe, you give him your own syringe and he fills it.

– Thomas

Hotel K's free market was at the other end of the spectrum from these organised drug worlds. No-one had blanket protection from the guards or exclusivity to sell. Arman would later become the number one boss when he aligned himself with Bali's most violent gang, Laskar, but in the meantime, he had to share the market, using only his ruthless ambition, and even his wife, Ratih, to build his business and beat the competition. Ratih had been caught with drugs and sentenced to two years in jail. Inside Hotel K she was famous for something else – her pink penis dildo. After news of a spontaneous cell check one day, she had scrambled to hide anything contraband and hurled her pink dildo towards the back window. But, in the panic, she missed. It hit the cell wall, and ricocheted out the door and onto the footpath, where it started jigging in front of a long line of girls waiting for roll call. The story of the dancing dildo titillated the jail, and earned Ratih a reputation as well.

Arman was less amused when he discovered his wife was having a lesbian affair with Nita, but looked at it pragmatically. He hoped it would split up Nita and her boyfriend, Ketut, marking the end of their business relationship and giving Arman a chance to consolidate with Nita. It didn't. But Ketut was later transferred to another jail and Arman lured Nita into working with him. Arman ultimately finished his underhanded scheme by stealing Nita's supplier and cutting her out.

Arman sold ecstasy to many people in karaoke clubs; many, many karaoke clubs take ecstasy from him, shabu *from him, so this time in Bali, many things actually came from jail.*

– Thomas

Austrian Thomas was another high roller who stirred up the market. He got pure and cheap smack from his regular sources, so started undercutting the others. It was a price war. Thomas sold both to inmates and his customers outside. When he received a delivery, he sent his regularly collaborating guard, Pak Giri, outside to collect it and bring it into Hotel K. This would usually take place at the start of the guard's shift at around 10 pm. All night, Thomas then sat in his cell weighing the smack into packets to match orders from outside customers and crushing it into a fine powder to put it into straws for prisoners to buy. Thomas used a cigarette lighter to melt the ends of the straws and seal them, often employing his cellmates to assist. Sometimes they would work for hours, filling up three or four hundred straws, which he'd sell for 50,000 rupiah ($7) each.

In the morning before the blocks were opened for roll call, Pak Giri would arrive at Thomas's window to collect several noodle packets, each filled with fifty straws, to take home with him. Thomas didn't want to risk inmates stealing it, so kept only one packet at a time in jail – which he guarded closely, often stuffing it into his underpants. Whenever he needed more straws, Pak Giri would bring them in. Pak Giri also smuggled out the bigger packets and delivered them to Thomas's outside customers. In a day's work, the guard could almost double his monthly salary.

How much did you pay Pak Giri?

It depends how much he brings in and out. Maybe if he brings in two hundred grams, and he makes two or three deliveries, he gets two million in his pocket [$270]. For an Indonesian, that's good. One or two million in his pocket, he's happy. All afternoon, he smiles.

– Thomas

Foreign inmates were forever phoning Thomas to buy a few straws of smack. He'd pay a local prisoner 5000 rupiah (70 cents) to deliver it to a foreigner's cell, so he didn't make himself too conspicuous by pacing up and down the pathways – although most guards turned a blind eye anyway.

Most of the guards, they knew already. If I was sitting with them, talking, I say, 'I want to use'. I go into the toilet, I use smack, I come out and talk again with him. No problem.

– Thomas

The Hotel K market was ruthlessly competitive, with the high rollers always watching their backs. While Arman was keen to take over Thomas's business, Ketut and his cohort guard, Fisheyes, were losing their existing smack business, and made bringing down Thomas their target. Fisheyes was one of the most dangerous guards. He always had his eyes on the lookout for a chance to sabotage other dealers who were outside his partnership with Ketut, or to confiscate their drugs to use and sell. Being an insider meant the sly guard usually got wind of the latest hiding spots and searched for drugs where other guards didn't even think to look.

One afternoon, Thomas was loitering between the tennis court and Block W with a bit of heroin in his pocket. He spotted Fisheyes slinking out of the steel door of Block W after a rendezvous with his inmate girlfriend. To avoid him, Thomas walked briskly down the path behind Iwan's workshop. But Fisheyes strode after him, shouting: 'Come here, come here!' He trapped Thomas behind the workshop and started frisking him. Thomas put his hands in the air while Fisheyes rifled his pockets and patted him down. Fisheyes found nothing at first, but then caught on. 'What's in your hand, Thomas?' Thomas held his fist high in the air and refused to open it. Fisheyes yanked at his arm. Thomas turned slightly and used his bony hip to knock him away. Then, in a split second, Thomas stuffed the packet of heroin in his mouth. Fisheyes was furious. He flew at Thomas and grabbed him around the throat, trying to stop him swallowing it. But Thomas was a pro and the evidence quickly vanished.

If he doesn't have evidence, he can fuck off. I say, okay, if you want to talk to the boss, I also want to talk. If you be quiet, I be quiet. I knew he sold shabu *and smack, and in the end he didn't make a problem for me. But he's an asshole. He's a very big asshole.*

– Thomas

But a couple of weeks later, Fisheyes stung Thomas. The guard was sleeping on a chair outside the printing factory as Thomas snuck past to hide his new supply of one hundred and fifty grams of *shabu.*

I got sent shabu *– it was Sunday or a holiday and one of my guards brought it in. I kept my drugs in the printing factory at this time. So I gave the* shabu *to one boy, who had a key to the factory and he put it inside. But this fucking bastard Pak Juli Fisheyes, he was sitting outside. One or two hours later, Ketut Dana says to me: 'Pak Juli wants to make problem for you. He wants to call the big boss to check the printing factory.'*

I say, 'Okay, you help me', because he was close to this bastard Fisheyes. They were smoking together, making money together, they were close. I say, 'Can you tell him, if he wants, I give him ten grams. If he shuts up'. Ketut goes and comes back. 'No, he don't want. He wants all of it.' So I say, 'I got it on credit, I can't give all. I'll give him twenty grams to shut up'. He goes again and comes and say, okay, he only wants thirty grams. So I give him thirty grams – much *money. This time is maybe 400,000 or 500,000 rupiah [$70] for one gram. But after a few days it was finished, and he kept coming back and asking me, 'Give me a little bit for smoking, give me a little bit for smoking'. He is a real motherfucker, actually. On one hand he use; on the other hand, he catches people who are not with him.*

– Thomas

Thomas realised it had been a set-up between Fisheyes and Ketut to take his *shabu.* Despite this, Thomas later smoked *shabu* with Fisheyes in Arman's cell. Fisheyes was one of several guards who would often sit in the cells and smoke with prisoners. *Shabu* was the drug of choice for working guards, as it gave them energy and made the mind race, unlike dope or heroin, which made them sleepy.

Many times he came in this room and was sitting there and smoking. So, I also came there, and I was smoking together with him. Because I am not one hundred per cent experienced in this shabu, *he lit the fire for me for smoking and I held the bong. But he still was a headache because he always wants something. He wants to buy half gram, or says, give me 200,000 rupiah. He always gave me a headache.*

– Thomas

Erratic drug censure in Hotel K meant drug users and dealers always had to stay on red alert. There were devious guards like Fisheyes and guards watching for drugs so they could get a cash sling to keep quiet. And there were always some guards who took it to the boss. But the constantly changing jail chiefs mostly opted to keep the prolific drug trade quiet, rarely choosing to involve the police. If a prisoner was caught with drugs, it was usually dealt with internally by confiscating them and locking the prisoner in cell *tikus*, until they paid to get out. Advertising the jail's thriving drug culture was not in the interests of the jail and its bosses.

Cunning prisoners devised a circus of stunts to get drugs inside. Prisoners got people to simply throw drugs over the wall in tennis balls, or cigarette packets weighted with a stone, coordinating the timing by phone.

He says, 'I'm here'. I say, 'Okay, throw'.

– Thomas

Some fished for drugs by casting a line over the wall with a nail tied to it for weight. After someone outside tied the drugs on, they'd reel it back inside. Suppliers posing as visitors often brought drugs into the blue room, in hollowed-out loaves of bread, hidden underneath a batch of cakes or tucked in their shoes. Local prisoners sometimes pretended to sweep the front courtyard so they could collect a drug package left under a bush. But the easiest, most efficient technique – the one high rollers mostly used – was to pay a guard, or a prisoner who had licence to come and go.

Police had no jurisdiction inside Hotel K without a warrant and were virtually impotent when it came to catching prisoners with drugs. In the time it took to obtain a warrant, the collaborating guards would phone their inmate dealers, warning them of the pending raid. By the time the police got inside, the bigger dealers were always prepared and would have disposed of their huge drug stashes.

Bali Police narcotics officers cancelled their planned raid of Kerobokan State Penitentiary on Thursday afternoon after prison officials warned them the raid might trigger a riot. Three truckloads of officers arrived at the prison's main gate around 3pm. The officers were ready to enter the prison to conduct a search for illegal drugs when the prison officials informed them the inmates were getting agitated and were likely to resist the search.

– *Jakarta Post*, 19 June 2009

Although prisoners had protection and insurance inside Hotel K, dangers still lurked for them outside if their customers were caught by the police. Aware of the heavy trafficking in and out of the jail, police set up surveillance directly outside the front of the jail, where they did have jurisdiction. Prisoners and guards running drugs in and out of the jail and doing transactions in the car park had to be careful.

There are many ways drug dealers use to deceive the police. One of them is by hiding the evidence in a torn slipper. This trick was used by suspect Sunardi, owning 1.4 grams of heroin. The prosecutor stated that Sunardi was captured in the Kerobokan Jail parking lot. Police got information that there would be a drug transaction in the parking lot. They executed surveillance and saw the accused showed a suspicious attitude. The police approached the accused and frisked him. At first the police found nothing on the body of the accused. But on seeing the slipper of the accused was open, the police examined it and found a small plastic package that was later tested and proven to be heroin.

– *Denpost*, 3 December 2005

The blue room was one of the busiest places for drug transactions. Drug deals were as common as blow jobs. Prisoners would take their drugs to a visit, to sell to their friends or customers. Many of the westerners regularly did a bit of trade to help pay their drug bills. But their customers put them at risk the moment they stepped foot outside the front door of Hotel K. Some avoided that risk by shooting up in the blue room toilet or popping an ecstasy pill before they left.

Suspect James Lobo, 24, was nabbed by police in the parking area of Bali's biggest prison after buying drugs inside, last Thursday. Police had been watching the prison after a drug felon involved in a case they were handling revealed the source of the stuff came from Kerobokan Jail. The police carried out surveillance, watching every visitor closely. At around 4 pm on Thursday, the suspect came to the prison with an excuse to visit. Thirty minutes later he came out. Several police approached the suspect because of his suspicious body language. When approached by the police, the suspect's behaviour got even weirder. When the officer reached in his pocket, a plastic bag containing putaw *[low grade heroin] was found. The suspect confessed he bought the illegal stuff from one of the prisoners for 400,000 rupiah.*

– *Denpost*, 27 May 2006

Brazilian Ruggiero had one strict rule for any friends who came in to buy drugs from him in the blue room; necessary for his self-protection.

I always say, 'The only condition I make is you put it in your pussy, not in your pocket. If you get searched and arrested, I get a problem'. Most of the time it's a girl coming in, my Swedish friend or American friend, they wear a skirt, they come prepared. They just … shhh . . . in an eye blink, it disappears up. A small little ball like this. Usually they take five, ten grams.

Bit dangerous, though, if it leaks?

Noooo. It's professionally done, professional. I'm not in jail for nothing, baby. I've done it many times.

– Ruggiero

CHAPTER 13
ROLLING THE DICE

I hate the fucking police, they fucked my life up. I don't do anything bad to anybody. I am not criminal, I am a normal person and I do business. I don't force anybody to take drugs. And if somebody has never used drugs, he can never get them for the first time from my hand. It's a normal business. They should make it legal, they should make it fucking cheap, so there is no criminal, so people can go in the shop and buy it. It is bullshit, actually.

I never do anything criminal. I came this way. You never know in your life where it is going, maybe you go this way, and you start a business, you don't think anything bad, or anything criminal. You just want to make some money; okay, you do something.

You didn't think it was criminal when you started selling drugs?

I knew it was illegal but I didn't think it was criminal. Criminal is if I steal something, if I hurt somebody, if I do something wrong, if I make corruption – because corruption is stealing, this is criminal. But doing business is criminal? I don't think it is criminal. Cigarettes are not good for health, alcohol is not good for your health, the chemicals they put in the food is not good for health. So they choose, the fucking government, they choose what you can do and what you cannot do. And normal sense, it does not make. What is the problem if we sit here and smoke ganja together? What is the problem? Who would it hurt? What's the problem? But if they catch you, they put you three years in jail, four years, ten years in jail. Bullshit.

– Thomas

***

The Denpasar Police apprehended a 35-year-old Caucasian man, Thomas Borsitzki, who is allegedly one of the top illicit drug suppliers in Indonesia. They found some 13 grams of pure heroin stashed inside a black-striped brown bag in his rented bungalow in Canggu area, 15 kilometres west of Denpasar. Borsitzki had been on the local police watch-list since the 1990s, after authorities began to suspect that he was closely connected with international drug smuggling syndicates.

– *Jakarta Post*, March 2002

For those involved in the drug business, it became an addiction to the game, the money and the buzz. It was worth the risks and the inevitable jail time. Most of the high rollers in Hotel K had done time before. Just as being inside didn't stop them playing, the moment they were released, they were back at it again outside. Iwan, Arman, Thomas and Nita had all been jailed more than once. Arman's convictions also kept multiplying while he was in jail. Nita was re-arrested for dealing only weeks after her release, while she was waiting in immigration housing for her passport so she could be deported. Nita was about to go home – go free. Instead, she went straight back to jail. With no cash left to make deals, she got a further ten years. She was suicidal, and for weeks didn't leave her cell in Block B. But when she started coping again, she also started selling again.

Thomas had returned for his second stint in Hotel K after ten years of business in a snakes and ladders-style drug dealing career; climbing, and then spiralling down to rock bottom, rolling the dice on his fate every day. After he was freed from Hotel K in the early 1990s, he was deported, like all non-Indonesian ex-cons, and his passport was red stamped so he couldn't return. He chose to fly to Bangkok rather than back home to Austria, and spent a few weeks networking. He bought a false German passport and then flew straight back to Indonesia. There he embarked on a life of constantly moving around to stay under the radar and invisible to police as he built a drug cartel that would, at one point, dictate the price of heroin in Jakarta.

Thomas had started his drug career in Austria during his teenage years, riding trains to Italy to buy a hundred grams of hashish to sell and smoke with his friends while they drove around to discos in the small farming village where he lived with his grandparents. 'I was already a little bit naughty when I was young.' By the time he was sixteen years old, he was smoking heroin, hashish and marijuana. By nineteen, he was facing a drug charge, but left Austria to begin a backpacking trip before it went to court. He flew to India and made Asia his new home. He dabbled in various businesses, but the drug trade was the one that would consume his life.

Soon after leaving Austria, he met an English woman in Bali who was ten years older than him. They had a child together, and both worked for an export company, sourcing clothes, statues, wood carvings and masks to send to England to be sold at North London's Camden market. Although Bali was their base, Thomas and his girlfriend were gypsies, endlessly moving between India, Nepal, Thailand and Bali. They used drugs regularly, and Thomas always flew with a smorgasbord of hash, dope and smack for their enjoyment, preferring to buy in Bangkok.

I didn't want to buy drugs in Indonesia at that time because it was always a little bit dangerous. Bangkok was very open. Everyone was using, tourists very openly using.

How did you carry the drugs on the plane?

I put it in my arse. At this time, it was not for business or anything. Only was fun and enjoy. I just pack in plastic and put some cream or something and push it up. When you first put it inside, you can feel it moving up, but automatically it goes right up and you can't feel it anymore. It's a safe way to carry.

After, I start getting to know people in Bali and start to bring maybe fifty gram, one hundred gram from Bangkok to Bali to try selling. This time I would eat it because it was too much to put up my arse. I first swallowed with water because I didn't know. But you cannot use water because your stomach is too full. You squash some banana and roll plastic ball of heroin in it so it's a bit slippery. Some use yoghurt, some use banana or something like that.

Actually, only two, three times I eat it myself. But when the business started to work, I didn't want to bring it myself anymore. So my friend in Bangkok buys the goods for me, and arranges a carrier for me. Mostly at this time I used Bali people.

I used other people to do the packing. This is their specialist job. You use fine sandwich plastic from the supermarket and put one and a half spoonfuls of heroin on the plastic, and fold it many times. It can't be rough. If one packet opens, you die. Then you use a cigarette lighter to melt it shut so it can't fall out. If you burn the plastic too much it turns black; sometimes this makes people feel sick and vomit. But if it's packed well, it doesn't make you feel like vomiting.

If they start to vomit, it's difficult to eat any more. You have to stop. You can't keep going. And if a courier can't eat a minimum of five or six hundred grams, they can't go because it is not worth the trip for such a small amount. They have to start again. So you wait until it comes out the next day, and eat it again. Maybe delayed two days.

I had one woman – she could eat only about three hundred grams. She could not eat more. But she wanted to go and we had already bought her ticket. Money already spent, so we put in her bra and we put inside her. She can't eat much but she makes it even by putting it elsewhere. They must carry six hundred and fifty grams minimum. I had maybe five or six women. One actually was good, she can eat a lot and she put inside and she was big inside. Was good.

Does the courier wash it before giving it to you?

Yeah! Expensive shit!

– Thomas

To safely move his drugs from Bangkok to Indonesia, Thomas used professionals, preferring to use Balinese, African and Nepalese people, who he found could usually swallow large amounts. Thomas built up his drug cartel over five years after his first stint in Hotel K, and climbed to the top of the lucrative drug business in Jakarta, doing incredibly well financially.

Maybe every month I sold five or six kilograms of heroin. I made $90,000, $100,000 a month, so I live well. I had good life. I couldn't use all the money. I could do whatever I wanted to do and the money still wasn't *finished. You can eat what you want, you can buy what you want but still you have money left for savings.*

– Thomas

Thomas decided to plan for his future and invested his vast amounts of cash. He flew to Singapore with $100,000 in his money belt, mostly in Singapore's top $10,000 notes to avoid a bulky stash. The first bank, wary of laundering dirty cash, knocked him back, but he easily opened an account in a Chinese bank, using his false passport. Then every few months his girlfriend would fly to Singapore to top up their savings and enjoy a bit of luxury shopping. By the time Thomas was arrested next, he had saved nearly half a million dollars and was well on his way to securing his financial future.

I was thinking, okay, I want to put one million dollars in overseas saving account in pound sterling – this time was about four per cent interest, $2300 interest a month for my security. I never wanted to buy car and house. To stay in one place, for me wasn't good. Two or three months, I change. So I was thinking it's better to put money in the bank – one million. This is my security. I thought, maybe if they don't catch me I work only five, six months more. And after that I thought, maybe I start to make another business – maybe driving a taxi.

– Thomas

Thomas was always careful not to be too flashy, but had bought himself a gold Cartier watch worth $30,000. When this watch was stolen, it could well have been an omen that the good life was about to come to an end for him.

My $30,000 Cartier watch was stolen in Bangkok by a Pakistani friend who I'd known for seven or eight years, who came to my home nearly *every day. I take a shower in the hotel, I put the watch on the bed, one gold ring on the bed, and when I come out he was gone.*

– Thomas

Thomas was wealthy, but he was living off his wits. The dice were always rolling. He had become accustomed to living on the run, always looking over his shoulder, using his instincts to evade police and moving fast when he felt the need. When his cartel was at its peak, he sensed it was necessary to get out of Indonesia and lie low in Bangkok for a bit. It was nothing specific, just a sense that things were a bit hot. But he didn't act on it. He hesitated. He was waiting on a delivery from his Nepalese courier, Buddhi, who had just flown in from Bangkok to Jakarta with a kilogram of heroin inside him.

It was a routine delivery. Buddhi breezed through customs, checked into a random cheap hotel and phoned its name through to Bangkok, doing everything by the book for his usual $500 fee. Thomas called Bangkok for the hotel name and then phoned Buddhi. He still hadn't expelled all the capsules, so Thomas arranged to pick them up around midday the next day, to give him time to pass the capsules of heroin and wash off the shit.

Pretty disgusting job, isn't it? Yeah, but money doesn't smell.

– Thomas

Meanwhile, a Chinese drug customer, David, was impatiently waiting for his smack order. Thomas broke a cardinal rule. He told him that at that moment his boy was in the hotel waiting to excrete the heroin and, in a costly slip of the tongue, named the hotel. His timing couldn't have been worse. Later that night, David was arrested with fifty grams of heroin. In trying to save himself, he gave up Thomas, supplying his home address and, most crucially, the sitting duck – the Nepalese boy waiting in the hotel. Police raided the hotel and arrested Buddhi, who instantly admitted that the heroin was for his boss, Thomas, not for himself.

At 6 am the next day, several Jakarta drug police went to Thomas's house, and set up a sting to get inside. Another one of his customers had been caught with a small amount of heroin and she had also told police that Thomas was her dealer. Police used her to knock on his door to lure him out. The moment he opened the door, police pounced. They charged in and tore his house apart. But, as usual, Thomas kept very little stuff near him. Police uncovered only twelve grams of heroin, but also seized an incriminating $80,000 in cash. Thomas tried to negotiate. 'How about we split the cash? And don't write any investigation.' They cops weren't interested. 'Okay, you take it all, take the 130 million but don't write it,' he urged. 'No, not possible,' they said. Thomas knew he needed to cut a deal fast or he'd have big problems. 'Okay, I give you 200 million.' 'No, not possible.' 'Okay, how much you need?' 'Not possible.'

Thomas was unaware that Buddhi was in custody and had pointed the finger at him. The Jakarta police boss had ordered his arrest. The case was already too big for these low-ranking officers to take his money, no matter how much they wanted to. But a knock-back in the first instance didn't necessarily end negotiations. In fact, it was just the start. It simply meant that Thomas would need to deal with the police superiors – and splash a lot more cash.

He hired the most expensive and the best lawyer around, whose non-negotiable start-up fee was $60,000. He was former president Suharto's family lawyer, and was used by Bali's former governor 'Mr OK' to exonerate him of corruption charges. This lawyer was known as a magician who could create life-saving magic, coming up with masterful ways to get his clients off the hook. He would always find some slippery little loophole for them to slide through. He found one for Thomas.

The Nepalese boy, the Chinese man and the lady all knew him as 'Thomas'. But he was not 'Thomas'. By this time he had switched from using his German passport to using a false English passport and having a new stolen identity. He was now Richard Edward Crawley. In one masterstroke, the lawyer had come up with the perfect way for the judge to drop the charges against Thomas for Buddhi's one kilogram of heroin, and the other two customers' grams, without red-flagging a bribe. The judge convicted and sentenced Thomas, or Richard Edward Crawley, to only eight months for the twelve grams they found at his home. Cash had saved Thomas from a life sentence, or even the death penalty. But the lawyer's fees and bribe money blew out his million-dollar dream.

If you have big problem, you need big money. I had to pay about $240,000 but I got only eight months for over a kilogram of heroin. I paid it to [my lawyer] and he paid it to the judge, the prosecutors and the police. He was a middleman. But by myself I can't contact the same way a good lawyer can do it. I never could have done it by myself, even with money. I couldn't have done it.

If it's too exposed, the judges and prosecutors are afraid. You can't talk too much. Newspaper and TV people came, but I sat in court hunched over with my head down. I didn't want them to take photos of me; I didn't want to talk to them, so the judge will not be afraid to deal. I knew if I had money I could pay, no problem, but only if you shut up, you're quiet and in court you're nice, polite to them. And hopefully they will receive your money, and they will help you, hopefully no problems. In the process, less you talk, less risk, more possibilities.

– Thomas

His Nepalese courier, Buddhi, wasn't so fortunate. He was sentenced to thirteen years jail, but riskily appealed and got life. He started his sentence in the notorious Cipinang Jail, where Thomas was also incarcerated. But Buddhi was then moved to Nusakambangan Island, and shared his days with hundreds of international drug bosses and drug couriers, including one of the most notorious: a black African man nicknamed 'Doctor', who got caught at an airport carrying a dead baby stuffed with heroin.

The Cartier gold watch was long gone as Thomas sat crammed into one of Cipinang Jail's isolation cells for the first three months of his eight-month sentence. It was smaller in length than a bathtub and he couldn't straighten his legs out properly. There were no breaks outside and no facilities to wash himself, only a guard occasionally spraying a hose through the door. After twelve weeks, he was moved out of isolation and into a small cell tightly packed with fourteen prisoners.

For the entire eight months, Thomas slept on concrete, which turned the skin on his hips and shoulders black. His body was also covered in weeping sores, a problem shared by all fourteen cellmates, and he scratched at a painfully itchy rash twenty-four hours a day. Several times the guards had viciously bashed him for as little as giving an insolent glance in their direction. With 3000 skinny and often heroin-addicted inmates loitering aimlessly around, the Cipinang yards resembled a concentration camp. Fortunately for him, Thomas was only doing eight months.

After his stint in Cipinang, Thomas was again expelled from Indonesia to Bangkok, where he spent a few months before returning to Jakarta on a new false passport. The heroin market was now dominated by a Nepalese friend of Thomas's, Man Singh, who would later be shot dead and named by Jakarta police as the boss of the Bali Nine. Thomas and Man Singh were working together, splitting deliveries of heroin to sell to their customers. The underworld grapevine hummed with the news that Thomas was back and it didn't take long for it to filter back to the police. Thomas was again spending his days looking over his shoulder, constantly moving around to stay under the police radar. Out of the blue one day, he received a telephone call from a drug squad police officer – one who had helped to put him away the last time. He was touting for business, offering immunity in exchange for cash.

He didn't want to catch me this time, he wanted to get my money. But this only works for some time. If you are friends with a policeman, he can't catch you directly. But other police will catch you. You pay and afterwards you still get caught. I didn't want to meet him.

The first time he rang I didn't know who it was, so I picked it up. 'Oh, this motherfucker.' Afterwards he called again, but I had his name in my telephone, so I gave the phone to my girlfriend. I tell her to say that I've gone back to my country. Then we moved quickly to Sukabungan, a village maybe three, four hours from Jakarta. So I stayed there, hiding. But it was very far away and also boring in this fucking village, so after, I changed to Bali again.

First I stayed in Seminyak. I feel no good, so I stay in Ubud. After I feel no good, I change far, far, far. Keep changing. Police were looking for me a long time, but always they see me and I get lost again. When police catch me, the police say, 'I follow you, I lost you again, I saw you, I lost you again'. I was a headache for them. I kept changing the place I lived. Also, when I go out on my motorbike I always use full helmet. I don't go to Kuta, Legian; I never go to busy places like that. Also, I go on the small streets. I knew police were looking for me.

– Thomas

It was yet another dealer's betrayal that eventually led police to his door again and to his second stint in Hotel K. One of Thomas's former Nepalese couriers, Kiran – brother of Bali Nine boss, Man Singh – exposed his location. The catalyst was an emergency phone call to Kiran from his wife, telling him that police were raiding their Jakarta house and warning him not to come home. So, Kiran flew from Jakarta to Bali and dropped in on his old boss, Thomas, who was instantly a little nervous.

I said to him, 'It's better if you don't stay in Bali, you bring problem. If you want, I have a friend in immigration who can check if you're in the computer yet, if not, you better leave now.' But he didn't want to listen. He came to my house, using my swimming pool.

– Thomas

Just as Thomas feared, Kiran brought the Jakarta Police to Bali – they tracked Kiran by tapping his phone and arrested him when he went to pick up three hundred grams of heroin from a hotel room. Typically, he spilled information in a desperate attempt to save himself, giving up Thomas's home address. But Kiran's betrayal didn't save him. He got twenty years and took his friend Thomas down too.

I was stupid, actually. For ten days I didn't know they'd caught him, and then my friend in Bangkok called me and say, 'Does Kiran know where you stay?'. 'Yeah, he came to my house.' 'He is no good, you better move,' he told me. I asked, 'How long have they held him already?'. 'Ten days.' I thought they must have finished the investigation and he didn't talk about me. If it was two or three days, okay. But ten days? I thought, no problem. So I didn't leave. On the eleventh day, they caught me – because he did talk.

– Thomas

It was dusk as Thomas turned his motorbike into his driveway on his way back from grocery shopping at Hero Supermarket in Denpasar. He switched off the bike, pulled off his helmet and in the next second, he was gone. Two officers sprang from the shadows and handcuffed him. More police quickly converged from every direction. They'd all been sitting in cars and nearby cafés, waiting for the notoriously slippery drug boss to show up. Inside Thomas's bungalow, police uncovered thirteen grams of pure heroin in a black-striped brown bag. One of the officers smugly asked Thomas if he recognised him.

He was the same fucking policeman who catch me in '92. It was the same fucking guy. I didn't realise until he says, 'You still remember me, Thomas?' … Fuck.

I only got caught with a small amount, but they say I'm part of an international syndicate, I'm the second in charge in Asia, and number one boss in Indonesia. But we are not mafia, we are not criminals, we are not anything, we are only friends. Okay, maybe we work together. We do business. He send, I sell. He make money, I make money. But no organisation or anything.

At this time I still had money, not too much anymore, but some. But the problem was, a woman who I was [with] for three years ran away as soon as I got arrested and took everything; she took the money, she took all my clothes. Everything. My prosecutor was Urip Tri Gunawan, he said he's a Christian so he won't make it too difficult. 'You pay eighty million rupiah and you get less than one year.' But the court gives me three years because I didn't have any more money.*

What was it like going back to Kerobokan again?

For me, easy to go inside, because I already know the guards. And I already know that after a little bit of time you can sell, you can have a lady. I knew a little bit already. When you first come, you don't know anything. The second time it's easier.

– Thomas

*Thomas's prosecutor in the Bali courtroom, Urip Tri Gunawan, was later sentenced to twenty years jail for taking a US$660,000 bribe. He was also the prosecutor in the drug cases of Mexicans Vincente and Clara and former Bali governor 'Mr OK'. The prosecutor's new nickname was 'The six billion rupiah man'.

The Corruption Court sentenced disgraced prosecutor Urip Tri Gunawan to 20 years in jail Thursday for taking a US$660,000 bribe to drop a major embezzlement case against fugitive tycoon Sjamsul Nursalim.

– *Jakarta Post*, 5 September 2008

CHAPTER 14

ANIMAL FARM

Jail is a place that drives you nuts. You go crazy. Can you imagine being locked in a room every day at 5 pm, when people are watching the sunset, locked in a fucking shit cell. You have to be locked up for thirteen hours day after day. It's not easy … it's very easy for sane people to lose their minds. Some people kill themselves, some people who don't use drugs, start using drugs in jail, many people. Many people get fucked up in jail.

– Ruggiero

You can't think too much or you go insane. If I think too much, I'm not happy.

– Thomas

Surviving Hotel K was not just about surviving the violence, the drugs, or the guards and inmates – it was also about trying to create a life in a small world that was constantly on edge. Every day, inmates were surrounded by some of Indonesia's worst psychopaths, who roamed the grounds of the jail looking for any opportunity to stave off the madness and boredom that life in Hotel K brought on them. Westerners were not only thrown into a violent environment, but into a culture that they often didn't understand. But they had to adjust – and many did this by trying to make their world a little more civilised, more comfortable and more like home. Bali Nine member Scott's parents gave him a vacuum cleaner. Schapelle's sister Mercedes brought her a small, fluffy dog named Stanley that she dressed in pink ribbons and walked around the jail. Argentinean Frederico installed a jacuzzi out the back of his cell. Brazilian Ruggiero built a pond with a Buddha statue sitting at its edge to meditate beside. Italian Juri had a wedding.

I rot my brain with computer games and TV and play tennis. I just feel stupid with what I'm doing. It's no way to live a life, really, but it's what I have to do. Same as any 10-year-old kid … eat, sleep, play sport and play games; that's all I do – it's ridiculous.

– Scott, Australian inmate

Many prisoners didn't judge others by their crimes. They were all in the same place and had to live together. A daily routine could include dashing from one cell to another for a smoke of *shabu* or a card game, organising drug deals or plotting to sabotage someone else's. Other ways to pass the time were blue room visits, sex, reading, a weekly yoga class, or, exclusively for the men, playing tennis, cricket or volleyball. Despite these activities life was a constant grind, but Hotel K – like any other pocket of society – had its characters with strange habits and hobbies that could make life more dangerous but also more tolerable and interesting, for themselves and other inmates.

Killer Saidin, the snake man, was one such character. Saidin had returned to Hotel K after originally serving a short time, and then being released on a legal technicality, for the late 1990s decapitation killing. Two years later he violated his parole by getting involved in a fight at a gambling night. Subsequently, his murder case was brought back to court and he was sentenced to seventeen years. Saidin was quickly promoted to *Pemuka*, the powerful position above *tamping*. He was in charge of prisoners, had keys to all the cellblocks and the run of the jail. He liked westerners and often hung out with Ruggiero and Juri, shared a cellblock with the Bali Nine and walked Schapelle to blue room visits.

It wasn't officially sanctioned, but Saidin slipped in and out of Hotel K's doors whenever he liked, often hiring a car and driving two hours to his home to stay with his wife and three young daughters for the night. Despite his crime, he was well-liked. Inmates didn't judge him for it and, if they did, it worked in his favour, giving him an aura of power. They all knew he kept his machete under a mattress in his cell as a souvenir of his gruesome crime – and that this sent out a warning not to mess with him.

He was lovely. He was adorable. You know, I have always been naturally attracted to the bad guys. Before I knew who he was, I always hung around with him. We smoke some shabu *together and we tell stories. And then someone said to me, 'You're not afraid to be with him?' I said, 'Why?' 'He's the biggest criminal here,' he told me. Later I said to him, 'Saidin, did you cut someone's head off?' 'Yeah, I did it. I would have done it again, the motherfucker, I would have lost my job if I didn't'. I said, 'I'm so happy to be your friend'. He said, 'Ruggiero, just by them [the Laskar gang] seeing you next to me, they won't touch you again'. Laskar wouldn't touch him, but he didn't have the power to stop them beating someone else.*

Why would the gang never touch him?

Because he would get his knife and cut another head off. He doesn't give a fuck. He was a maniac. Everyone knows his knife is still there. He's the type of guy who doesn't talk much, but you don't fuck with him. Leave the guy alone . . . he's psychopathic. Completely cold blooded. I nickname him Gi Gi as in 'guillotine' because he cut the head off. It was a private thing. Not many people dared to call him 'guillotine'.

– Ruggiero

Saidin was security for VIPs and dangerous inmates. He was called if someone overdosed and he broke up fights – but his specialty was catching snakes. One morning when a two-metre cobra slithered into one of the women's cells through a bathroom drain in Block W, Saidin got a phone call asking him to come quickly. He knew the drill; it happened often enough. He ran down the path and into Block W. Instantly he knew which cell it was, as a group of women stood outside, yelling and pointing. Saidin walked down to the cell and went inside. The snake's head was up; it was angry and ready to bite. Saidin walked back out. He'd have to wait until it settled or he'd be bitten. He had an affinity with snakes, and knew when to leave them alone. He sat chatting to the women, keeping an eye on the cobra through the door. As soon as he saw its head drop, he went in, slid his hands under its middle and slowly up to its head, then scooped it up, curled it around his neck and came out. The women leaped back to let him pass.

As he casually walked to his cell, he decided to keep this one as another pet. He already had five cobras that he kept in his cell inside large plastic water bottles under his bed or in the bathroom. They were his pets. Every couple of weeks, Saidin left Hotel K to drive to Denpasar and buy four white rats from a pet shop to feed his snakes. He would take the cap off a bottle, and put the live rats in each container for the snakes to swallow live and whole. Most days he took one of his snakes for a walk, wearing it around his shoulders, even wandering into the blue room. Often he let the snakes out in his cell for a play, or put them out in the sun. They'd vanish into the long grass at the back of the cells, usually returning through the bathroom drain a week or so later. The westerners were fascinated by Saidin's ability to tame snakes and regularly took photos. His four cellmates had gotten used to living with snakes. But one afternoon, one of them became a little too blasé.

Inmate Nanang was drunk on *arak* when he took one snake out of its water bottle, and let it run around his body, teasing it by sticking out his tongue, breathing 'Haaaaa' into its face. The snake didn't like it. It sprayed venom into Nanang's eyes, and then bit him on the neck. Nanang screamed in pain, dropping the snake and clutching his swelling neck, struggling to breathe. Saidin got an emergency phone call and sprinted to his cell. Nanang was lying on the floor, barely conscious, with the cobra on the loose in the block. Saidin carried Nanang out, with the help of his cellmates, and drove him to Sanglah Hospital, where he stayed with him for two weeks until he recovered.

A convict at Kerobokan Prison, Nanang, 30, on drugs charges was rushed to Sanglah Hospital because he was bitten by his pet cobra. The snake bite wound on the neck of the dark skinned man had been treated by paramedics. According to his family who visited him in hospital, Nanang has always been a snake lover. He enjoyed keeping poisonous snakes of all types in his house before he went into Kerobokan Prison four years ago. His favourite reptiles were cobras and green snakes. It looked like he never stopped his hobby even though now he lives in Kerobokan Prison. Apparently, Nanang keeps quite a large cobra in his prison cell.

– *Denpost*, 2 June 2004

To Saidin, cobras weren't just pets. When he was bored, he chopped them up and fried them. He'd cut off the head first, then slash a knife along the belly and gut it, taking out the heart and liver to eat raw and wash down with a glass of *arak*. Wasting none of his precious snake, he fried the flesh and ate it with rice and chilli sauce.

If the westerners heard I was killing and cooking some snake, they would all come and say, 'Give me some, give me some'. They'd sit in the cell eating it, and drinking arak. *We drank the blood like a shot. It doesn't taste good, but has good health benefits. Lots of vitamins. Like medicine. But the fried meat is delicious. Like chicken meat.*

– Saidin

If westerners weren't keen to eat snakes, there were plenty of other exotic items on the prison menu. Inmates would catch geckos and grill them. During the rainy season, they would also catch frogs, piling them into a bucket and skinning them to fry on gas burners in their cells. Saidin also regularly ate rats that he caught and bludgeoned in his cell.

Rats are very delicious. I would grill the whole rat first and scrape it to get rid of the fur. Then I'd chop the head and legs off, cut it in the middle to open it up and then cook it again with some spices. You leave the skin on. The skin is nice, just like suckling pig, nice and crunchy. Whenever I saw a big rat in my cell, I chased it and hit it with a piece of wood, a broom stick. Anything.

– Saidin

I've eaten some weird stuff since I've been arrested. I ate bat in Kerobokan, it was very nice. I had it with vegetables. I also drank cobra blood and ate dog. First time the dog was nice, second time it was disgusting, I swear I would never eat it again. The meat was too hard. First time, maybe, it was a better race of dog. And not long ago a guy made a goat head soup, it was really nice, but very strong. Not many westerners had the guts to eat that kind of stuff.

– Ruggiero

But it wasn't only rats, snakes and dogs that kept the prisoners' minds occupied.

Hotel K prided itself on being a rehabilitation facility and gave prisoners the chance to run businesses. Iwan had his workshop, a killer named Tommy had opened a printing factory, Australian beauty school student Schapelle had requested permission to open a beauty salon and Bali Nine member Matthew was teaching English. Not only did these activities fill the empty hours, they helped shave time off their sentences. When drug dealer Thomas returned for his second stint, he went back to his Austrian village roots and planted a vegetable garden. He was taking a forced break from drug dealing because he had no cash to buy from suppliers. His savings were long gone. He threw himself into his garden, which ran for about fifty metres behind two blocks. Just as he had with his drug business, Thomas gave it one hundred per cent. Every morning he spent hours diligently watering his crops of lettuces, spinach, eggplant, *sawi* and cherry tomatoes.

Thomas liked being busy in his garden, where he could retreat into his own world. He sometimes walked around it, spraying insecticide with a metal can on his back and a hose draped over his shoulder, laughing out loud.

I felt like an astronaut. I was laughing to myself.

– Thomas

Always keen to do business, Thomas organised to sell his produce to a supermarket chain in Denpasar. Every morning he noticed that inmates had stolen from his garden, but he always still had plenty to sell to the supermarkets and cook for himself each day. But his vegetables weren't making him much money. If the supermarkets ordered a box of spinach and two boxes of tomatoes, the guards would deliver it, collect the fee and take fifty per cent. Expenses like seeds, fertilisers and insecticides all came out of Thomas's half. At the end of a month, he would be left with 25,000 rupiah ($3) for his efforts. So when the Swiss consul, who looked after Austrian citizens in Bali, offered to invest and buy lettuces for his up-market Swiss restaurant in Kuta, Thomas leaped at the chance. The consul invested 500,000 rupiah ($70) and Thomas planted hundreds of lettuces.

Late one afternoon, Australian Mick, Scottish inmate Robert and Thomas sat drinking *arak* by the tennis court. Mick casually mentioned he'd read somewhere that the Chinese used human shit as fertiliser. Robert's ears pricked up. 'Must work – look how many people they have to feed,' he said. It had been a throwaway comment from Mick before he ambled off to his cell for a late afternoon joint. Thomas left to shoot up, and think about it. Robert, seeing everything through a drunken haze, worked himself into a frenzy of excitement. He raced over to a couple of locals and offered to pay them in *arak* if they helped him smother shit over Thomas's vegetable patch. They agreed, and grabbed a few plastic buckets and sticks to tie to the handles.

After shifting the concrete slab on top of a septic tank, they ladled buckets of steaming human shit and carried them across to pour over Thomas's vegetable garden, spilling the stinking slop all over their hands and feet. They emptied three septic tanks. By the time they had finished, the lockup bells were ringing. The women were already padlocked in their cells, and the vapours of hot shit were wafting over the walls and into their block, causing agitation. They were fighting and accusing each other of making a foul smell. But, as the stink grew inescapably stronger, they fast realised it was coming from outside. They didn't have a clue what was causing it. But it was so nauseatingly vile that they all sat holding their noses or smothering their faces with pillows for the rest of the night.

The next morning, Mick casually walked across the jail yard to pick up a blank art canvas from Iwan's workshop near the vegetable garden. He was completely oblivious to the nasty little disturbance he'd caused, but halfway across the smell hit him hard in the face. 'This is your fault Mick,' a guard yelled across at him. Mick yanked his T-shirt up to cover his nose, quickly realising that it was his idea that had inflicted the stink on the jail. It clung to the air for more than a week.

But the human compost worked well and Thomas's lettuces grew abundantly. He continued to use the shit as fertiliser, but more sparingly, only a bucket or two at a time. It gave them all a laugh to think of the tourists sitting in the expensive Swiss restaurant in Kuta, eating their delicious crispy green lettuce, and having no idea it had been grown in Kerobokan Jail using human shit.

Although the vegetable garden kept Thomas busy, he hadn't stopped using smack. But, with very little cash, he was using *putaw* (low-grade heroin) and sometimes sharing needles. He regularly relied on charity to get food and cigarettes. After about a year, he was dealing again. It began gradually, after a friend had given him a few grams to sell in jail. He used his cut of the profits to invest in more. He started juggling the two businesses, often using his patch of earth to hide his drugs when he wanted a break from carrying them in his underpants. He would dig a hole with his hoe, put the heroin inside and cover it up, leaving it for a couple of hours rather than risk carrying it around. But eyes were always slyly watching and he lost his stash several times. After digging around for it, he'd eventually have to concede it had been stolen.

One afternoon, Mick walked into Robert's cell and saw him chasing the dragon with a couple of local inmates. There was a huge bag of smack on the floor. 'What the fuck? That's a lot,' Mick gasped. Robert quickly put a little in some plastic and passed it up to him, saying, 'Take it, take it and leave'. 'Okay, thanks,' Mick said, incredulous that stingy Robert had given it to him so willingly. 'It was like Christmas.' But when Mick spotted Thomas agitated and muttering, 'I've been robbed again. My smack is gone, thirty-five grams of smack gone,' Mick instantly understood why Robert had been so generous, and why he had shooed him out so fast. He hadn't wanted Mick to create a fuss and attract a crowd of westerners.

I was so fucking jealous. It was, like, 600,000 rupiah a gram.

– Mick

Mick seized the opportunity to get more smack. He walked back to Robert's cell and asked casually, 'Where did you get it from, Robert?' 'I bought it,' he said. 'Mmmm . . . where did you get the money from?' Mick asked, menacingly now. 'A friend sent it from Hong Kong,' he replied, scooping up another gram, putting it in plastic and passing it to Mick. 'This is for you,' he said. The stash of stolen smack was worth $3000. Robert's cellmate had pinched it from the garden, and during the next few days they sold it across the jail. Inevitably, Thomas found out, but there was nothing he could do. The locals fought in packs and Thomas didn't stand a chance of winning.

The westerners could steal from and cheat each other but still be mates. Soon after stealing his smack, Robert went to Thomas, suggesting they try to grow magic mushrooms in his garden. They grew like crazy in Bali, with light rain and a sprinkling of cow shit. Thomas was keen. But the jail boss, aware of their intent, refused their request for permission to bring in cow shit. That only made them more determined. Several of the other westerners were now excited by the idea of growing their own drugs. Typically, they found a way to defy the rules and get the cow shit into the jail.

Villagers were working on building a new cellblock, and dozens of them arrived in the back of a truck each day with their building equipment. An extra bag of shit wouldn't be noticed. So, Thomas, Frenchman Michael, Englishman Steve and Robert kicked in 30,000 rupiah each. For the next ten days, the villagers arrived with a bag of cow shit for Thomas to spread over an empty patch of dirt. Like kids on Christmas morning, Steve, Michael and Robert raced over to the garden every day to see if a plantation of magic mushrooms had sprung up during the night. But they were always disappointed.

Thomas spent months trying to grow the mushrooms, even building a hothouse using bits of wood from Iwan's workshop to make a box, putting plastic on the top, and then covering it with grass to hide it from the guards. But still, no magic. In a final attempt, Thomas put a bucket of soil in the oppressively hot machine room that housed a large generator for Iwan's workshop. This also failed. Then, without any nurturing whatsoever, mushrooms started to sprout in a small flower garden in front of the mosque. Robert's cell was opened first in the morning and he paid a boy 3000 rupiah (40 cents) to run out and pick the lot each day. He occasionally gave the others a few.

You eat these mushrooms, you fly. In Kerobokan, we ate them raw. You eat fifteen or twenty, and you're smiling and laughing all day.

– Thomas

Thomas was having more success selling drugs than growing them, though. After a year of working in his vegetable garden, he gave it up and switched to dealing only and making small wood carvings in Iwan's workshop.

Another way that prisoners beat the boredom of everyday life in Hotel K was by breeding creatures such as fish or birds. Thomas bred catfish in his watering ponds. Another inmate farmed ducks. He kept about one hundred next to Thomas's vegetable garden, but his ducklings were regularly eaten by rats and *muses* (a nocturnal Indonesian animal with sharp teeth and a long tail). The long wild grass between the two jail walls was riddled with cobras and there were usually a few prisoners, besides Saidin, who would catch them and turn them into pets. One local inmate caught a cobra and put it in a box, but accidentally killed it by feeding it a poisonous toad. A Chinese inmate fished in the ponds all day for green frogs to eat. He baited a piece of string with grasshoppers and used a stick as a rod, moving from one stagnant pond to another each day. He sometimes even fished for them in the bathroom drains. During the rainy season, when the jail overflowed with large pools of water, several prisoners used makeshift fishing lines to catch eels, frogs and fish.

Whether they were mad or just plain bad, Hotel K had a strange mix of prisoners. There were some seriously sick people, who, in most jails, would have been isolated, but in Hotel K, rapists, paedophiles and killers lived side by side with someone who had stolen a can of Diet Coke, or who'd been dancing at a club with an ecstasy pill in their pocket. Among the worst were a dentist who'd performed eighty-seven illegal abortions on foetuses, some as old as eight months, at the back of his clinic; another who'd killed twenty people in Timor – ripping the skin off their skulls; and a young man who'd hacked off his girlfriend's head after finding her cheating. When police pulled him over on his motorbike for a traffic offence, they discovered the girl's head dangling in a plastic bag from his handlebars.

Another Balinese man, Tanjung, was in Hotel K for the murder of five people. He had been working as a taxi driver in Bali when he went on a two-week holiday and let a friend drive his taxi. But when he returned and went to pick up the car, the friend refused to give it back. Tanjung went to his boss to complain. But his boss blew Tanjung off, telling him, 'You know what . . . you always scratch the car, damage the car, the guy drives better than you. You don't work for me anymore.' Tanjung walked away quietly, but he was seething – and plotting his revenge. A day later he borrowed a car, bought drums of petrol, drove to his boss's house and knocked on the door. As soon as the man answered it, Tanjung bashed him. He then stole the house keys, locked the doors from the outside and, with the terrified family stuck inside, he walked around the outside pouring petrol. Then he lit a match. The boss, his wife and their three young children were burned alive. Tanjung stood listening to their screams, not leaving until he was sure they were dead.

In Hotel K his psychopathic tendencies flared at the slightest provocation. One afternoon he was running one of his regular illegal gambling games, throwing three dice from a little Chinese cup, when a female guard turned up. She confiscated the dice, the cup and the cash, and walked off. Tanjung flipped. He snatched a piece of wood, and sprinted after the guard, screaming that he was going to split her head open. It was only the other prisoners struggling to hold him back that stopped him.

The guy's skinny, but it took a good six people to hold him. He is a fucking maniac, he's very dangerous. Never know when he can flip. These guys are totally brainless. They have all the characteristics of a psychopath.

– Ruggiero

CHAPTER 15

WITH FRIENDS LIKE THESE

High on almost all inmates' priorities list was making a quick buck. It followed that gambling was another favourite pastime in Hotel K – although gambling was illegal in Indonesia. Many prisoners were doing time for playing cards or betting on cockfights, but, like the drug dealers, the gamblers continued carrying out their crimes inside. Almost every night, girls were playing cards for money in their cells. In some of the men's blocks, inmates set up mini roulette tables and the card sharks ran poker games, frequently aligning themselves with guards to rip off new inmates – often, wealthy Chinese. Night-shift guards would release the players from their cells, and they would sit together at a table playing poker, giving each other signals in order to strip new unwitting inmates of their cash.

Whatever an inmate's vice, in Hotel K there was bound to be a way to feed it. Most inmates welcomed the distraction.

In jail it's boring. You wake up; you see the same face day after day after day after day. Same food, day after day after day after day, people talk the same shit, day after day after day.

– Ruggiero

When African inmate Benoit invited Ruggiero to spend a night with him in his cell, promising a surprise, the Brazilian thought, 'What the hell?' Benoit wasn't your run-of-the-mill prisoner. He wore heavy gold chains around his neck and wrists, and dressed in faux-designer Louis Vuitton or Armani shirts. He aspired to be a music mogul, dressing as if he were already in Los Angeles.

No one would fuck with him because he's a fucking Godzilla. He's a fucking King Kong.

– Ruggiero

When the lockup bells rang, Ruggiero walked across to Benoit's cell. He was busy hanging black curtains on the barred door and windows, making the cell pitch-black. As soon as the guard locked the door, Benoit turned off the fluorescent cell light, then switched on a red light and opened the locked bathroom door. Strung across the ceiling were fine strings with many $100 notes hanging off them. Ruggiero instantly realised it was a money-making factory. 'If the Queen of England can make pounds, I can make fucking dollars, man,' Benoit bragged. The show was just starting. He took a piece of black paper out of a box and, in one swift movement, ran it through a tray of clear liquid then hung it up on the string. Ruggiero excitedly stood watching. Next, Benoit started blowing the black piece of paper with a hair dryer. Before Ruggiero's eyes, the black faded and it morphed into a $100 note. The dazzling night-time show completely convinced him that he had seen money growing on those bathroom strings.

We made many hundred-dollar bills that night. We made a good $10,000.

– Ruggiero

As part of the show, Benoit had explained that the black paper was a negative and by imprinting it with a real one hundred dollar bill, and then developing it, using rare and expensive chemicals imported from Switzerland, he could make cash. He boasted that he could make one genuine-looking fake hundred dollar bill from every real one. Ruggiero was convinced, and quickly spread the word. This was exactly what Benoit had intended. He needed a jail buzz to snag investors.

Benoit was one of three Africans doing time for a fake American-dollar scam. All three were now acting in sync in Hotel K to find investors among the wealthy drug bosses. Benoit was working with Afong and the third African, named Karim, was also doing private bathroom shows for select audiences. The word quickly spread, luring instinctively sceptical criminals into the makeshift darkrooms. Drug boss Iwan sent a guard to check it out for him. Other guards also heard the news and were knocking on the cell throughout the night, begging, 'Please make us the money'. The Africans had credibility because their crimes and court cases had been high profile in Bali, with the local press reporting they had been caught making *billions* of dollars.

Three suitcases containing basic material, paper which had been 80 per cent processed, two bottles of liquid used in the making of the fake money were confiscated. The fake money was estimated to be around five billion dollars.

– *Denpasar Nusa*, 11 January 2002

The Africans told potential investors that if they paid 500 million rupiah ($70,000) to import the rare chemicals from Switzerland, their money would be doubled overnight. The first to give it a go was one of *Pemuka* Ketut's drug bosses, who was doing three months in Hotel K for *shabu* possession. He invested no more than twenty five million rupiah ($3000) to test the scheme's veracity. Iwan and Arman held off, waiting to see the results. Meanwhile, Karim was targeting another inmate, Toto, whose brother was a wealthy drug boss outside. Toto and his cellmate Den went to Karim's cell to watch a dip, hang and blow show. At the end of it, Karim gave them one of the $100 notes to take away and have exchanged in a bank to prove the scam was legitimate. Two weeks later, Toto finished his sentence and walked free. He soon found a wealthy friend of his brothers to invest $70,000.

We thought it was real, I'm not joking. Toto and I believed it because Karim made the money in front of us . . . like magic. Then he gave us that money to exchange. Success – it was real. So we believed him. He knew Toto was a big shot. It's Toto's brother who takes care of Vincente. He has a lot of cafés, restaurants and hotels in Bali. It was easy for Toto to find investors.

– Den

The three Africans only had one chance to lure investors before their smoke-and-mirrors scam was exposed. They knew that as soon as people realised they were not getting any cash back, the news of a hoax would spread like wildfire. Once exposed, they wouldn't be able to con the same captive market. Karim almost lost Toto and the investor when the other two were revealed as con artists. Four weeks after Ketut's boss had handed over the $3000 to magically be turned into $6000 there was still nothing. Day after day, Afong and Benoit continued to make excuses.

Finally the drug boss had to admit he'd foolishly been duped. He was furious. He told Ketut to punish Afong. The stocky, tattooed killer walked into the African's cell and made him very sorry. He left him quivering in the corner, with a boot imprint in the side of his head.

Afong, he's a homo from Cameroon. He cheated the boss of Ketut.

– Den

Karim had to go into crisis management mode to keep Toto and his rich client on the hook. He strategically distanced himself from the other two Africans, acting furious that they were ripping people off and giving the fake money game a bad name.

Karim say to me, 'Don't make friends with Afong and Benoit. They are number one motherfuckers. They will cheat you of the money'. In front of people they are enemies. But, actually, they are in the same group. They are all working together. It's the same business, but nobody knew. We still believed Karim because Mick stayed in his room. So we did a deal secretly and nobody else knew.

– Den

Karim threw in a late change of plan to save himself from the same brutal fate that Afong had suffered. He told Toto and the investor that he could not manufacture such a vast amount of money in his cell, so an African friend of his from Jakarta would do it outside. Toto and the investor fell straight into Karim's trap. They met the Jakarta friend and contrived to do a deal directly, cutting Karim out of the deal and saving on his cut. Karim's plan was sophisticated in its simplicity. He knew their criminal instincts would ensure they'd cut him out of the deal if they could. This was his insurance.

The investor – Toto's brother's rich friend – transferred 400 million rupiah ($53,000) to a bank account ostensibly to pay for the chemicals, which would be couriered from Zurich to Bali. After four days, a parcel arrived, and Toto, the investor and the African from Jakarta checked into a hotel room, to use as the darkroom to make the money. The investor handed over a final cash payment to the African. The African then got to work, putting the black paper into an aluminium box and pouring in the chemicals. Then they had to leave it to soak in the dark. He stressed to them that there must be no light, so no-one should open it for twenty-four hours. The three of them then left the hotel, and planned to meet the next day to blow dry the sheets of black paper and turn them into hundreds of crisp $100 bills.

The next afternoon, Toto and his investor showed up, but the African didn't. They waited for around two hours until they could no longer deny they'd been played like idiots. The furious investor flung open the aluminium box. Inside was a soggy wad of disintegrating black paper, which he scooped up and hurled at the wall, screaming, 'Motherfucker!' The pair stormed out and went straight to the blue room at Hotel K to confront Karim. Karim simply used his insurance tactic, claiming that he'd been the one who was ripped off when they cut him out of the deal. But it was obvious this was an act, when he suddenly became flush with cash.

After that case, Karim became rich. He didn't have money or anything before, he just ate noodles everyday. No visits for a year and a half. After that, his girlfriend came from Australia, bringing lots of things. His life started to change just within fifteen days, one month. So where did the money come from?

The investor was really pissed off with Toto. Toto was fucked, but he thinks, 'Oh well, that's not my money'. Actually, it was not Karim who is stupid. We are stupid to believe he can make money. But we didn't know the reality. We see in the newspaper that these black people got busted for billions of dollars of counterfeit money. Then they show us how they make money. But the reality was they put [on it] some kind of chemical to dye real money black, then bleach it out and the original money comes back.

– Den

If the duped inmates had read the follow-up press stories about the Africans' cases, it would have saved them a lot of wasted time. Although, time to waste was something they all had in vast amounts.

The Head of the police research unit explained that after preliminary tests on the evidence, which were papers and liquid, the result was nil. The black liquid could not turn the sheets of black paper into dollar notes as said before. It's true that the black liquid is still going through further tests at forensic lab, but the result later will only be used as comparison. 'Because we're convinced already, based on proof after tests were done, there's not the slightest indication pointing at dollar note counterfeiting,' he explained.

– *Nusa news*, 15 January 2002

Karim escaped any reprisals after one lame attempt to plant photocopied dollars in his cell and alert the guards to a counterfeiting racket, failed to arouse any interest. But often prisoners who did the wrong thing were subjected to bashings or humiliating punishments – dished out by guards or other inmates. There was an open drain filled with sewage, inside which inmates were sometimes forced to swim. The psychopathic killer from Timor who had ripped the skin off his victims' skulls worked as a debt collector around the jail, and used the drain to coerce payments.

It was a river of shit; all the oily stuff from the kitchen and the toilets. The guys who didn't pay their debts were forced to go in there and swim to the other side, head under. The debt collector hangs at the side with a knife. The guy swimming is covered in shit.

There was one guy who borrowed money from one of the westerners and he wouldn't pay back the money, so they forced him to swim about forty metres in all this human shit. I went and watched and had a great time. Shame I couldn't take any photos.

Did he come out covered in shit?

Yeah, from head to toe. And then after they come out, they say no shower, you sit in the sun for a little while. Then the smell is going to stay with him for a while.

You could die from the diseases you catch?

People don't give a fuck in there.

– Ruggiero

CHAPTER 16

AN EYE FOR AN EYE

I saw a guy get his eyeball cut out with a knife. This was Laskar against Laskar. His name is Bambang. Don't know what he did. But all Laskar fight against one Laskar if he fights with the boss of Laskar. All cowards. When he came back from hospital he had a patch. I started calling him Johnny Depp. He's a crazy motherfucker. The day he left prison, he killed someone outside.

– Ruggiero

Overnight, Hotel K's world turned more dark and sinister after eight men from Bali's most violent gang, Laskar Bali, including its number one boss, checked in. There were already more than a dozen gang members inside. Laskar instilled fear in prisoners and guards. Their well-known violent activities on the outside – and now the inside – had everyone jumpy. Stabbings, bashings, rapes and killings became a bigger part of life. The guards no longer had any power. Laskar was the law.

Suddenly when they went to jail, Laskar Bali owned the jail.

– Journalist Wayan Juniartha of the *Jakarta Post*

Kerobokan was waaay *more violent when Laskar came inside. What happened was that the guards just retired. They let them do whatever they wanted . . . as they pleased.*

– Ruggiero

One afternoon, Nita was escorting inmate Sari across from Block W to the blue room. Standing on the top of the steps to the hall was a Laskar gang member. 'Oh, you're pretty,' he said menacingly. Both women quickened their pace. 'Come here, I want to talk to you,' he yelled. Nita felt an icy shiver run down her spine. You couldn't disobey Laskar. The two women stopped. The boy pointed at Sari, saying, 'You come in here', then looked at Nita and barked, 'You wait there'.

Sari walked up the steps and disappeared into the hall. Moments later, her anguished screams pierced the air. Nita wiped away her tears as she stood there uselessly, feeling a stinging hatred for the vicious gang that now terrorised Hotel K. There was nothing she could do to help Sari. Even when a female guard came over, both stood helplessly listening to the sobs. Half an hour later, Sari came out, dishevelled and distressed.

She was crying. I ask what's happened. What did they do? She tells me that three men force her to do sex with them.

– Nita

Nita ushered Sari towards the blue room, suggesting she still go for a short visit to see her friend. The female guard slipped a light jacket around her trembling shoulders. A few minutes later

Sari left the blue room too traumatised to be among strangers. She gripped Nita's hand as she walked back across the jail. The rapists were smugly watching them from the top of the hall steps. Sari was doing three months for petty theft. One of the rapists was her new jail boyfriend.

Back in Block W, all the women were feeling Sari's distress as she lay silently in the corner of her cell. No-one could comfort her. If they offered her a glass of water, she ignored it. If they stroked her arm gently, she pulled away. For two days, she didn't move. But when she finally got up, she walked straight out the door without a word and across to the guards' table. She was bitterly angry at the evil bastards who had raped her and wanted to report them to the police. But the guards shook their heads. Sari checked out a week later. No-one was punished.

The guard told her it's better to keep silent, otherwise the gang will hit you. I also tell to the security, but they don't want to get involved in this matter.

– Nita

The incident sent fear through Block W. The women were scared to walk the perilous path across to the blue room to collect their mail. Many now rigidly stuck to the footpaths, avoiding the short cut past the hall. As part of her job as *tamping*, Nita walked back and forth escorting prisoners several times a day; now she always took the long route, usually pretending to buy something at the canteen so that the Laskars loitering in the hall didn't see her fear.

Jail life is more dangerous than before because inside the jail is a very powerful gang. This gang is more powerful than the security inside the jail. If the gang commands you, you must do it freely without any complaints or they will hit you. Being block leader I have to do my job seriously, but dealing with the gang is very hard for me. I talk sometimes to the woman security, who is very close to me, but she can do nothing more than us.

– Nita

The women were not even safe in their own cellblock. The gang could go wherever it wanted.

One afternoon, a young, drunken Laskar recruit walked into the women's block and approached Australian inmate Schapelle Corby. She had returned from performing in one of Hotel K's regular PR stunts – swinging open its doors to journalists and TV cameras to show the women doing a tightly choreographed exercise routine on the grass, in stark contrast to the hellish anarchy that really existed. Schapelle was sitting outside her cell when the inmate sat down opposite her. 'Come and sit with me,' he said. 'No thanks.' He angrily slapped his leg. 'Sit here.' 'Sorry, no thanks, I'm busy.' She turned away and walked into her cell. 'Schapelle, Schapelle, Schapelle.' He kept calling until she appeared back in the doorway, then hurled a brick at her. It missed her, but hit the bars and broke in half. He threw several more, but she'd retreated into the cell. He was angry. 'If that's not big enough, how about this?' he yelled, throwing a large rock and causing the nearby inmates to scurry into their cells.

He then turned and screamed abuse at a female guard, who burst into tears, frightened and powerless to do anything. A couple of Laskars finally took him out of Block W. But within half an hour, he was back. The guards could do little but lock all the women in their cells early for their own protection.

In the men's block too, the gang instilled fear. Around 6 am one day, *Pemuka* Saidin was doing his patrol when he received a phone call telling him to come quickly to the gang's cellblock,

C1. Inmate Beny was dead – hanging by a thick plastic rope over the squat toilet. The cells inside the block were already unlocked and inmates had gathered to look. Saidin told everyone to stand back. No-one was to touch Beny until the police arrived. They soon turned up and untied the plastic rope, and Saidin and an officer lifted the body down. Most of those inmates in the block knew the truth. Beny had been strung up by the gang.

If you kill yourself, there are visible signs. I think they overdosed him first and hanged him while he was unconscious, but still alive.

– Inmate

North Sumatran inmate Alpones Simbolon – nicknamed Beny – had been well-liked among the westerners. He often talked philosophy with Mick, or shot up with Thomas, who he'd known since their stint together in Hotel K ten years earlier. Beny had an Australian ex-wife and teenage son, and an Indonesian wife and a young son. His local wife and their 12-year-old boy had often visited him, with the boy even staying overnight in Beny's cell occasionally. Beny – dubbed a 'drug trafficking big shot' in the local papers – had been caught with more than two kilograms of heroin, and had been next to face the death penalty after Frenchman Michael and Mexican Vincente. He had hoped to do a deal and get fifteen years, but like the other two had received life. He admitted to friends in Hotel K that he'd been dealing up to six kilograms of smack a month.

Inmates had different theories about why he was dead, but none believed Beny suicided. It was a paid hit. Some thought Beny, a heroin and *shabu* user, had been murdered for a spiralling drug debt and it was a warning to all. But those closest to him were convinced it was because he knew too much, was using too much smack and had become loose-lipped; something not tolerated by drug bosses. The night of his hanging, several prisoners heard Beny shouting as one of the Laskar gang hit him.

A cursory jail investigation deemed his death suicide. But the police suspected foul play, telling the media there could be a link between Beny's death and a syndicate that was possibly behind the Bali Nine. Beny's body was exhumed and autopsied.

Police are investigating a possible link between the suspicious death of a convicted drug dealer in a Bali jail and the syndicate believed to be behind the Bali Nine. The body of a man convicted in 2002 of trafficking 2.2kg of heroin has been exhumed after he was found dead in Bali's Kerobokan Prison last week. Dealer Alpones Simbolon was apparently hanged in the washroom of his cell last Tuesday. His death was originally treated as suicide, but Indonesian police said that there was a possibility it might be linked to the same syndicate as the Bali Nine.

– *The Daily Telegraph*, 25 April 2005

When the autopsy found there had been drugs in Beny's system, the police investigation was closed, with no further word of a link to the syndicate. But local journalists and those inside Hotel K had no doubt that Laskar Bali had been paid to kill him.

After Laskar entered the jail, there were one or two unsolved murders inside the prison. Although the prison authorities said it was suicide, a friend of mine who is very close to Laskar, said they were Laskar jobs.

– Journalist, *Jakarta Post*

Beny's death cast a shadow of sadness over the westerners. Scottish Robert walked around for days in his usual drunken haze muttering, 'Why did they have to kill him? Why?' It was a sentiment shared by all.

***

Out of five major gangs in Bali, Laskar was the most violent. The up-market tourist areas of Seminyak and Legian were its turf. Laskar was in charge of security in all the nightclubs, bars and restaurants, also selling ecstasy in most of the major tourist clubs, such as Bounty, the Hard Rock Café, Paddy's and Double Six. Four or five Laskar members were security at each club, and had the ability to call on its five hundred or so members if a situation escalated. It was a shock when the top bosses of Laskar, including number one Agung Aseng, were sent to jail. They normally had immunity, working with police to evade punishment.

Usually the Bali police tried not to disturb the Laskars. Here is how it works in [the] Balinese underworld; the gang kills someone, the police announce informally to the gang leaders that they have to surrender the person who killed.

Please make our job easy, the police say. The leadership of the gang will hold meetings to decide who will be sent to the police to confess as the killer. They will never send the actual killer because the actual killer is an asset to the gang. A killer will increase its reputation and power.

This is the story behind the story that never made the newspaper or [reached] the public. Denpasar Moon, supposedly a karaoke bar but it's open until six in the morning, is right across the street from a military complex that oversees Bali.

The security of this Denpasar Moon is not by Laskar. On this night, there is a violent argument with one of the security and one of the guests.

It turns out that the guest has a good relationship with Laskar, with Agung Aseng, the head of Laskar himself. He calls Agung Aseng. The Laskars arrive in two open jeeps, carrying swords, spears, lances.

And they attack Denpasar Moon security. One of the on-duty military men at the regional complex (First Corporal I Gusti Ketut) hears the commotion. He goes to check, he wants to know what is happening, he approaches Denpasar Moon, and is stabbed and killed by Agung Aseng and his men while he was trying to break up the fight.

I was there several hours after the murder of this military guy, and already several young soldiers were gathering and speaking about revenge. The commander of Bali military summonsed all his officers and told them he will not tolerate any revenge, because the image of Indonesian military is still very low and they should not create an incident that will further tarnish that image.

But his subordinate, chief of the Denpasar military, was a very young, very tough, no-nonsense guy. He calls the chief of Denpasar police and says, 'Do you have a suspect yet?' Of course they didn't have a suspect yet because they had to sort it out with the gang first. The military knew Laskar did it; they knew Agung Aseng was there.

So this young military guy informs the Denpasar police chief, 'Okay the one who commit[s] the crime is Laskar and . . . the guy's name who was involved in the attack is Agung Aseng. I expect all the suspects to be arrested within twenty-four hours; otherwise I and my men will arrest them. And if I do the arrest, you can be sure that none of them will be alive to stand trial'.

It was not an empty threat. A group of military soldiers in plain clothes was already surrounding Agung Aseng's house under direct order from him.

The police chief knew the house was surrounded and called Agung Aseng, saying, 'Please surrender'.

Agung Aseng surrendered. The Denpasar police chief called the Denpasar military chief . . . 'We've got the suspects'.

So, normally there is some arrangement with the gangs, but when you deal with an angry army guy, you don't have any choice. Agung Aseng got three or four years. It's common knowledge that each night he's still able to leave the prison, stay at his house, or control his men who are working in the streets of Legian and Seminyak. Eight Laskars got sentenced. And, suddenly, when they went to jail, Laskar Bali owned the jail. I think most of the guards are frightened of the gang, afraid for their own lives and their families' lives.

– Journalist Wayan Juniartha of the *Jakarta Post*

***

From the first day Agung Aseng entered Hotel K, he took over, strutting about while talking on a mobile phone, walking into the boss's office, out the front door, doing whatever he liked. The guards knew the power of the Laskars and just stood back to let the gang take control.

I remember once I was at the front door and Agung Aseng came to the guards' door and asked, 'May I come in? May I come in?' . . . He was supposed to be in jail. He'd been out for two days and came to spend the night in jail.

Nobody dares close Agung Aseng's cell door. Every night he had a party, barbecue, smoke marijuana, supply whisky for the guards. Every night. Outside every block there is a small garden. After 5 pm everyone has to go inside the block and the block is locked. But not his. His was always open. And whoever he wants to come, he tells the guards, 'Go and pick him up at his block'.

– Ruggiero

He brings a woman to his room; he brings his people, his friends from outside and inside. Free. No limits. Mostly, he went out to sleep at home. Every morning he would come back just to close the eyes of the government. In Kerobokan, everybody is working for Agung Aseng.

– Den

If the guards tried to impose authority, they were bashed. Trying to lock boss Agung Aseng in his cell one night caused a guard to be viciously beaten. Two other guards stood by watching, helplessly. Assisting him would only have meant them being bashed too. Another guard was beaten up by an angry Laskar inmate for refusing to let him walk out the front door. The inmate was not punished.

The guards and their families lived under threat; all knew Laskar could mobilise its members with a phone call. Just as they did at nightclubs, a Laskar pack would descend on Hotel K to answer a call. Several times, dozens of Laskars turned up inside Hotel K to bare their teeth. A rumour that Agung and his men would be moved to a prison outside Bali brought more than twenty gangsters.

They were sitting on the lawn, drinking arak *there to protest. The guards could not do anything. Maybe twenty, thirty people came. Sometimes they came to one block, they sit [on] the grass and drink* arak *and guards cannot speak, because how many people in Laskar – a thousand people. Guards don't want to die.*

– Thomas

Laskar was jail mafia, brutally enforcing its own laws, sometimes collaborating with the guards to bash inmates. If a prisoner was caught escaping, failing to pay drug bills or had committed atrocious crimes, the Laskars would take the Hotel K law into their own hands. During an afternoon visit, a Laskar member doing time for killing a man dragged a new inmate through the blue room and into the large office atrium. He forced the inmate to his knees and lifted his hand ready to crack him across the skull, then stopped. He caught a glimpse of Schapelle and her visitor watching him through the door. He left the prisoner trembling on his knees and walked across to explain that the inmate was a paedophile. He was about to get his first prison bashing.

Laskar also did personal security jobs for prisoners. If someone had a phone, an MP3 player, cash, or anything else, stolen, they could pay Laskar to get it back. The Laskar enforcers were always keen to do a little business on the side. One westerner paid the gang to punish a new inmate who had ripped him off a year earlier. The new inmate had promised to use his court connections to get the westerner's sentence cut on appeal. The westerner was desperate. He paid him 175 million rupiah ($23,000), but his sentence was increased by two years. The local man had stolen the money. So when the new inmate was caught with hashish and put in Hotel K, he was a walking bullseye. Several times the Laskars hurt him badly, trying to extract the stolen cash for the westerner inmate.

They locked him in the room and beat the shit out of him.

– Inmate

While the Laskars often had a reason for their violent attacks, a lot of the aggressive young recruits, often high on drugs or drunk on *arak* and power, terrorised inmates just for the hell of it.

They are brainless. Big guys, big body, small brains, probably small cock. Totally brainless people.

– Ruggiero

Ruggiero's outspoken nature and hot Latin temperament didn't serve him well with the gang. He clashed often with Laskar, initially refusing to swallow their constant harassment. But it was a losing battle.

I had already been beaten up so many times by the gang there, because I fight against Laskar a few times. It was very uneven. Kick me in the face, hit me with a stick. Because I wouldn't take any shit from them. I buy ten beers and they want to confiscate five. They do whatever they want.

One day I was playing tennis with the Australian Chris, and Laskar Bali came and broke the racquets. They were drunk. If someone brings me food – say, two apples – they take one. If I punch the guy to get the apple back, ten Laskar guys punch me; in the end, I say, 'Keep the apple'. It [got] to that stage. They are all maniacs. The problem is, Balinese are cowards. You don't fight one on one. One on one is okay. The biggest monkey there, no problem. But they don't do one on one.

– Ruggiero

It wasn't just the inmates and guards who Laskar terrorised – there was also anarchy within its own ranks. Gang member Bambang had his eye gauged out with a sickle and his arms slashed, before he was dragged a few hundred metres up the road outside the jail and his body dumped in a ditch. A passing motorist spotted him, covered in blood and unconscious but still breathing, early the next morning.

Laskar's biggest and most lucrative job in Hotel K was providing protection for drug dealer Arman. The dealer and the gang had struck a deal to make them both lots of money, by turning Arman into the sole drug dealer, crushing anyone else who dared try selling to the inside market. Laskar enabled Arman to fulfil his wish to become Hotel K's drug lord. He was selling huge quantities of drugs inside and outside, paying Laskar for protection, and prisoners and guards to work as couriers, supplying bars and clubs across Bali.

Arman was making at least 100 million rupiah [$13,000] a day, sometimes 300 million [$39,000]. Many times I saw the guy folding up a whole lot of money. He sold shabu, *heroin, ecstasy, ganja, hashish, cocaine, everything.*

The whole block worked for Arman. All the guards got money from him. So, by any chance, if the police intend to come inside here to search, he was the first one to know about it. There were ten telephones inside the block. It was very well-organised. But it was Laskar who gave him such autonomy, you know. Of course he paid Laskar. They go inside, they go in the block, they could have a hit on the pipe, whatever, and they go back out. They take ten grams, twenty grams, outside to sell.

It was a big business. They sold one hundred grams of shabu *a day inside and outside. The market inside is one tenth of it. He sold inside maybe ten, fifteen grams between just the foreigners who buy one gram a day. They buy smack or* shabu *every day. Plus there's all the people inside who are buying to sell in a visit. Many of my Swedish friends come: 'Can I get two grams* shabu*?' 'Okay.' She comes in, I give her a kiss, give to her, she gives me money and goes home.*

The guards love it. They carry money outside, get paid one million. Bring drugs inside, get two million. Their wage is one million a month. But they bring one little thing inside and they get two million. Fuck, I'd do it every day. They cannot stop corruption in a place where the salary is so low.

– Ruggiero

For sure, one hundred per cent, Arman paid the jail officers. Everybody knew he was continually busy in his room, always smoking, smoking, and no problems. The guards go and smoke in Arman's cell. There were quite a few guards in Bali who like shabu. *Mostly, in Bali they didn't like heroin; most guards like ecstasy and* shabu *because afterwards they're still fit, no sleeping.* Shabu *is vitamin A – it makes you active.*

– Thomas

Agung Aseng mainly went to jail to collect the gang's huge weekly payment of protection money. Cash flowed as freely as the drugs and everyone was in for a cut, including police. A rumour circulated the jail that *Poltabes*, a Denpasar police station, was supplying confiscated drugs to Arman to sell for them. This was confirmed one afternoon when Englishman Steve Turner bought a few ecstasy pills from one of Arman's boys, who walked around the jail selling pills from his pocket. Steve was sitting on the grass with a group of westerners when he looked at the pills and leaped up yelling, 'They're mine! It's my shit, he's selling my shit'.

Steve, dubbed the 'Ecstasy King' in the press, had been caught at a Denpasar post office, claiming two packages sent from London. He was asked to open them in a routine inspection; the first package contained nearly three thousand pills inside a shampoo bottle; the second held another three thousand pills wrapped in two shirts. Police then raided his home and found two thousand more tablets hidden in his ceiling. Steve's tablets were all stamped with distinctive heart, deer or butterfly logos and were much bigger than local pills. During his court case, it made news that hundreds of the pills went missing from police evidence. In fact, more than three thousand pills vanished, and that afternoon in Hotel K, Steve instantly recognised the pills from Arman's boy, as his own.

The case of British man Steve Turner, 38, was also leaving a trail at the police department, where some evidence of ecstasy tablets went missing. The original number of ecstasy tablets was 8175, now only 7847. When the evidence arrived at court, 328 tablets were missing. The case ended with the questioning of two police officers about the matter.

– *Denpost*, 30 June 2003

Inside Hotel K, Arman's drug business was booming, but life had consequently become more violent for inmates. Anyone else caught dealing to the internal market was bashed. Anyone who couldn't pay their drug bills was also punished. Groups of muscle-bound Laskar enforcers constantly prowled around after those in debt, making threats, smacking them around a bit as a warning or, if that had already failed, bashing them viciously. With Laskar and Arman pushing drugs and offering unlimited credit to westerners, many inmates let their drug bills spiral out of control. If they couldn't pay up when Arman called in the cash, the consequences were deadly.

The guys get fucked up on smack or shabu, *or whatever, and they give them more and more and more and more. Just give drugs, drugs, drugs to the foreigners and they lose control of the bill. Eventually they have to pay fifteen million, twenty million. Then if they couldn't pay, they'd beat them up. One time what they did to the Australian kids you wouldn't believe, and this Italian kid, they beat him up.*

– Ruggiero

If they know that you are a drug user, they force you to buy drugs from them.

– Nita

Many of the westerners who lost control of their drug bills got cash from their parents or friends to avoid being bashed. Juri's elderly parents had moved their lives from Italy to Bali so that they could visit him daily, doing anything they could to make his life more bearable, including giving him money, unaware their hard-earned cash was spent on drugs. Juri lied in any way necessary to get cash from friends and family for his heroin bill, acutely aware of his fate if he failed to pay. Everyone had seen what had happened to Dutch inmate Aris.

Aris had been loading up his drug tab for weeks. He had a huge pile of credit notes that Arman's bookkeeper gave him each time he scored. Arman had given Aris thousands of dollars of credit because Aris had promised to get MDMA powder sent from Holland for him. Arman and Iwan would use it to make thousands of ecstasy pills in Iwan's workshop. But with no sign of the powder, Arman called in his credit. Aris didn't have the cash, and had let his bill run out of control, spending money he didn't have. Now he had nowhere to run. The Laskars beat him almost to death.

They took Aris, the Dutch guy, and tied him to the bars like Jesus Christ with some electric cable, took a stick and beat him hard. They beat him very hard. Laskar are all animals, they are very savage. This guard, Pak Mus, saved him. It was apel *[roll call] time and I told him, 'He is down the block, being beaten. Stop the shit, Pak Mus,' and Pak Mus brought him back. Nothing happened to the guys who were beating him. They probably would have hanged him there if Pak Mus didn't go.*

– Ruggiero

Typically, Hotel K wanted to avoid bad publicity, and refused to send the badly injured Aris to hospital because too many questions would be asked. Instead, Aris was locked in his cell. For two days he complained of dizziness, and for two weeks he couldn't stand up. He wept from the pain. It prompted Mick to raise cash from a few of the westerners to buy Aris a gram of smack to ease his agony. His wife was being refused visits so that she couldn't see his atrocious injuries and report them. To stop her daily attempts to visit him, she was told that Aris didn't want to see her; that he had another woman. But she didn't believe it. She knew something was wrong. She was distressed and threatened to phone the Dutch consulate. The Laskars gave Aris a mobile phone and instructed him to call his wife.

'You tell her you have a girlfriend, you don't want to see her, and don't make a fucking problem,' one of the Laskars told Aris. 'Okay, no problem,' he quickly agreed. He was in no shape to argue; his eyes were puffed into slits and his body was black and blue. He told his wife the lies. She broke down crying, refusing to believe him. 'No, no, I'm coming to see you. I love you.' Aris felt her pain. But he was surrounded by Laskars and, for both their sakes, he had to make her believe him. 'I don't love you anymore. Leave me alone, get on with your life,' he told her. A long wailing noise came through the phone and then it went dead. She didn't visit him again.

But Aris got off lightly. He had lived. It was a dark secret among the inmates that the deaths around the jail, set up to look like suicides – such as Beny's, rarely were. Suspicious deaths were common in Hotel K. At 7.30 am one day, guard Agung Mas had unlocked the women's cells and was doing the day's first roll call. She mentioned to Nita that she'd felt there was something strange about the main hall when she'd walked past it earlier, and was going to take a closer look. Unusually, she left Block W's steel door open, so Nita trailed behind her, and

Schapelle, who'd overheard the conversation, also tagged along in her pyjamas. This was a rare chance to walk in the prison grounds and out of the claustrophobic Block W on a fresh, quiet morning; anything slightly different was a relief.

But there was no chance to enjoy it. Through the hall window, they saw a prisoner hanging in a noose in the centre of the room. One end of a sarong was tied around his neck, and the rest of it was twisted up and tied to a rafter poking through the broken ceiling. His feet were dangling centimetres off the floor.

The female guard, Schapelle and Nita all knew the prisoner. It was Agus, who'd been a Hotel K inmate for a couple of years. He'd arrived fit and well-built, but inside jail had deteriorated into a skinny heroin addict. He'd been a gregarious drink-seller in the blue room, often telling new inmates to be careful of drugs in Hotel K because he was now an addict, but had never once touched any drug before checking in.

Now, hanging in the hall, he looked normal, almost as if he were sleeping. His skin was still its usual colour. The only hint of something sinister was his tightly clenched fists and the fact that his block was still locked. The question of how he got out of his locked block during the night would never be asked, let alone answered. Schapelle and Nita stayed calm, numb to the kind of chilling sights to which they'd become far too accustomed inside jail. Very quickly, they were surrounded by a crowd of men as news of Agus's death spread through the blocks. Schapelle and Nita turned, and pushed past to go back to Block W. A female guard was standing at the block's door to stop a stirred-up bunch of women from walking outside for a look.

The inmates all knew this was a murder. The rest of the blue room drink-seller boys were shaken and upset. Not only was it a stark warning to pay their drug debts, but they had lost their good friend Agus. This was the real and dark heart of Hotel K – no matter what PR stunts it turned on for photographers and reporters.

Life goes on and, after a few months, a killing inside the hall happened again. One prisoner man was hung with a sarong and plastic string. Everybody was shocked. According to the security, he kill himself by overdosing on drugs. Police came and investigated the case, and took the dead body outside the jail for an autopsy. According to news from the security, somebody killed and hanged him in the hall. The condition and situation of the jail is very dangerous.

– Nita

Nita knew more than anyone how dangerous Laskar was, but got mixed up with them when she crossed Arman. She'd agreed to supply him with a fifty-gram sample of *shabu* from her supplier in the Philippines so he could trial a new source. But Nita no longer had a *shabu* supplier in the Philippines and all she was ever going to get from the deal was a smoke of *shabu*. Nita called her cellmate Sassa's boyfriend, Antonio, in another Bali jail, telling him she had a French customer wanting to buy fifty grams. But Antonio ripped Nita off. He sent fifty packets with only half a gram in each. Not realising she'd been short changed, Nita passed it to Arman, who'd already paid the twenty-five million rupiah ($3300). She hadn't weighed it and had smoked a gram with the girls in her cell. It didn't take long for the drug lord to weigh it, cast an eye over it and see that it was only twenty-five grams. He also recognised it as his own *shabu* – Antonio had originally bought it from Arman. Nita and Sassa would suffer a vicious reprisal.

Arman sent the enforcers down to Block W. Seven men strode through the steel door, carrying a plank of wood and calling out for Nita and Sassa. Women scampered out of their way as they stormed along the path. They found Nita and Sassa cowering in their bathroom. Both women were grabbed roughly by the arms and dragged out, terrified. On the grass between the hall and the front wall of Block W, Nita was attacked. They took turns kicking and punching her body, legs and feet. Nita crouched down, trying to shield her face with her hands. Sassa stood watching and sobbing for her friend, terrified of her own fate, while a Laskar roughly gripped her arm so she couldn't run. Finally, they let Nita go. She stumbled away, with blood covering her face and her legs shaking violently. There was nothing she could do to help Sassa. The men had grander plans for her; she was young and ripe. They stripped her naked and gang raped her while a crowd of about twenty inmates stood around watching. An hour later, she walked back into Block W, clutching her stomach and crying. Her shirt was on back-to-front and her trousers were undone. As she walked along the path to her cell, women silently watched, backing away to let her through. No-one wanted to be next.

Nita spoke to the jail boss, telling him she was scared for her life. He advised her to move jails. It was too dangerous for her to stay in Hotel K and he couldn't protect her; Laskar had all the power. Nita would soon be transferred.

CHAPTER 17

SEX ON THE BEACH

Jail is a gradual killing-you process. Slowly, by slowly, your clothes get more odour and you don't care about much anymore. You get less and less contact with the outside world and you have less money, so it's not easy.

It takes away something from you?

Yeah, but I punch back all the time. They will never break me down.

– Ruggiero

Money is powerful. If you have money, you can go outside the jail to meet your friend; [go] shopping. Just ask permission to the head of the jail and pay money, and they allow you to go out.

– Den

One morning, Ruggiero was on a high, but it had nothing to do with drugs. He grabbed cash from inside a secret drawer that he'd built into a table and walked across the yard to the front door. The jail monotony was going to be broken today.

He was heading out for a trip to the dentist – or that's what he was doing officially. As soon as the police escort showed up, Ruggiero climbed into the car and they took off. The car didn't turn right towards his dentist in Denpasar; it turned left and went straight to Canggu Beach.

Ruggiero could stay out enjoying life until 5 pm. The Brazilian had done this at least twelve times – whenever he had the cash. It was an expensive day, usually costing more than $200, split between the right people, but a sanity-aiding trip outside Hotel K was worth it. On the way, Ruggiero phoned his girlfriend, confirming he was en route.

When they arrived, the three police and the guard sat at the beach bar, eating nasi goreng and drinking cans of soft drinks, putting it all on Ruggiero's tab. Ruggiero sat with his girlfriend, enjoying a plate of his favourite garlic prawns and drinking a glass of beer. After lunch, Ruggiero held his girlfriend's hand and walked down to the water's edge and along the sand. Small things had become so indescribably precious to him.

The more times Ruggiero went out with the police and behaved, the more lax the security got. The first few times were strict. He really had gone to the dentist with a quick side trip to the beach on the way back to jail. But as the police started to trust him, he was given more freedom, until the dentist was just a cover. The same police chief took care of him each time, bringing with him two other obliging officers. On earlier trips, Ruggiero had been banned from entering the water, in case he escaped or drowned, but one afternoon the police chief finally allowed him to go for a surf.

I got to know this one policeman, he became my good friend. I say, 'Oh, go to a bar with me', we went to a bar . . . then after a few times he allowed me to take a dive in the ocean. One day I even took the board and went for a paddle in Canggu. They were shit waves, very bumpy. But it was pretty big and they were afraid I was going to be sucked out into the ocean and wouldn't show up again. They said afterwards, we're afraid you're going to drown.

– Ruggiero

On another occasion, Ruggiero phoned his girlfriend, asking her to meet him at a nice little four-star hotel, not far from Hotel K. 'Can you bring me a bit of *shabu*?' she asked. 'Yeah, of course, no problem,' he said.

The next morning, Ruggiero walked out the front of Hotel K with *shabu* in his top shirt pocket, and greeted the three police. Officially, he was being escorted to the dentist again. He got in the car and they sped off to the hotel to meet his girlfriend. While two of the police sat by the pool, drinking soft drinks on Ruggiero's tab, he and his girl paid cash to use a room. The officer who'd drawn the short straw sat outside the door.

Later that day, Ruggiero went for lunch at Echo Beach to meet some mates he had phoned earlier.

When I arrive at the bar, there is, like, ten friends there. I call everybody to say, 'Come'. I take some coke and make lines in the toilet. Everybody drinks whisky, everyone is waiting for me.

– Ruggiero

Some afternoons he took his girlfriend to the beach – but he needed to use a little ingenuity to have some private time.

We had a little corner of the beach that had some privacy . . . a bush. We go behind the bush. I say to the cop, 'I am Ruggiero, you can trust me completely, I would never escape, I wouldn't do that to you'. He's been out with me, like, six times. And the guard from jail, also the same guard. He could trust me because they knew I wouldn't do anything.

Then one day I took a rope, like, a fishing rope, I say, 'Listen, I find a very nice spot, behind a nice bush, where I intend to spend some time with a girl'. The guard always wants to see me [so that he knows Ruggiero hasn't done a runner].

So I climbed a little branch that was free, I tied the rope on my shirt up there. I said, 'Listen,' – because I had my hand phone with me – 'whenever you want to – instead of seeing me – just call my number'.

So I was there with my phone, he calls me … I am in the bush with the girl, and I do like this [pulls the rope that shakes the shirt on the branch].

They see the shirt shaking. So the police know I am there.

I did this the first time. The second time I took this rope, very thin one, and I put the thing up and I made a joke. I went far away, like one hundred and fifty metres, along the beach. I disappeared and took the rope and the phone with me, and he would call me. And then, when it was time to come back, I say, 'Motherfucker, I don't want to come back. Catch me if you can'.

Then when he went down there, there was nothing. Where is he? I was over here … I came back. It was just a joke. 'Don't do that to me again,' he told me.

– Ruggiero

But whatever fun Ruggiero had, there was always a reality check when he was taken back to jail.

There's two sides of the coin. You know. Sometimes fuck … so nice outside, then back in jail. The time outside runs so fast. I have my friends … many of my friends don't like to go to [the] jail, it's not a nice place to go, so I call my Swedish friends and people come out to the beach, and have big party and drink whisky, sometimes I take some coke and we have a line inside the toilet.

I'm in jail and I'm the one who brings the drugs.

– Ruggiero

But letting prisoners out for a few hours could represent a risk for the guards and police involved if they got caught. In fact, the consequences for several of them could have been dire if Ruggiero had lost the plot on the occasion that he was allowed out and given a fully loaded machine gun.

You know the craziest thing? Once I went out to the hotel and my girlfriend wanted a photo with our guards. No problem, they say. So there is one guard on one side of me and my girlfriend, and the other guard next to me and the other taking the photo. And the one who was taking the photo had the machine gun. And he put the machine gun down to take the photo.

I say, 'Wait, wait, wait, get the gun for the photo, it would look nice', so he gave me the gun.

I'm holding the machine gun for the photo, then I was pointing it straight at the other cop. I say, 'This cannot be loaded'. After he took the photo, I said, 'Man, is this shit loaded?' He said, 'Yes'. I said, 'Are you joking?' I take the clip out and it was fully loaded, and the gun was in my hands. The guy gives me a fully loaded machine gun. He said, 'Give it to me, man'. He was a very nice guy, but I say, 'You stupid man, don't ever give a prisoner a gun'. But they say, 'You're a very nice guy, we can trust you'.

Did they always carry machine guns?

Yeah. I'm a dangerous guy, man! Well, they made me that; I didn't know I was dangerous fuck[ing] big dealer, four grams of hash. But they had to do it.

– Ruggiero

Days out were common enough for westerners, so long as they paid up. And it was a win-win situation for prisoners, guards and police. Prisoners could forget the hellhole that was jail for a few hours, while for the guards and police, it was an easy day's work, with a free lunch and a nice cash bonus.

The system was simple if the prisoner had cash to pay to the right people. To get out the door, they first had to pay the jail doctor between 200,000 ($27) and 500,000 rupiah ($67) for a dental referral letter and the head of security 200,000 rupiah ($27). The doctor's certificate needed to be signed, and usually the inmate paid a local to do this. The dentist would charge a fee of about 300,000 rupiah ($40) for his signature. Nothing was free. But the biggest expense was the police. They took a fee of around 800,000 rupiah ($106) between them, and all their food, drinks and petrol expenses were paid for by the inmate. That was the deal.

Inmate Juri had been outside several times. He had enjoyed a swim in a hotel pool, and a few drinks with his parents and his fiancée, Ade.

I went to the hotel with my fiancée, one time with my sister. One time, my friend from Italy came. There's a swimming pool, we make like a small party. I went to the beach one time … I went home first and at one o'clock in the afternoon, I say to the police, 'Why you don't take me to the beach?'

And they say, 'No, we cannot, we have uniforms'. They didn't want other police to see them. I say, 'No problem, I'll give you T-shirts'. 'Yeah, okay, if you give us a T-shirt'. I give them T-shirts, shorts, everything, and they used my father's thongs. They put the guns in one bag, big beach bag. And my mum carries the bag with the two guns, and we go to the beach in a taxi. There were two police and one guard. They leave their uniform in my parents' house, but the guns they bring. They give to my mum to put in her beach bag.

– Juri

Juri, his mum, his fiancée and the police in their casual gear, took a taxi down to Kuta's busiest beach strip. Juri wasn't sure if they would let him swim, as he'd heard from Ruggiero that the police didn't often let prisoners go into the water. But, when they pulled up Juri asked, 'Hey, can I go in to swim?'

'Yeah, but can you swim?' asked the policeman.

They were concerned that they would be in trouble if he drowned.

'Yeah, I can swim,' he answered laughing.

'Just go then, why you asking? Go!'

That was it. Juri ran and dived into the ocean and for an hour or so, he felt like a free man, splashing about in the water, drinking beers, enjoying the tropical island like the tourists around him were doing. But, unlike them, he wouldn't be going back to shower at a nice hotel.

When Juri arrived back at Hotel K at about 6 pm, it was not easy for him to walk back through the door, into the dark, seedy world, while he was still smelling of sea salt, tingling from the thrill of the waves, and so freshly reminded of the beautiful life that was lost to him. But he would do it again; the days out were worth the torment of coming back.

Mick spent many afternoons sitting in a bar in the tourist area of Sanur Beach, where he had often stayed on holiday. He would go there to drink with friends. Several times the police didn't bother taking their guns – they handcuffed him until he got into the car and opened the cuffs as soon as they drove off. He enjoyed seeing the sea, drinking beer and talking, feeling like a normal human being again.

I washed my face with seawater. Walked in the water a bit.

– Mick

Mick went out eight to nine times, all up. Sometimes he didn't go to the beach, he just walked around the streets, soaking up life on the outside. He had several chances to escape from bars and clubs he went to, but a lack of money and the chance of getting caught stopped him.

Twice I really could have escaped, but I didn't have the money. I needed $US2000 or $3000. The point is, you have to set things up.

– Mick

Occasionally, things did go wrong for a prisoner and his or her minders. In a case that hit the news and embarrassed the jail, two of its guards and a prisoner were caught at a brothel, all three using its services.

A prison inmate, who was supposed to be safely locked up in Bali's Kerobokan penitentiary, was nabbed before dawn on Sunday at a brothel in the Sanur area, Denpasar. Apparently, the escapee had spent the night with a prostitute. In a strange turn of events, two prison guards were discovered to have not only helped the suspect escape from jail, but also participated in the night's escapade.

– *Jakarta Post*, November 2001

In another incident, Taiwanese prisoner Tommy, who'd won the trust of the guards, paid the necessary fees for a day out. He didn't have a police escort; only a guard and *Pemuka* inmate Saidin. The three of them broke the rules and split up, arranging to meet back up at 5 pm near the jail. Tommy had ridden off on a hired motorbike. They'd done this before. But on this day, Tommy didn't return. Saidin and the guard spent two hours waiting for him to show. At 7 pm they walked back into the jail and broke the news. The security boss phoned local hospitals in case Tommy had crashed his motorbike. Finally, at 9 pm, they put out an escape alert. But Tommy had been a free man since 10 am and had already taken a flight to Jakarta. The Taiwanese man was never caught; he made it home. It was bad news for the westerners, with their days out aborted for a while.

It was a lot easier for the Indonesian prisoners to go outside. Many, in fact, went in and out if they had a job outside. Several long-term prisoners, especially men, appeared to have free reign to walk in and out of the front doors whenever they liked, paying cash for the right to an unofficial day's leave.

In most prisons, you would think, those convicted of the most serious crimes would get the least freedom. But in the strange and chaotic world that is Hotel K, this seems to work in reverse. Often an inmate serving time for murder will stand at the front door, acting as doorman. The Laskars, Saidin, Ketut and Iwan all acted as though Hotel K was a normal hotel. Some of them had official licences to come and go for their jobs. One prisoner who was in for murder walked freely in and out to the gym around the corner from the jail every day.

But when the wrong police caught him outside, he was severely punished.

They took him to Polda *[police station] and bashed and bashed and bashed him for twelve hours straight with big poles of wood with nails hanging out of them. They put a T-shirt over his head so he couldn't see and fifteen policemen bashed him. He came and showed me his back and it was just like Jesus had come off the cross, it was just open wounds. He told me they hit him with a belt bucket on [the] back because he went outside. They didn't break any bones, but they did hit him in the head. He was okay after a while.*

– Inmate

Some of the ordinary Balinese prisoners were also allowed out for jobs such as sweeping the car park, buying cigarettes for the guards, or taking out excess slop prison food to give to someone to feed their pigs. Some worked cleaning the guards' homes. Often these local inmates took the chance to go home to their villages for the afternoon or to eat lunch at a local café and go shopping. Others were allowed weekend release. Depending on who they were, and how connected they were, all sorts of freedoms could be granted.

For a small sling to the guards and an excuse, such as selling their jail artwork to a nearby gallery, local inmates could usually get out for a few hours. It was a safe bet they'd return, as their family villages and homes could be easily located. So locals got a lot more freedom than inmates from other parts of Indonesia or westerners. Even those Balinese prisoners without jobs could slip out for the day by spending a little cash and climbing onto the rubbish truck.

Whenever they bring the rubbish out, they put maybe two people inside the truck, and they go out of the jail and then go their own way all day and in the evening they come back. It was Balinese people. They sit normally in the truck. It was business for the jail. They would pay, of course; maybe 400,000 each. Every time the truck was going out, two or three people would go out for a holiday.

– Thomas

Whatever it took to have a few hours away from Hotel K, most prisoners would seize the chance. But for all of them, it was a bittersweet taste of the life lost to them over the walls of Hotel K.

The first time I stepped outside of the prison wall, I felt nervous because it was the first time I'd experienced it for a long time. It felt like a dream and I even pinched myself on the cheek to check whether it's real or not. I could breathe so freely and really take the fresh air as deep as I could, and didn't care about the pollution because it's quite bad traffic in the tourist area. I got out from the darkness into the light, even though it was only for a moment. But I felt it was a beautiful blessing, and I felt so lucky because not everyone got the chance to enjoy it.

– Trisna, Balinese inmate

CHAPTER 18

RAIDS

The guards don't want the police to come inside. It's their kingdom.
– Thomas

Juri sat on the blue room floor, stroking his fiancée's face and talking, enjoying their time together as they sat crammed in among hundreds of people. Ade had just returned from a trip home to Timor and they were sharing a tender moment. It ended abruptly when Juri leaped up, gasping, 'Shit'. He ran across the room, darting around the sitting bodies. Ade turned to see what had made him jump. Striding in along the far wall was an endless line of police carrying machine guns. Juri was in the toilet, frantically wrapping a gram of smack that he'd had in his pocket in a piece of foil from his cigarette packet before slipping it up his arse. Hotel K was being raided.

His phone rang just as he finished. 'Juri, come fast, they're searching our block,' Chinese inmate Patrick blurted. Visitors were being ushered out by guards as Juri sprinted through the blue room, across the jail yard, past hundreds of police and into his block. He slammed his cell door shut and looked for anything incriminating. The police were outside; he had seconds. He snatched up a card he used for chopping smack, a bit of aluminium foil and a lighter, and hurled it all out the back window. Just as he turned back around, the door opened and three police officers walked inside.

Juri stood there breathless, watching as they searched his cell. He suddenly realised he'd forgotten his bong. It was sitting under the table, tucked behind a box. It was only a matter of time before they found it, but there was nothing he could do. They were tearing his room apart; stripping the sheet off his mattress, searching a pile of clothes and squeezing out toothpaste. Then they found it.

There was a momentary uproar as the police started talking excitedly and yelling to others to come inside. Three more police entered the small cell, along with friendly guard Pak Mus. 'You use. We catch you,' the policeman said to Juri, pointing to the bong for emphasis. 'It's not mine,' Juri said. He was desperate. He didn't want another case against him. He started talking fast. 'This belongs to a Dutch guy who used this room before me; he's just left the jail. Pak Mus, that's right, isn't it?' he said, turning to the guard for help. 'Yes, this is true. Juri doesn't use,' Pak Mus said. He saved Juri. The police didn't charge him.

I was lucky that time.

– Juri

The whole jail was active. No-one knew if the police would come to their block, but they had to be prepared. Prisoners in the other ten blocks were still running around, yelling, 'Police coming, police coming … clean … clean!'

Prisoners everywhere were clearing their cells, frantically picking up and disposing of drugs, bongs, foils and syringes that were lying around. They were throwing them out the back cell windows, burying them in the dirt, hiding them in secret compartments and shoving them up their arses. A group of prisoners gambling at the roulette tables near the temple packed up fast, carrying the tables into the back of the Hindu temple and stashing them away.

Typically, police were searching the blocks one at a time. Specialised police went inside, while at least a hundred and fifty armed police surrounded the block, prepared for a possible prisoner attack. Usually the raids were done in the evenings, so the prisoners were already locked in their blocks. But this day, more than nine hundred criminals, most with a bitter hatred for police, were roaming freely about.

Brazilian Ruggiero was in his cell, sleeping away the hot afternoon, when he was suddenly woken by an inmate running around the block, screaming, 'Police, police, police, police!' Ruggiero leaped up and shut his door. He swept around the cell, scooping up his knives, phones, chargers, headphones, and anything else he could find that was contraband, and putting it all in a secret bunker that was cut into the floor. He didn't have any drugs, and his laptop and some cash were already hidden in the false bottom of his wooden table. By the time the police opened his door, he was ready. He gritted his teeth as he stood watching them pry and pick through all his personal belongings, flicking through his Buddhism books, rifling through his clothes, looking through his crate of beer and flipping the mattress. This was jail and he was used to raids, but he didn't like them. They were humiliating and intrusive, and sometimes ridiculously excessive. When a female police officer stuck her fingers in his fresh cheese baguette, his patience snapped. 'Bitch, don't touch my baguette!' he snarled. The police left his cell without finding anything and, fortunately for him, left behind his full crate of beer, which he'd bought from Laskar member Alit Balong, who was in the cell next door.

Police swept through the rest of the cells in Ruggiero's block, and found drugs in only one room. That morning another prisoner had discarded several marijuana seeds and a twig in his ashtray while rolling a joint, and had forgotten about them. It was a costly mistake. He was arrested, charged and, after going through another court case, had two more years added to his sentence. This sort of incident was why the prisoners took raids very seriously.

For this raid, police had secured their search warrant after arresting guard Pak Giri. Police had followed him the night before, after a tip-off. Pak Giri had left Hotel K after his shift, ridden his motorbike to a karaoke bar in Denpasar, stopped in the car park, turned off the bike and pulled out the key. The next instant, several police officers rode up beside him and surrounded his bike. An officer told Pak Giri he needed to search him for drugs. The guard argued that he didn't have anything with him. But, after patting him down, they found a plastic bag in his sock. It contained just over four grams of heroin. Police then escorted Pak Giri to his house, where they'd been told he stored drugs for Hotel K inmates. Under the tiled floor beneath his bed, they found a candy tin stashed with two plastic bags, one of cocaine, weighing fifty-two grams, and one of heroin, weighing almost nineteen grams.

The suspect confessed that he got those illegal drugs from a prisoner. He also mentioned that the said prisoner is keeping drugs in a large amount in his cell. Next, the police raided Bali's biggest prison on Tuesday. Unfortunately, the prisoner's room was already empty.

– *Denpost*, February 2006

The prisoner was Hotel K drug lord Arman. The police knew he was a big-time dealer from his cell, because people arrested outside with drugs continually confessed he was their supplier. Since checking in, Arman had added to his criminal record a number of new cases for possession of thousands of ecstasy pills. As the jail's notorious drug lord, Arman also took the rap for his biggest ecstasy supplier, Iwan, who sat back quietly in the shadows of his furniture workshop-cum-ecstasy factory. It was widely known among inmates that Arman was Iwan's agent. Arman acquired the new drug charges for many reasons. Prisoners were often caught couriering his drugs outside. Dealers working in clubs and pubs selling his drugs often got caught and quickly gave him up. There was no loyalty.

Arman was even set up by one of his formerly most trusted men, who had been caught with three hundred and forty-three of his ecstasy pills. The man did a deal with the police to have his charges dropped if he worked a sting on Arman. So, he ordered 2000 pills and went inside Hotel K to pick up the package. Arman gave his trusted dealer a red bag filled with T-shirts, which the dealer passed to the police as soon as he walked outside. Underneath the T-shirts were the 2000 pills. The confiscated 2343 tablets, priced at 175,000 rupiah each, were worth four hundred and ten million rupiah ($55,000).

The biggest case against Arman began when one of his suppliers in Jakarta was caught with 35,000 yellow ecstasy pills with Popeye logos that had been smuggled in from Holland. The supplier's house in Jakarta was searched and police found a list of drug deliveries, including one to Bali for 7000 pills, and an airway delivery note. Jakarta police flew to Bali, and waited at the cargo office for the drugs to be collected. Two men, Aldi and Prana, arrived in an old Honda Accord and were arrested as soon as they tried to pick up the package. They confessed that their friend Ayung, a prisoner in Kerobokan, was due to meet them at a restaurant at 4 pm to take the package.

'The suspect who was supposed to be in Kerobokan Prison at the time, arrived in a taxi around 4 pm. The police nabbed him when he got out of the taxi and entered the restaurant. When Ayung (prisoner) was interrogated, he claimed that the stuff belonged to Arman Maulidie and that the plan was indeed to take them to Kerobokan Prison,' stressed Bali Police spokesman AS Reniban.

– *Denpost*, May 2006

After every outside arrest that led a trail to Hotel K, police were able to secure a warrant to raid the jail. But in their endless raids of Arman's cell, they only once uncovered drugs. One of Arman's men had tipped off police that he kept a supply of drugs hidden underneath a cleverly designed false squat toilet, purpose-built to hide drugs. Previous raids had always failed to uncover them. But, with the inside information, they found a huge stash in his cell toilet, including cocaine, heroin, inhaling equipment, ecstasy pills, several currencies of cash – twenty-nine million rupiah, US$500, €5000 and A$500 – and even a shotgun. Arman confessed it all belonged to him.

Each time Arman faced new charges, he was arrested and taken to the police station, but the charges often disappeared, costing him tens of thousands of dollars. He paid $94,000 for one big ecstasy case against him to go away.

But there were times when Arman's cash didn't work, when a case was too high-profile or the wrong police were involved, and he was taken to court on new charges. There were always several cases pending against him, and his ten-year sentence escalated to twenty-six years during his time in Hotel K. But it didn't deter him. He was making $10,000 a day and could come and go whenever he liked. Before the raid prompted by the arrest of Pak Giri, Arman had had his usual warning phone call from a guard, who told him the bad news that Pak Giri had been arrested, that he'd been named and that police were now on their way to search his cell. Arman was pissed off and alerted his men. They started quickly taking his drugs out of the ceiling and from a concrete bunker in the cell, putting whatever they could into a sealed box and dropping it into the sewerage drains, to retrieve later. They also threw drugs, bongs, foils and straws out through the window at the back of the cell. It was a basic rule not to hide drugs in the cell during a raid. If the drugs were found in a neutral spot, police would confiscate the drugs but no-one would get charged.

Some inmates seized this opportunity and ran behind the cellblocks to scoop up as many drugs as they could before the police arrived. In a raid a month earlier, police had found a prisoner, Abdul, a motorcycle thief, lying in a ditch behind Arman's block, overdosing.

All inmates knew of the tactic of throwing drugs out the window, and Abdul wasn't the first to scurry around scooping them up. But when he saw the police, he didn't have time to hide them. He panicked, and started trying to swallow all the evidence. By the time police got to him, he was having a seizure, with foam pouring out of his mouth. In his clenched fist, they found a gram of heroin, and in his pockets, twenty-five ecstasy pills. He was rushed to Sanglah Hospital, but died on the way.

What was catastrophic was a convict, involved in vehicle theft cases, named Abdul Habib, jumped into a ditch behind Block E. Quickly police came to the rescue. Apparently the man had just swallowed 25 inex *[ecstasy pills]. Habib was rushed to Sanglah Hospital. Sadly though, he couldn't be saved and died around 5 pm from a drug overdose.*

– *Denpost*, 28 December 2005

During the Pak Giri raid, police found four hundred grams of smack behind Arman's block, which they confiscated. They meticulously searched his cell, but typically found nothing. Police also raided Iwan's furniture workshop, looking all around his machines. But Iwan had also received a warning phone call and the place was clean. In an earlier raid, he had thrown a tin of 1000 ecstasy tablets on the rubbish heap, but then couldn't find it. With Thomas's help, he spent hours looking in tin after tin on the rubbish heap. Eventually, he had no choice but to accept the loss of $20,000 worth of ecstasy tablets. But a local inmate, who worked nearby in the garden, couldn't believe that a tin filled with 1000 ecstasy pills, worth more than he'd ever make in his life, could really just disappear. He spent two days searching through the garbage and eventually found it. Incredibly, the very honest criminal gave the tin back to Iwan and asked for nothing. As a reward, Iwan gave him a bit of cash and a job in his furniture factory.

He was stupid to give it back to Iwan. What did he get … a job working for 20,000 rupiah [$2] a day.

– Thomas

In the Pak Giri raid, police spent three hours in the men's blocks, finding some drugs and bongs and arresting six prisoners. They confiscated knives, kerosene stoves, mobile phones, chargers, DVD players, porn DVDs and ledgers of drug sales. They even discovered the three illegal roulette tables that had been hidden in the rarely searched temple. This was a full jail sweep, after Pak Giri, to help win himself a bit of favour, had disclosed to police the widespread drug use and dealing inside Hotel K. When the ex-guard was later sent from the police cells to serve his time back in Hotel K, he had to get protection from *Pemuka* Saidin.

During the raid there was also an uneasy tension in Block W. The women were locked up in their block, sitting in their cells, waiting for their turn to be searched. An hour earlier, female guards had come around, telling them not to wear anything sexy in front of the male police officers. Anyone wearing skimpy outfits threw on more clothes.

Australian Schapelle Corby was always a focal point. Dubbed 'Ganja Queen' by the local press, she was a celebrity prisoner after her case made international headlines. She was wearing a singlet and pyjama bottoms. The guards told her she was still looking too sexy, so she put on a bra and her pink fake Chanel sunglasses. All the women had been busy preparing for the raid; hiding their phones, DVD players, chargers and money. In one cell, the women piled all their contraband electrical equipment into a bag and gave it to one of the female guards for safe-keeping. Now they waited.

It began with three loud bangs on the steel door. Police burst in with machine guns, sprinting into the block and yelling and screaming, spreading out to every corner. In front of each cell, several police officers stopped and stood with their guns poised. The women had been ready for it, but it was still an abrupt, brutal change of pace. For those who hadn't seen a raid before, it was frightening. Even the guards were running around the cells, yelling, 'Get out, get out, get out!', ordering all the women to line up for call.

Once they were standing in their lines, two women from each cell were ordered to go back inside and collect all the keys for the locked cupboards, boxes and drawers. When they returned, police were given bundles of keys to use and started ransacking the cells, picking through clothes, books and toiletries, and throwing everything into huge, jumbled piles in the middle of each cell.

Several police were using videos cameras to film the raid and occasionally turned their lenses on the line of women. Most turned away, covering their faces, not wanting to be exposed on the television news that night. Schapelle, in particular, hated it, as she was always a target, with photos of her easily selling to the media for big bucks. As she sat in the roll call line, she tried to stay hidden behind a small tree, wearing her sunglasses to mask a nasty eye infection.

Another foreigner, the Bali Nine's Renae Lawrence, saw that police had found the bag stashed with electrical goods that the guard had been looking after, including her new portable DVD player. She wasn't happy. 'Excuse me, that's mine,' she said, picking it up. 'No, no, we're just checking for drugs,' a police officer said. 'Okay, no problem, I don't have any,' she said, putting it back down. Police checked it and said, 'Okay'. Renae took it back. She was the only inmate to stand up to the police. They took phones, chargers, cash, and gas burners and teaspoons that could potentially be used to heat heroin – although the majority of female inmates only used the gas burners to heat food or boil water for a cup of coffee.

After a long couple of hours, the raid finished and the police vanished from Block W as fast as they had arrived, streaming out through the steel door and sweeping en masse across the jail lawns towards the front door. But it wasn't over for the police. Things were about to get nasty. Behind them in the men's blocks, angry inmates, who were usually locked up during raids, were ready to ambush them. On cue, about eighty men charged at the police, running in a pack, screaming, 'Motherfuckers, motherfuckers!' and pelting rocks and stones. The swarms of police started running towards the offices.

All over the world, people hate police. They're the number one enemy.

– Juri

The bitter hatred for police that naturally existed in a jail was exacerbated by their blatant hypocrisy. Most prisoners knew that many police were doing drug deals, using drugs, and even selling the drugs they confiscated from Hotel K.

Word of mouth in jail was that Arman was selling for some police.

– Saidin

The angry stone-throwing was mostly by locals. Brazilian Ruggiero had joined in only for sport – until he spotted the police officer who had arrested and beaten him three years earlier. Anger tore into his guts. He ran like fury and hurled a stone as hard as he could. It missed. But it felt good. He was in the line of rock fire, and ran back for cover.

Hundreds of rocks were now flying through the air. In a frenzy, the locals were chanting 'Motherfuckers!' and furiously hurling stones. Windows were smashing. Police were sprinting towards the exit. One got hit in the back of the head. Another was struck in the neck. It was a war zone. It was mayhem.

Three police officers suddenly turned and fired their machine guns into the air. Prisoners instinctively froze. For an instant, the yard was still. But the inmates quickly erupted into loud hissing and booing, again screaming, 'Motherfuckers! Motherfuckers!'

as they started to run. Most police were in the offices by then. Several prisoners chased them right through to the front door, screaming and lobbing stones into the car park.

It was nice. It broke the boredom.

– Ruggiero

CHAPTER 19

KEROBOKAN CREW

Every day was a party. When they lock us in the block every day, we had beer, arak, *we danced like maniacs. One day I took ecstasy – me, Gabriel and Aris, we were dancing like maniacs – the local people think we're from another planet. We start dancing while the block's open, then they lock us inside.*

– Ruggiero

Of course, in jail we have good time as well, but you can die every second, every minute, you can get killed from someone. You make a small mistake, that's it. You say one wrong word to someone, you can get killed. From morning, we use Xanax, alcohol, smack, whatever. You forget everything, don't get stressed.

– Juri

With Bali being such a popular holiday destination, with people from all over the world flocking to its beaches and night-clubs to enjoy the party lifestyle, Hotel K inevitably filled up with guests from the farthest corners of the earth – Austria, Germany, China, France, England, Canada, Mexico, Brazil, Peru, Australia, Argentina, Nepal, Taiwan, Japan, Russia and Sweden.

Bali is a tourist spot. There, tourists get arrested. Not too much culture, but there was always interesting foreigners in Kerobokan. Everyone is crazy here. Gabriel, Aussie Martin, the guy from Greece, the guy from Russia, from England, from America, from Italy, Argentina, Canada, France, so at least we had crazy people from different parts of the world. Just being a foreigner makes them already more interesting, because the guy from France is going to tell me something about wine; the guy from Hawaii tells me about the surf, the guy from Japan tells me about … da da da, Aussies tell me some stories about Aussieland.

Did you have any fun times together?

Yeah, of course. We have three different tribes of foreigners: the ones who like smack, the ones who use other drugs, and the ones who like to drink, and then there are ones who like everything. I was [in] the drinking tribe. I'm the beer man. I think I've been an Australian in another lifetime.

– Ruggiero

Juri was another who liked to party with the foreigners.

Yeah, we have a good time … many, many times we have good time. Sometimes, like one New Year Eve, everyone's cells are open. You can go everywhere, the jail became like big discotheque. Everyone's cell open until the night after. Twenty-four hours. Every block. You can just walk everywhere. You can smoke joint, take ecstasy. Everything. Everything. It was crazy.

– Juri

Most afternoons, the westerners would gather on the grass outside their blocks, drinking beer, smoking dope and listening to techno music on a portable CD player. Mick would play with an inmate's pet musang (a small cat-like animal), blowing dope in its face to get it stoned; Juri would sleep in the sun after smoking smack in his cell; Ruggiero would drink beers and cook up a barbecue for everyone, pulling beers out of his crate and passing them around. 'Do you want any drugs?' he usually asked his guests. 'Yeah, I wouldn't mind a line of coke', they would say. Ruggiero enjoyed playing host, often taking out his guitar and singing. Scottish sailor Robert would usually be passed out drunk on the concrete bench or retelling his story about losing his ship on the China Seas. One of Arman's boys would walk around selling ecstasy pills from a plastic bag in his pocket, with most digging into their pockets or taking a credit note to buy one or two.

American big-wave surfer Gabriel was often drunk and high, and would sit around in his bright pink hibiscus-flowered surf shorts and metallic blue sunglasses, with his wavy, long sunbleached hair hanging down his bare back. He sat with his phone in one hand, a beer in the other and a cigarette dangling from his lips. This was a typical wasted afternoon.

But, in an instant, a relaxed day could turn very tense. One afternoon, the Kerobokan crew was lounging about in the sun when Mick caught a glimpse of Gabriel up in the watchtower. They all turned to see him sitting up there in his blue sunglasses, drinking a can of beer. Freedom was just a jump away. A sudden energy and excitement rippled through the group. But they all bet the American wouldn't have the guts to do it.

Gabriel had been mulling over his escape plan for several days. He could just walk through a hole in the inner wall, climb up into the watchtower and jump. It was easy. But the plan would only be viable until the hole in the wall was filled. It had crumbled a few days earlier at the spot where the guard who smuggled in *arak* had dug a small tunnel under the fence to pull the plastic bags of booze through. Torrential tropical rains had washed away more soil, turning the tunnel into a ravine, and causing the old concrete wall above it to collapse – not for the first or the last time. In a snap decision that afternoon, Gabriel had thrown a few things into a little black backpack, torn two sheets off his bed, walked through the hole in the wall, and across the snake-riddled grass and up into the unused watchtower.

We call it the monkey post. If the guards hear this, they don't like it. But it's what prisoners call it. It's mostly empty. The guards don't sit in the watchtowers, they sit near the kitchen playing cards or drinking, passing the time.

– Thomas

Had Gabriel not been so high and drunk, he might have had second thoughts about his escape plan, particularly as he had only five months left to serve. But in his addled state of mind, he made a decision he'd live to regret. He finished four cans of Bintang beer while he waited for two men lingering on the street below to disappear. When they moved he was ready to fly. He abseiled down the two bedsheets he had tied to a concrete post on the tower. When he hit the ground, he tore down the sheets, slung his backpack over his shoulder, and started walking up the road. With his dark sunglasses, his pink hibiscus-patterned surf shorts and his long hair, he looked more like a tourist than a Hotel K escapee. But before he could hail a taxi, freedom was snatched from him.

A mob of twenty Laskars, guards and local prisoners had seen him escaping and left the jail to chase him up the road. One prisoner tore around the corner on a motorbike and aimed it straight at Gabriel, hitting him hard and knocking him flying into a rice field. The prisoner dropped his bike, ran over to Gabriel and started kicking him in the guts. Within moments, they had circled the American and were viciously kicking and punching him. Gabriel didn't stand a chance. Typically, the Balinese were fighting in a pack. All he could do was shield his head with his arms. By the time they dragged him back down the road and into Hotel K, he was barely conscious and had deep bloody gashes on his head and face.

Laskar, guards, people in the street – they were all bashing him. You know how it is in Bali; when they catch a thief, they all beat him up until he dies, then throw him in the garbage truck. They are mean people. They are cowards. If I fight with someone and I have a friend who wants to join me, I say, 'No, I fight one on one'. Not two on one. They fight as many as possible against one.

– Ruggiero

On the way inside with Gabriel, the group pushed past Juri's mum, who had arrived for a visit, giving her a nasty shock when she saw the familiar face of her son's cellmate covered in blood. It was a stark reminder of where her youngest child was living. In the blue room, visitors and prisoners had watched the flurry as the mob had sprinted from all directions across the jail to the front door and out into the street. Brazilian Ruggiero had run towards the front door too and had seen them carrying his long-time friend inside. He trailed behind as the Laskars took Gabriel through the blue room and into the security boss's office, where they threw him down on the tiled floor. Gabriel lay motionless, slipping in and out of consciousness as they continued attacking him; beating him with a stick, kicking and punching him. Ruggiero stood near the door, catching glimpses of the vicious attack and becoming more and more agitated and distressed.

His head was broken and they would come and kick his head. Then this one guy, this motherfucker who smoked so much shabu *his eyes don't focus, has an iron hammer and he bangs the soul of his feet and his anklebone. A kind of little torture. It was too much. I couldn't stay still anymore. I went in the room and said, 'Motherfucker, you have to hit me too'. Then they pushed me out. But they didn't touch me. They broke his anklebone. They are mean people, they are very mean.*

– Ruggiero

The atmosphere in the blue room was tense and excited. People were standing up and looking through the windows into the room where Gabriel was being attacked. They could hear screams, thumping and whacking. It was not done covertly. When prisoners left the blue room to go back to their blocks, they walked right past the wide-open door, and could see Gabriel sprawled on the floor being bashed with short iron bars.

It was a vicious beating. The inmates knew it might not stop until Gabriel was dead. The mob wouldn't mean to kill him, but most were high on ice so wouldn't know when to stop. Gabriel needed outside help fast. Foreigners had consulates and this was exactly when they called on them. Ruggiero and Mick both phoned the US Embassy for help, telling them to come quickly. Within fifteen minutes the consul arrived, marching angrily into the room. He was suddenly in the line of fire, getting punched, until they realised who he was. Schapelle convinced the Block W guards to let her go to the canteen to buy a bottle of Fanta. She took a detour to peek into the room. Gabriel was in a terrible state, unconscious and bleeding on the floor. The consul was still being pushed and shoved, arguing that Gabriel had to be taken to hospital. The guards were refusing to allow it. Schapelle raced back to Block W and phoned her sister, Mercedes, asking her to call the Red Cross and the Australian Consulate, fast.

The US consul kept arguing with the Laskars and guards, and eventually they agreed to allow Gabriel to go to hospital. None of Gabriel's mates knew if he would survive the night.

His escape plan was totally fucked. He saw the wall was down and a couple of days before he went, he said to me, 'I'm going to go, man, look, the wall is down, you can get out'. I said, 'Okay, man, I hope you do it'. But it was 1 pm … full traffic on the roads and he jumps from the wall. He just decided to go, he was off his face.

– Ruggiero

Gabriel was a 42-year-old American building contractor, who had moved to Bali to enjoy surfing and partying. Every day he rode the waves, high on heroin. It was a perfect Bali life for him, until one afternoon when the police raided his villa, and found sixty grams of smack hidden in his pillowcase. Gabriel didn't stop the partying lifestyle in Hotel K. He lived in an alcohol and drug fuelled haze, addicted to smack and falling into spiralling debt. Blue room drug sales earned him a bit of cash, but he mostly relied on his mum in California for handouts. But she had suddenly cut off the cash flow when she learned Gabriel was using it for drugs. Arman called in his credit; Gabriel couldn't pay. He was being threatened. He was desperate. His mum wouldn't send more money; his lacklustre escape attempt had been a stunt to rattle her so that she would send more cash. It worked. She did. But he hadn't anticipated that the price he would pay would be a vicious attack, or that they would shave off the long hair he'd had for twenty-five years.

After a few hours in hospital having his wounds stitched up, Gabriel was sent straight back to Hotel K and thrown into a tower isolation cell. On her way across the jail to church, early the next morning, Schapelle could hear Gabriel's faint moans and calls for help. She was being escorted by guards, so could do nothing. On her way back, Gabriel was quiet. Schapelle looked at the ground, trying to be inconspicuous, as she loudly called out to him that she was trying to get help for him. Later she organised a little care package and sent it to him via a prisoner, with a small note saying that she was praying for him.

Gabriel's leap from the tower was costly for the other western men. In a security crackdown that lasted several months, all western men were moved into the same block, and locked in their cells all day. Their only outings were for visits, or to have a sneaky twenty minutes in the sun if they paid the right guard. Gabriel's escape had been embarrassing for Hotel K, particularly as it had come only two months after the Taiwanese inmate, Tommy, had escaped.

The wall also had to be fixed and the westerners were asked to pay for it, like they paid for most things, even the septic tank being emptied.

They are crazy. They want me to pay for something that holds me in, stops me going free. The guys who came around asking had balls. They also wanted us to pay to put more barbed wire around our block. 'You guys pay for the barbed wire.' 'Yeah, kiss my arse.'

– Ruggiero

For months the gaping hole in the maximum-security jail's inner wall was covered by tacked-up sheets of metal. A murderer ran to freedom through the wall a couple of months after Gabriel's failed escape attempt.

A convict at Kerobokan Prison, Rudi Setyawan, who was serving an 11-year sentence for murder, escaped yesterday at around 3.30 pm through the prison's southern wall that collapsed last year. 'The wall was temporarily covered with sheet metal material. After he managed to sneak out of his block, he headed towards the temporary wall and ran away,' said Prison boss Bromo. 'We hope to find him,' he stressed.

– *Denpost*, 19 March 2005

The locals often found ways to escape over the walls or under them, through sewerage drains. But most were recaptured within hours, often in brothels or their family villages, and were sent back to Hotel K and brutally bashed.

A Kerobokan prisoner, Ketut Agus Suarjana, 28, was caught by prison guards yesterday after enjoying 13 hours of freedom. Agus was thought to have escaped at 5.30 am and was caught at [6.30 pm] when he was about to cross a road near a shopping complex in Denpasar. According to a source in prison, Ketut Agus Suarjana escaped after climbing a wall near the emergency gate using a rope and black cloth tied together.

– *Denpost*, June 2002

Another inmate climbed over the wall, using a bamboo pole with grooves for footholds. He was caught as soon as he landed outside, and suffered the same fate as Gabriel. He was dragged past inmates and visitors, including Schapelle and her sister, Mercedes, in the busy blue room, in soiled underpants, with bloody welts across his back and with a shattered, bleeding nose. The prospect of escape was not worth it unless the plan was foolproof. But the lure of freedom was strong.

Escape was something every westerner daydreamed about for a while. Schapelle visualised a helicopter flying over Hotel K, dangling a swing that would scoop her up and take her home. Mick's vision was a bit more realistic. He imagined sawing through the bars, pole-vaulting the wall, and riding on a motorbike into the Balinese sunset. He got as far as having a blade brought inside the prison in a French breadstick.

But foreigners rarely actually tried to escape. They were aware of the brutal consequences if they didn't make it. Local inmates, many of whom hated and were jealous of the westerners, were quick to seize on the chance to bash them if they saw them trying to escape. If westerners did escape, life afterwards would never be free. They would be fugitives, running, looking over their shoulder, unable to see their families. Most inmates longed for the day they'd walk free; anyone with money never stopped trying to do deals, to work the system to find loopholes to slide through to get out early. The quest for freedom was part of life. Many spent years convinced they were going to go free in a month or two.

Clinging to hopes of imminent release was the way many survived. If they imagined truly being stuck in Hotel K for fifteen or twenty years, or for life, they would go crazy. But the hope wasn't merely wild fantasy. It was often realistic. Unlike most countries, where an inmate's sentence was set, no-one really knew how long they would serve in Indonesia. The system of twice-yearly remissions for good behaviour was erratic. For a sling of cash, an inmate could sometimes get six months slashed in a year. In Indonesia, where killers often walked free after two or three years, anything was possible.

Sentences could be radically cut. Juri's was reduced from life to fifteen years. Frenchman Michael's was cut from life to twenty years. Sentencing could also mysteriously be changed in the paperwork. Englishman Steve Turner waved a $35,000 wand to magically convert his six-year sentence into three years. The judges publicly sentenced him to six years, while quietly writing three years in the official paperwork. This avoided questions being raised over why he was doing three years for possession of thousands of ecstasy tablets, while poor locals routinely served four years for possession of one or two. Gabriel's eight-year sentence was cut to two years and Argentinean Frederico's from five years to two in their court papers before they reached Hotel K. Everyone's sentence was potentially pliable. This gave even those on life and death sentences something to cling to – the hope that the prison doors could suddenly swing open and set them free.

But, in the meantime, Hotel K was home and the inmates had to adapt. Using drugs and getting obliterated every day was, for many, a way to fill the endless hours. The westerners checking in and out of Hotel K were a disparate bunch, but often well-educated, wealthy and from loving families. If many were unlikely friends outside, inside they were bonded by geography, lack of choice and the shared pain of being locked in Hotel K.

Some days we had a good time, we were a good family – not homogenous, we had some very weird species, very rare species. This day was the best. I took acid. Gabriel had a speaker [that] he put outside, and [he] put on Red Hot Chili Peppers. Aris is a fucking punk dancer, you know, full of tattoos and no shirt. The locals look at us like we're from another planet, and guards come and think 'Who the fuck are these guys?', and eventually some of the Balinese start to join us. It was a comedy. It was really a comedy.

– Ruggiero

The afternoon parties' food and drink were upgraded during the three months that millionaire Australian yachtsman Chris Packer spent in Hotel K, for having unregistered guns on his boat.

He paid a guard [to] go to his boat often and bring him the stuff; bring him wine and whisky and filet mignon steak, spare ribs, lamb chops, prawns, etc … and give it away. Chris had very good taste in booze, he had some excellent wine. We had all the good stuff. He spoiled us. He is a very nice guy. If there was ever a gentleman behind bars, it was him.

– Ruggiero

The freedom they had within the walls of Hotel K fluctuated greatly depending on how strict or amenable the presiding jail boss was and which shift of guards was on duty. But when they had the chance, the Kerobokan crew went wild.

One night, Swedish inmate Lars threw a birthday party for himself, providing copious bags of *arak* for everyone in his block. The partying started in the early afternoon sun, and continued in their cells after 5.30 pm lockup. A couple of hours later, the fun finished abruptly. English inmate Steven had fallen asleep under the table, and when Filo couldn't wake him up, he decided to splash *arak* across his bare back and arms. Filo was larking around. He was high and drunk, and didn't think. He threw a match at the Englishman's back. It exploded. Steven leaped up, screaming. Fire was scorching up his arms and across his back. He was in agony. He ran around the room screaming, flapping his arms, trying to put the flames out. Filo stood back, gaping in shock. Two cellmates were watching in horror from the floor. Lars threw a glass of water on Steven's back. A blood-curdling scream ripped across the cell; the water felt like razor blades slicing his back. For several more seconds, the fire burned into the inmate's skin. Once the alcohol was burned up, the flames died and Steven collapsed, unconscious, on the floor. His badly burned arms and back were blistering before his stunned cellmates' eyes. Guards and a *tamping* turned up quickly. The whole block had heard the screaming. Steven's cell was unlocked and he was driven to Sanglah Hospital, which had a special burns unit that had been installed after the Bali bombings. For two weeks he received treatment for third-degree burns and was then returned to Hotel K, wrapped in bandages. He was angry. Filo guiltily paid the hospital bill and apologised. But Steven was left with permanent gruesome scars and a recurring nightmare of almost being burned to death. His four cellmates were sent to cell *tikus* for several days until they paid to get out.

Filo is devilish. He was playing. It wasn't intentional. They [take] smack together, get drunk together. They were friends. Shit happens. They're off their faces on smack and alcohol, and in jail. Nobody's too sane in jail. We're all a bit crazy. This place is weird. Jail is jail, you know.

– Ruggiero

Filo is a psychopathic French guy who just wanted to see if arak *burns or not. He was drunk. He didn't expect it to burn like that.*

– Mick

The French guy is a little bit strange. If he's stoned, he's out of his mind. He had loads of money; well, anyway, enough money. You could see his face was like a naughty boy's.

– Thomas

The endless dramas that played out in the men's block helped the days, weeks, months and years pass for the inmates.

There was always something brewing. One night, Arman, who could sleep in any cell he liked, was staying in Vincente's room in order to use some cocaine. The prisoners were locked up for the night, but Arman called the guards to unlock French inmate Michael from his cell, and escort him across to join their party. One of the Laskars, Asman, known for carrying a gun in his pocket, and who had total freedom to walk in and out of Hotel K, also turned up.

Asman phoned Ruggiero, asking him to teach him to make freebase cocaine – a procedure that involved mixing the drug with water and baking soda, and cooking it on a spoon to turn it into crack. Ruggiero wasn't too keen, as he was watching the US Open on TV. He was also tired of joining in the same inane drug-induced conversations. But he turned off the TV and went anyway. By the time he arrived, the others had smoked a lot of *shabu*, and Vincente was freebasing.

We're drinking beer and Arman doesn't drink anything. I say, 'Arman, take care, man; you don't do sports, you're not fit and you are going to smoke this shit'. Then he smoked the thing. Boom! When I went to the toilet, he was standing against the wall; pale, grey, one step from overdosing. I got some salt to put on his tongue. I undress him, put him in the shower; he almost overdosed. He used shabu, *but this day he smoked* shabu *and freebase cocaine. Makes you stoned. Like, boom! He doesn't drink. When you do a line of coke, you drink beer or whisky, and he didn't even drink a sip of a beer, so he was very dry … crazy.*

– Ruggiero

Tall, lean and muscular Dutchman Aris was one of the stranger inmates, usually walking around hallucinating on LSD, and notorious for changing his look. He'd turn up with different hairstyles, from punk to being bald, or shaving his facial hair in a lopsided style – taking off his right eyebrow and the left side of his moustache – just for the hell of it.

Aris was an LSD freak from Amsterdam.

– Thomas

Scottish sailor Robert – father of Black Monster's baby – was often seen having sex behind Iwan's workshop or in the back of the church, with a girl straddling his lap.

He was horny like a goat. He sees any hole, he wants to go in.

– Mick

Most days, Robert was drunk by lunchtime, stumbling around and abusing people, drinking *arak* from a plastic cup, a cigarette dangling from his lips. The front of his trousers was often dripping wet from where he had pissed himself. He was an aggressive drunk, indiscriminately screaming, 'Fucking idiots!' and provoking anyone walking past, including the Laskars, who would bash him senseless. By the time the afternoon lockup bells were ringing, he was usually sleeping on a concrete bench, or on the grass, with a cigarette between his fingers and had to be carried back to his cell.

Once he was drunk in the grass, and we put frangipani on his neck and took photo. He didn't move much … he was like a statue.

– Mick

Robert's very nice, but when he gets drunk he's a pain in the arse. He was always drunk, giving shit. Kind of Scottish … he doesn't give a fuck. He's a wild man. Extremely strong, he just grabs you. He drives everyone absolutely nuts. He's crazy. He got beaten up many times. They punch him and he screams, 'You fucking faggot – you don't hurt me!' Fuck. To make it worse, he says, 'Listen, you punch me, but your cock is still small; I have a big cock,' and pulls down his pants. Fuck. He's one of a kind.

– Ruggiero

American Gabriel was also a bad drunk, recklessly taunting a killer one afternoon just for the sake of it. He was drunk. It was a bit of fun. It was also a mistake. You could never forget where you were. The inmate pulled out a knife and slashed Gabriel across the chest and arm, cutting a tendon and temporarily paralysing his right arm. The killer complained to the jail's security chief about Gabriel's taunts, and it was Gabriel who was sent to cell *tikus* for punishment.

Frenchman Michael and English Steve were called 'the veggies', always sleeping in their cells after shooting up. Italian Juri was well-liked, and seemingly was always happy and smiling and high on heroin. Mexican Vincente was considered to be aloof, rarely mixing with the group, and known for psychotically going from casual laughter to a screaming tirade in a split second. Dropping cigarette ash in his cell or placing your sandals in the wrong spot could set him off.

He was an angry man. Like a psychopath, he would flip out over little things. People didn't like to get close to him.

– Mick, former cellmate

Australian Mick swung between bursts of hot anger and quietly reading his metaphysical books, painting pictures and practising yoga. He was seething at being locked up for fifteen years for hashish possession, swearing the basket of almost three kilograms of stuff that police found in his half-built Bali holiday house was a herbal medicine. But the courts had refused to permit it to be tested independently.

'I'm so confused, it's a shocking situation, it's like a dream, it's not reality,' Fardin told AAP by telephone from prison in Bali. 'The problem is they just don't want to lose face. It doesn't matter whether it's hashish or not hashish, they just want money.'

– *AAP*, 25 July 2002

Mick had refused to plead guilty, dumping his lawyer when he asked for cash to pay police and the court. He had written fifteen to twenty letters to anyone he thought might be able to help, including the Indonesian President, human rights groups in Jakarta and Australia, and the Australian Government, explaining that he was not getting a fair trial. He received only two letters back, both from human rights organisations – the Australian group simply said that it could not interfere in another country's justice system, and the Jakarta group told him to push harder for re-testing of the stuff. Mick argued furiously in court for the re-testing but the judge refused point-blank. In sentencing, the judge went in hard. For possession of under three kilograms of what the judge suddenly and inexplicably claimed was not pure hashish but a hashish-sand mix, Mick and his girlfriend, Trisna, went down for fifteen years each.

I couldn't believe it at first. I felt like I'd been in a time machine. Was it karma? Action reaction? Did I do something and was not aware of it? I wanted to make sense of what had happened. What action had I done for this reaction to come to me?

– Mick

When the governor of Bali was in Hotel K one day, giving an Independence Day speech to inmates, Mick desperately wanted to talk to him about his case and give him a letter. He waited in the shade for the governor to finish his speech, and then approached him. The governor swept straight past, completely ignoring the inmate. Mick called out, 'Governor, please can I talk to you?' Two of his bodyguards turned and blocked Mick, saying, 'Not today'. Mick's hot temper flared. 'You fucking corrupt bastard. I want to talk to you about your corrupt courts, your police!' he yelled at the governor. The governor started to run. His bodyguards left Mick, to join their boss. Mick charged behind, yelling, 'Stop, you corrupt bastard!' The bodyguards turned and blocked him again. Mick went ballistic, screaming, 'You fucking corrupt bastard. Stop! Stop!'

The governor was by then sprinting through the blue room, past a crowd of police, consular officials and politicians who were all walking towards the door. As the governor flashed by, the room suddenly stopped. Bewildered, everyone turned to watch the scene. Mick was still running and screaming, 'Fucking corrupt bastard!' as the governor flew breathlessly out the front door and leaped into his car. Mick stood in the doorway, screaming almost dementedly with rage and from a desperate sense of injustice. He had no-one to help him. No-one would listen. Three guards held him back as he watched the governor's shiny car cruise out of the car park.

The guards were not angry. I think they felt sorry for me.

– Mick

Mick didn't only vent his rage at the authorities. Being locked up each day and feeling such a sense of injustice caused his grip on reality to warp, and subsequently he would lash out. One afternoon he offered to cut Ruggiero's head off, for $5000. His fury had been unleashed when Ruggiero failed to pay $35 for a pearl necklace he had sold him. Blinded by anger, he imagined that he could cut off Ruggiero's head to punish him, and also earn $5000 to pay his way out of Hotel K. His decapitation idea had come to him when wealthy Argentinean inmate Frederico was angrily muttering about Ruggiero being a 'fucking arsehole'. Frederico believed Ruggiero had organised to buy drugs from him in a police sting – to help save his own arse – and was therefore responsible for his arrest. Such set-ups were common and Ruggiero had been arrested a few days before Frederico.

Mick went across to Frederico's block, and caught him and another inmate walking out. He told them his plan. 'This piece of shit put you in here; do you want me to kill him? I'll cut his head off.' Frederico liked the idea. They walked down to the canteen to buy cigarettes and discussed it. Frederico would talk to his Israeli girlfriend about getting the cash out of his bank account. But by the next morning, it was off. Frederico's girlfriend instantly saw that it was a crazy idea and refused to get the cash. Ruggiero had already heard about the bounty on his head from the other inmate, who had been a good surfing buddy of his for years. The next morning, Ruggiero went to Mick's cell, paid him the cash for the pearl necklace and apologised for the delay.

The tough guy became a pussy cat. I really would have cut his head off. At that time I was an animal man – my perception of life was different.

– Mick

The westerners regularly fought with each other, although the fights often finished as quickly as they started. Robert was constantly being belted by someone for yelling, 'Fucking idiot, fucking idiot!' like a drunk parrot. Thomas and Gabriel brawled over unpaid smack bills. Mick beat up English Steve and threatened French Michael for not paying money they both owed Thomas for smack, because Thomas owed Mick. Michael's mum paid the bill and there were no hard feelings.

One afternoon, a blind-drunk Ruggiero sprinted up to Mick, who was sitting on the grass, quietly drawing, to try out a Jiu-Jitsu kick. Mick saw the skinny Brazilian coming at him, and at the last second stuck out his leg, sending him flying.

He always wanted to practise his Jiu-Jitsu. Some people already had a headache with it; they didn't want any more of his fucking practice.

– Thomas

I was always out of my head, I was always drunk. I didn't feel anything. I didn't want to feel anything. I was numb. I didn't give a fuck anymore.

– Ruggiero

It was an international mental institution.

– Mick

Their aggression was a result of frustration, the claustrophobic lifestyle, and the sense of injustice that many felt. But it was exacerbated by the poison they drank every day, like it was water. They had discovered that rapist Garen, who was the main *arak* dealer and who got supplies from the guards, mixed it with methanol and crushed mosquito coils to give it extra kick.

There was a rapist called Garen, a rapist who was like a celebrity. In my country, a rapist cannot leave his cell because people kill him. Not here. He was a disgusting fat guy. He was the one inside selling arak.

He mixed it with burning mosquito coil and methanol. We drank two or three bottles every day. I didn't know it was mosquito coil, I found out after. You can't see green pieces inside. I just knew that I wanted to fight with everyone.

– Ruggiero

Some westerners tried doing something useful during their endless days. Mick painted pictures for French Michael's mum to sell, and Ruggiero wrote and sent emails on his laptop at night, and was also studying Buddhism, which was slowly helping him to manage his fiery temper. Robert was an engineer by profession, and in the mornings, before he started drinking, did electrical wiring jobs around the jail. Many of the men played tennis. Several of the Bali Nine prisoners, including those on death row, played for hours every day in the hot sun. Bali Nine boss Myuran Sukumaran sometimes employed a tennis coach to come inside and give him lessons. Hotel K opened its doors to the media for a couple of days, for a tennis match between westerners – the aim being to present Hotel K as a humane rehabilitation facility. Afterwards, Australian Scott was told by the guards to talk to the journalists. So, with his cap on back to front, and looking more like Lleyton Hewitt than a death row inmate, he talked to an excited scrum of reporters and cameramen.

After I finished my tennis match, I felt really funny – like a celebrity, kind of – because after you finish a tennis match, you feel good with yourself. I was glad with the way I played, anyway. Then someone came up to me with a microphone, and then the guard made me speak to them even though I didn't really want to.

– Scott, death row inmate

The struggle to have some semblance of a normal life was constant. Juri was looking down a long dark tunnel of life behind bars when he proposed to his Timorese girlfriend, Ade. They had been together for years before Juri's arrest, and were still in love and going strong. So, Ade agreed to have her wedding in Hotel K.

Like most weddings, it took a lot of organising, although choosing the venue was easy. Their wedding planner was Alit Balong, one of the Laskar bosses, who walked around Hotel K in traditional Balinese dress and carrying a machete. If the westerners wanted something done, they could pay Alit a fee and he could usually do it. He had keys to the blocks, sold crates of beer and Coca-Cola from his cell, and could organise for male inmates to have visits with female inmates. Juri's family bought all the wedding food and drink from him.

Just pay him and he can do whatever he wants.

– Juri

Juri and Ade had invited more than one hundred guests, including western inmates and family. Most of the Kerobokan crew came, including several of the Bali Nine, Schapelle, and French Michael and his mum, Helene. The Laskars took charge of security to keep uninvited guests out of the cordoned-off garden area.

Ade's dress and Juri's suit were both designed and cut in Italy, and made from Italian raw silk. Juri's two older sisters and both his parents were excited that the only boy in the family was getting married. Juri's parents spent a fortune trying to give their son and his bride the perfect wedding, despite its grim location. They would have done anything to give their son some happiness.

That marriage was the funniest thing I've ever seen. The best man was Steve. I think he and Juri smoked about a gram of smack before they went to the altar … and they were falling over. And, besides this smack, Steve liked to squash Xanax pills and mix with the smack, and sniff together.
– Ruggiero

As the vows were read at the altar of the prison's Christian church, with Ade in her white meringue-style silk dress and Juri in a silk suit and tie, best man Steve lolled around like a rag doll, only standing because Ruggiero was gripping the waist of his trousers.

I held him so he could stand up. But I let go and he fell. Juri was destroyed. They were full on smack. And best man Steve was sweating. But we were all having a great time. It was real comic theatre. Robert was drunk, pissed.

And then comes the priest, and everybody was sweating and the father of one of the Aussie kids taking photos. And then, okay, now the ring, but Steve couldn't find it. I say, 'Find the ring, man'. 'I'm sure I had it here,' he says. Eventually, he finds it.

Then there was a new guy who had just arrived there, Simon – a Dutch guy. He had a very nice girlfriend. He had just arrived in jail and was a very horny bastard. While the wedding was going on, they busted him shagging another inmate in the toilet.

I said, 'Man, I have to give you a medal because it took me one year before I could lay my hands on a lady here. You've been here one week, already shagging at the wedding inside the fucking toilet'.

How did they catch him?

One of the guards wanted to take a leak. Knocking on the door, saying, 'Come on,' and then he heard some noise. He didn't see the guards coming. But then everything was arranged; he gave the guard 150,000 rupiah.
– Ruggiero

CHAPTER 20

ROOM 13

It's like a dog kennel. I have never experienced anything like it. I wouldn't wish it on my worst enemy.

– Chris, inmate

It's like we are always dancing on razor blades.

– Mick

The human spirit somehow adapts to the most extreme situations and people can endure hardships that once would have seemed inconceivable. Being locked up in a small cell for fourteen hours a day – day after day, week after week, month after month – with people you don't much like or trust, is a nightmare that none of the westerners in Hotel K could ever have been prepared for.

After Gabriel's botched escape attempt, the westerners were all put in cells together to increase the security. Scotsman Robert, Austrian Thomas and Australians Chris and Mick were moved into Room 13 in Block B – a drunk, a junkie, an ice freak and an angry madman.

In Room 13, the four westerners fought tirelessly – they stole from, drugged, bashed and abused each other. Every night, the cell erupted with battles, but the arguments died down just as quickly as they had started. The inmates could share a joint amicably, despite having been screaming abuse or throwing punches thirty minutes earlier. They didn't hate each other. They were just four men who were squeezed together in a tiny concrete cell for fourteen hours a day.

The cell, including the toilet area, was about four metres by three metres, and the men had to be creative to fit into it. They slept on three levels – Chris on the top bunk; Mick in the prize position, on the bottom bunk next to a small barred window; and Robert on the floor. He'd drawn the short straw. Most of his mattress was directly underneath the bottom bunk, with the end poking out at the foot of Mick's bed to give Robert a bit of headroom. Thomas also slept on the floor, at a right angle to the others, with the edges of his and Robert's pillows touching. During the day, Thomas's mattress was pushed up on its side against the wall, to clear the doorway.

When Mick, clutching an armful of his belongings, first arrived at his new cell on the afternoon of Gabriel's escape, he looked around and felt sickened by the filthy concrete box.

It was a pig house. Very dirty; the bathroom was so black, you think you're still in darkness, with thirty years of shit dried on the floor. Local guys had lived there before and they never clean. They live like that. It was maybe not cleaned for thirty years. It stank worse than shit.

– Mick

Mick still couldn't comprehend how his life had spiralled into such a dark hole, so far from his former life in Sydney. He'd driven a Mercedes, lived on the beach in Maroubra and regularly dined at Sydney's top restaurants. He had worked hard creating a lucrative smash repairs business, sold it because of his bad lungs, and invested his cash in uncut Australian opals. He was selling them in Japan and Singapore, staying in five-star hotels in Asia and building a holiday house in Bali when he was arrested for possession of drugs.

He spent hours down on his hands and knees in Room 13, scrubbing the slimy floor and scraping the black gunk and dried shit off the toilet, using the only cleaning product he had access to – laundry detergent. After a couple of days, he gave cash to Juri's father to buy him bleach and disinfectant, and eventually the grime vanished and the foul stink faded. Mick also organised for the dirty-grey whitewashed walls to be freshly painted, white tiles to be laid on the bathroom floor and a new toilet to be installed. Killer Saidin did the ceramics jobs around Hotel K, but was so busy that he deputised his boys to do the job, charging Mick about $100. Mick also had a slim wooden cabinet custom-built in Iwan's workshop that would hold food, books, a TV and DVD player. By cleaning up the filth in Room 13, he was trying to salvage a little dignity and avoid sickness.

Westerners usually put some effort into sprucing up their grim cells, which suited the guards – it gave them another business, of selling the best cells. Often, as soon as a renovation was finished, the guards threatened to move the westerner unless they paid to stay. Guards also charged new prisoners extra cash to be put into a renovated cell. It was fast, easy money, as westerners almost always found hundreds of dollars to avoid the grime-covered, shit-splattered cells.

They use us … they put us in shit room and every time they move us, we fix, we paint, we decorate, and then they move us again and they sell this room to someone else. Each time they move us, we lose everything. Each one of us has made about three rooms. Since I got arrested, I've decorated eight rooms, maybe. I make wooden shelves, paint it, clean the sink, put tiles on the floor, paint, decorate, put in a table for the computer, put in a nice bed, nice mattress.

Did they do that with all the foreigners?

Yeah, yeah. Frederico was even worse. Frederico is more crazy … behind the block, he started making a little swimming pool – a little jacuzzi. He put tiles down and when it was ready, the guards say, 'Sorry, you're not allowed to go out the back anymore'. They just waited for him to finish the project and kicked him out. That's what they do. They see us as their ATM machines.

– Ruggiero

Even after Mick had renovated Room 13, life inside it was a living nightmare. The four men were locked in at 5.30 pm, and spent the next fourteen hours cooped up together in the oppressively hot and claustrophobic cell. But no matter how intolerable it got, how much they frayed each other's nerves, there was no escape.

On a usual night, Thomas went straight to the bathroom, to shoot up privately. He'd once given a seedy little show – finding a vein, sticking in the needle, and pumping it in and out to boost the hit – but Mick had warned him against ever doing it in front of him again. 'If I see a needle, I'll put it right up your arse,' he yelled. 'Don't do that shit in here again.' So, Thomas used the bathroom, aware that Mick would carry out his threat. After shooting up, he'd drift out and collapse onto his mattress, fumbling around for a cigarette. He'd light it and leave it dangling precariously between his lips, sitting blissed-out with his eyes shut, ash falling onto his lap, until the cigarette burned down to a butt. Several times Mick or Chris leaped out of bed to grab a cigarette that was smouldering on the mattress after having dropped from Thomas's lips. His mattress was covered in small black holes.

Chris usually came in drunk and stoned from an afternoon session of drinking *arak* and smoking *shabu*. He was a skinny ice addict, who'd been caught at a cargo office in Denpasar trying to send 42,000 ephedrine tablets packed in water bottles and stashed in a flower pot with concrete mix on top, and one kilogram of ephedrine powder to Australia. He'd admitted to police that they were the raw materials for making ice and ecstasy, and that their intended destination was Australia.

Mick also turned up drunk and stoned from many of the afternoon party sessions. He would make a coffee and then sit on his bed, rolling a joint and passing it around, or smoking some smack, sharing it with Robert and Chris. He would then draw, or read one of his books on metaphysics, pulling down a dark blue sarong he'd tacked to the upper bunk for some sense of privacy. Unfortunately, it wasn't soundproof.

Robert was, of course, a loud, drunk, bombastic nightmare, often arriving covered in blood from a bashing and with his trousers dripping with piss. Most afternoons, the Scotsman was picked up from a concrete bench, or off the grass, and carried to his cell by three or four *tampings*, waking in fits and screaming, 'Fucking idiot, fucking idiot, put me down!' before passing out again. In the cell, he and Chris fought like cat and dog, shouting abuse across the room, both completely out of their heads. Mick would angrily kick the bottom of Chris's bunk and tell them both to shut up.

Throughout the night, Robert would have outbursts of yelling 'Fucking idiots!' and ranting in his foghorn Scottish-accented voice about sailing the China Seas. Mick would start off by saying, 'Robert,' in a schoolmasterly tone, shutting him up for a minute or two, and then Robert would start again. It would soon escalate into Mick screaming, 'Shut up, you stupid fucking Scottish bastard!' or leaping to the end of the bed and throwing a few punches. But nothing worked. Until sunrise, Robert intermittently broke everyone's sleep – every night.

Some nights, Mick set up his easel and canvas near the door. He'd sit with his brush in one hand and a beer in the other, a cigarette in his mouth, quietly painting until 4 or 5 am, often using his sleeping cellmates as models. He used the nights to regain a bit of sanity, despite the cacophony of croaking toads, high-pitched screams of feral cats and Robert's disruptive outbursts.

One of Arman's boys would walk around each night, selling a smorgasbord of drugs from a tray for a set price. 'What do you want?' he'd call out, taking orders. Prisoners would yell for pills, smack, ice, dope, whatever they felt like. The boy would fill the orders, piling the drugs onto his cardboard tray, and go around like a waiter, passing the drugs through the doors. He accepted credit if anyone was out of cash, writing it down officially in a note book that he carried. All night, people would call out for more drugs – it was a twenty-four-hour service. If the boy ran out of anything, he'd call Arman, who'd send somebody with supplies.

Sometimes I was sitting painting and needed a smoke to give me inspiration. I'd pay 100,000 rupiah [$13] for some dope rolled in newspaper. If Chris was awake, I'd give some to him.

– Mick

On sex nights, there was frenetic activity outside Mick's window until daybreak, as inmates dashed past, buying mosquito coils and cigarettes through the window of Room 12. The cell was used by local prisoner Wayan to run a twenty-four-hour convenience store, selling such things as energy drinks, chocolate, biscuits, cigarettes and noodles. Wayan had bought the business from another prisoner for ten million rupiah ($1300) to run during his four-year stint in Hotel K for murder. The killer was a former professor of business development at Bali University.

He caught a guy screwing his wife in a car out the front of his house. He stabbed him to death. He was a little bit of a mongrel, actually.

– Mick

Only two prisoners were authorised to run little shops from their cells, catering to all blocks; they had paid to have this exclusively, and the guards enforced it for a fee. Dutch inmate Aris shared Room 9 in Block A with a local prisoner who was covertly selling cigarettes and drinks. The guards were tipped off, but raided Room 6 by mistake. Aris's cellmate shut down his illicit business anyway, as the guards would be back, and it wasn't worth losing his cartons of cigarettes to them and being punished.

Every day at around 7.30 am, Room 13 was unlocked, and Chris, Mick and Robert ambled out. In his previous cells, Mick had usually woken early and angry, desperate to get out, standing at the padlocked door, and wildly shaking and kicking it, screaming, 'Let me out of this fucking place, you fucking monkeys!' The guards always scurried to open his cell first, to stop the tirade.

I would be out of my head. I had to get out of there. I was furious, I just wanted to get out and kill a couple of people. I was like a tiger in a cage. Mad. If I did a bit of a run in the yard, the guards would watch me. They always watched me. If I had a knife, they'd watch me. Others had knives, no problem. But I was madman.

– Mick

By the time he was living in Room 13, Mick had adapted a bit, and his late-night art sessions meant he often slept until mid-morning. But just knowing that the door was open and that he was able to step outside the tiny cell was a relief.

In his sober morning state, Robert was useful and likeable. He enjoyed using his hands, and spent time doing things like building wooden boats in Iwan's workshop, making a lamp-shade from a Vietnamese farming hat that he hung on the wall above his mattress, and fixing an old Nokia phone to run on an ill-fitting Ericsson battery that he taped to it.

He also, of course, worked as Hotel K's electrician, wiring up cells with power. He spent days working in Room 13 to give it round-the-clock electricity, increasing the allotted twelve hours of power. Using a single power point on the wall, he spun a web of wires throughout the cell to give all four of them power points to run a reading light and a fan by their beds. His wiring job was effective but crude. Cables for the four lights and fans turned the cell into a tangled electrical minefield, with unearthed wires hanging off the walls and crossing the floor. Every day, someone would walk into Room 13 and get a shock. Given the low voltage, it was more a nip than a bite, but enough to cause a jig. Mick thought it was hilarious.

One afternoon, a new prisoner arrived and asked the guards, 'Which room can I have some fun in?' They told him Room 13. Exhausted from being at the police station, holding his little bag and a pillow, he looked around Room 13, saying, 'Hello, hello'. He took a step inside and put his foot on a wire, jumping like a spring, and still clutching his bag and pillow. 'Be careful of the wire,' Mick warned, laughing. The new inmate put his bag down on the floor and went to take a shower, being careful where he trod. But coming back, he forgot about the wires, and stepped onto one with his bare foot. He jumped, cursed, and walked straight to the window, shouting, 'Please, please, take me out, take me out!' The four cellmates smirked. 'Don't worry, you'll get used to it,' Chris told him. But the man, who was a big German body builder named Wolf, paid 200,000 rupiah to move out the next morning.

It had actually been a bungled wiring job that had set Robert on his path to Hotel K. He'd been friends with Englishman Steven – the inmate whose back was burned by Filo – in Hong Kong and had offered to rewire his apartment so that Steven could use his neighbours' electricity. This would save him a fortune, as he used copious amounts of electricity to grow a hydroponic marijuana crop in his lounge room.

Not long after Robert's shifty rewiring work, the apartment building's caretaker and a police officer arrived at Steven's door. The caretaker knew something fishy was going on when she saw the electricity bills and that only Steven's account was being charged. And his bill was astronomical. The police officer found Steven's crop and he was charged – thanks to Robert having tweaked the wires back to front while he was drunk.

Steven and Robert flew to Bali for the next instalment of their farcical adventure. To pay the fine that the Hong Kong court would inevitably impose for the marijuana crop, they planned to make some fast bucks by selling two kilograms of hashish. They sat in a McDonald's in Kuta, eating Big Macs, and waiting for their first buyer to show up. When he did, he passed the cash and Steven slipped him the hashish. In the next instant, they were gone; the buyer was an undercover cop. Police sprang from every direction and snapped handcuffs on the stunned duo. The police had covertly surrounded the store. Steve and Robert admitted to the police that they brought the hashish from Hong Kong, where it was only $3.50 a gram, to sell in Bali.

Two British nationals who lived in Hong Kong were arrested trying to sell 457 grams of hashish to an undercover policeman … The friendly looking Robert said this was his first visit to Bali. 'I met Steven in Hong Kong as I work there as an engineer. He invited me to come to Bali, but it ended up like this,' said Robert sadly.

– *Denpost*, March 2002

One afternoon, Robert, Chris and Thomas were already inside Room 13 waiting to be locked up for the night when Mick arrived and noticed the floor was soaking wet. 'What's this?' he asked. 'Fucking Robert, he piss on the floor,' Thomas replied. Mick instantly flew into a psychotic rage. He punched Robert on the cheek. Robert slurred, 'Fucking idiot!' and threw a punch back. He missed. His flailing fist went into thin air as Mick ducked. Mick didn't miss a beat. He turned and hit him hard in the ribs. It knocked the breath out of Robert, who fell to the floor. Mick gave him a deadly look, saying, 'You make one more noise out of your mouth and I will fucking kill you, Robert'.

A guard locking the rooms couldn't have failed to hear the fight, but simply snapped the padlock on the door shut and walked away. Robert sat quietly on the floor. Mick was trembling with anger. Thomas moved to start cleaning up but stopped abruptly when Mick yelled ferociously 'Clean up your own fucking piss, you stupid Scottish bastard!' On his knees, Robert grabbed a T-shirt and provocatively started spreading the piss across the tiles. Mick exploded. He leaped off his bed and attacked Robert, punching him in the face, the ribs and the stomach. Robert hadn't given up. He tried to block Mick's fists, yelling, 'Fucking idiot!' and provoking Mick even more. 'Shut up, you fucking bastard!' Mick yelled back. 'Fucking idiot, you're supposed to be a spiritual person. But you're a spiritual person in my arse, Mick!' Robert shouted back. Mick grabbed a piece of wood and screamed, 'I'm going to kill you!'

Thomas, who had just dashed into the bathroom to shoot up, ran back out, holding his syringe and smack in his hands, and pleading, 'Please stop, Mick'. He was desperate not to bring the guards back. Mick ignored him and slammed the piece of wood into Robert's stomach. Chris jumped from the top bunk, grabbing hold of the wood before Mick killed Robert, telling him to stop. Mick was still raging, but let go. He walked across and sat on his bunk, angrily snatching down the dark blue sarong. Robert spent the rest of the night as quiet as a mouse, and the next morning apologised to Mick for pissing in the cell. His cheek and neck were visibly bruised.

I was a crazy man. I couldn't handle it anymore. I see this guy, Thomas, shooting himself with smack, his eyes going crazy, and he falls down on his mattress. I don't know if he's alive or dead. And this shit Robert getting drunk every night, pissing on the floor – a 40-year-old man. And Chris was always drunk and smoking ice, loudly arguing bullshit crap with Robert all the time. We were living in a dirty rat hole, and on top of this dirtiness, to be with this Scottish guy and next to you this stupid guy putting a needle in his arm – I felt disgusted and dirty.

– Mick

In addition to its colourful occupants, Room 13, like all the cells, regularly had things crawling around it. The inmates could wake up some nights with a trail of big red ants crawling across their pillows, or with several rats scurrying across the floor or over Thomas's and Robert's mattresses. They came through the door or the bathroom drain. Mick started leaving out chicken scraps sprinkled with chilli to try to eradicate them, a trick many prisoners used. Many times, Mick watched a rat snatch a bit of chicken, run a bit, and then drop the morsel on the floor as its mouth started to burn. Mick was often woken by one of the many mangy, furless and sick feral cats that ran in through the barred door, across the cell, up onto his stomach and out of the window.

During the day, Mick, Robert and Chris spent little time in their cell; going inside only intermittently to grab a beer, a book or a quick lie-down. Mick was furious when he walked in one day and found American Gabriel lying topless and sweaty on his clean sheets, watching TV. Mick tried to keep the cell clean and fresh, and yelled at Gabriel to get off his bed. Some days, a few of the guys would sit around on the floor chasing the dragon, blowing smack into a junkie cat's face whenever it slunk inside. The pet *musang* would also sometimes come in, and cheekily snatch a banana from the small table and scamper out. They'd all sit around watching, entertained by small things.

By the time Thomas was in Room 13, Arman was the drug lord and the Austrian was no longer allowed to sell. But Thomas was still getting deliveries from one of his Bali contacts, who needed to move smack being flown in from Nepal. He used Thomas to sell it for him. Just before lockup one afternoon, he got a delivery of half a kilogram.

Pak Giri stood outside the door, pulling the smack from his

shoes and his pockets. Robert was watching and slurred to Mick, 'Shit, it's a huge bag'. Mick wasn't impressed. 'Thomas, don't you bring that shit in here!' he yelled from his bottom bunk. 'You get caught and we're all fucked up.' But Thomas walked inside, clinging to the bags of smack and mumbling, 'Don't worry, I'll sell it fast,' and quickly stashed it under his pillow. During the night, he laboriously filled hundreds of straws with it, as he talked to Mick, who was sitting up painting, about his life in Austria.

While drunkenly rambling around Hotel K the next afternoon, Robert told Englishman Steve Turner – Juri's best man – about the delivery. As usual, Steve was out of it on Xanax, but somehow he had an inspiration; they could steal the heroin. He knew that Thomas protected his smack like a mother protects her newborn, but Steve was thinking creatively. They could spike his coffee with crushed Xanax pills so he'd sleep like a dead man, and then Robert could pinch it from underneath his head.

That afternoon, Robert staggered back into his cell just before 5.30 lockup, carrying a cup loaded with a lethal mix of Nescafé, sugar and twenty-four crushed Xanax pills – enough to knock out an elephant, let alone a skinny heroin addict like Thomas. Robert switched on the kettle, which would take thirty minutes to boil at lockup time as everyone was using power, and waited. The other three were busy: Thomas was shooting up in the bathroom, Chris was smoking ice on the top bunk, and Mick was reading on the bottom bunk. None of them took any notice of Robert hovering interminably over the kettle, until he started moving erratically in and out of the light, casting shadows.

'Get out of the light,' Mick yelled as the shadows flew across the pages of his book. 'It's not a fucking bus stop.' Robert was jigging from one foot to the other, desperate to use the bathroom but not wanting to leave the spiked cup or piss on the floor again. 'It will boil in a minute,' he mumbled, before feverishly muttering his mantra, 'Fucking idiot, Mick, fucking idiot, Mick'. Mick pulled down his blue sarong and pretended not to hear him.

Minutes later, Robert asked, 'Thomas, you want a coffee?' Thomas, who was sitting cross-legged on his mattress with his eyes closed and a cigarette dangling from his lips, replied, 'Sure, thanks'. Robert gave him the cup, and then ran to the bathroom. Thomas took one mouthful and spat it across his mattress. 'Fuck, did he piss in that?' he asked, putting the cup on the floor near their pillows.

Robert came out of the bathroom five minutes later, so drunk and stoned that he'd forgotten all about his plan. He climbed onto his mattress, and sat against the wall with his legs stretched out under Mick's bunk. Mick passed him a joint. Robert took a couple of puffs and handed it back, then lit a cigarette. He spotted the cup of coffee on the floor and reached out for it. Thirsty from all the smoke and booze, he gulped down half the cup. Within sixty seconds, he was out.

When Mick looked up from his book, he instantly grabbed his sketchpad. It was a sight too good to waste. Robert was asleep, sitting slumped against the wall with a burning cigarette hanging loosely from his lips, and his glasses skewed awkwardly across his nose. Mick sat on his bottom bunk sketching Robert for forty-five minutes. He was the perfect model; still as a statue, unflinching even when hot ash fell onto his neck. When Mick was finished, he plucked the dead cigarette butt from his model's mouth, switched off the light and went to sleep.

When Room 13 was unlocked at 7.30 am, Robert hadn't moved a muscle. He was still sleeping against the wall with his glasses on the end of his nose. But no-one took any notice, except for English Steve, who was initially shocked to see Thomas up and about. Steve walked past Room 13 a number of times throughout the day, calling out, 'Robert, Robert!' He finally asked Mick, 'Why's Robert still asleep?' Mick answered casually, 'He's probably still drunk,' a bit surprised that anyone was interested in Robert's sleeping habits.

Robert didn't wake up that day, or the next. He slept for two days and nights, only coming to forty-eight hours later, confused and angry.

He was like a bear coming out of hibernation. He was hungry and thirsty, looking for food, stumbling around, gasping for water, saying, 'I feel dizzy, I can't see properly. I need water'.

– Mick

Robert later confessed his devious Xanax plot to Mick. 'You fucking idiot, Robert,' Mick rebuked him, 'you could have killed him. Why did you use twenty-four tablets?' Whimpering like a child, Robert said he'd only wanted to use two pills but that Steve had convinced him to use twenty-four, to knock Thomas out in the first one or two mouthfuls. When it dawned on Robert that the plan had worked perfectly on him, he was furious with Steve, walking around for days like a madman mumbling, 'Fucking idiot, Steve, fucking idiot'.

Robert – sometimes he was too much, I tell you. If he's not drunk, no problem, but if he's drunk, he's such a fucking asshole.

– Thomas

For Thomas, guarding his smack was a full-time job. He even had to take it with him when he used the bathroom. A couple of times a week, Robert would sneak two or three straws to smoke with Mick and Chris. Mick would watch from his bunk Robert's sleight of hand, as Thomas sat on his mattress, filling his straws, counting them, taking one out for himself; always busy with his stash. When Thomas turned away for a split second, quick as a flash Robert's hand would dart across, snatch a straw or two and shove it under his own mattress. By the time Thomas turned back around, Robert would be slumped against the wall, pretending to sleep. Thomas often thought he'd miscounted his straws.

One morning, Thomas almost lost the half kilogram stash that he had tucked under his pillow. It was almost 9 am, but the four cellmates were still sleeping after drinking and taking drugs until late the previous night. Mick was woken by a prisoner shaking him vigorously, saying: 'Mick, Mick, wake up'. 'Oh, shit.' The cell floor was under a few centimetres of water. Mick yelled out to Thomas, whose mattress was soaked. The instant Thomas's eyes opened, he grabbed his stash from under his pillow and leaped up, stepping straight onto a wet electrical cable. He got a shock and did a frenzied jig in the middle of the cell as he clung to his smack. A moment later, he turned and yelled abuse at Robert for his stupid cables. Robert threw back, 'I'm not your baby-sitter. Watch where you walk'. It turned out that someone had left the bathroom hose running during the night.

The events of that morning prompted Thomas to start stashing his drugs in a hole in the ceiling, which Chris had made one night during a drunken escape bid. Thomas employed Robert to stand on his shoulders and put his plastic bag of drugs through the hole, into the dark, dirty roof, pushing it out of sight, and tethering it by a piece of string to a nail he'd hammered on the ceiling. Whenever Thomas wanted it put up or taken down, he got Robert to climb on his shoulders. Robert would jump down, saying, 'Okay, give me my wages,' and Thomas would give him two or three smack straws. It was a good arrangement until Robert tried another prank. One afternoon, he was standing precariously on Thomas's shoulders, blindly flapping his hands around inside the ceiling, trying to locate the string attached to the bag.

He says, 'Oh, it's gone, it's gone. Somebody took it, maybe.' He was looking everywhere and saying, 'Oh, it's not here, I cannot find it. It's gone'. He kept checking it and couldn't find it. I thought, fuck, it's better that I go up and check upstairs.

– Thomas

Thomas walked out and found a *tamping* prisoner with a key to unlock the small gate in front of a ladder to the roof. They both climbed up into the ceiling and found the bag of drugs about one metre from the hole in Room 13.

I suspect it was Robert but I cannot say one hundred per cent, but it cannot automatically fly over there. He put it there, maybe, because in one week I was going free and he can take it.

– Thomas

Chris and Mick knew that Robert had tried to steal the smack. Chris had heard a clunk above his head while he was standing near the bathroom. As soon as Robert told Thomas that the stash was missing, Chris realised what the clunk had been. Thomas had been too busy concentrating on keeping Robert balanced on his thin shoulders to notice. Mick had heard a faint noise, but didn't pay any attention. Chris told Mick about it later, and Mick told him to shut up.

But Robert was the least of Thomas's problems. The Laskars had started coming into the cell, asking for cash. Arman had found out about Thomas's recent deliveries and was not pleased. He wanted Thomas to pay him the sales profit. Several times Thomas had obeyed the rules and given his new supply to Arman. But he'd become sick of giving his cheap, quality smack to Arman and making no profit, and was acutely aware that he'd need cash when he checked out shortly. But now Arman wanted the money he considered due to him.

They came in my cell and asked, 'When do you give us money?' They asked and asked and asked. I said, 'I don't know, later on, later on, later on'. Every day they came and gave me headache. They beat me two or three times and say, 'Okay, tomorrow we come back again'. Ah, make me a headache.

– Thomas

One morning, the talking was finished. Laskar heavies turned up in Room 13, telling Thomas that Arman wanted to speak to him over in his cell. Thomas knew this was bad news, but had nowhere to run. The Laskars walked outside, and waited for him out the front of the block. Thomas grabbed his plastic bag of smack, ran into Michael's cell, where Mick was sitting and talking, and said, 'Please hold this, Mick'. Of course, once Thomas left, Mick and the other cellmates opened the bag, saw the smack and started chasing the dragon.

You cannot work against Laskar. If you work against Laskar, it's a problem. Guards were afraid, everybody is afraid.

– Thomas

Thomas walked into Arman's cell and four bulky Laskars started knocking the skinny Austrian around as Arman stood against the wall, watching. They were throwing punches and demanding money. Thomas was still defiant, 'I don't have, don't have,' he kept saying. He took blow after blow, in the face, in the neck and in the stomach. He didn't try fighting back, as he didn't stand a chance. He was surrounded; they were huge. They took turns smashing into him. Somehow he was enduring it until a fist struck his face especially hard. He felt his nose crack. Another fist hit it again fast. He fell down screaming, but they didn't stop. It only got more frenzied as they smelled blood. Thomas was now crouching, trying to shield his broken face with his arms, with blood pouring from his nose. Fists and feet were coming at him furiously. 'I want my money,' Arman yelled angrily. It was enough. He was surrounded by thugs, it was not going to stop. 'Okay, okay!' he cried in defeat.

You cannot fight back. How you fight against three or four people … and more coming? [You're] fucked up if you fight back, you're fucked up.

– Thomas

Thomas agreed to give Arman the rest of his stash as payment. Arman knew that Thomas was leaving in a week and agreed to accept the stash, as it was better than nothing. Arman sent a boy to go with Thomas to collect four grams of smack. Thomas left Arman's Block E and walked into the sunshine, sore, dazed and bloody. He felt the tip of his nose with his fingers. It was squashed flat and he gently pulled it out, trying to straighten it. He could feel his eyes starting to swell.

Thomas took the Laskar boy to Michael's cell in Block B, where several inmates were now high on some of his smack. He grabbed his plastic bag off the table and gave it to the boy, and then went across to his cell. He was a shattered mess. One of the prisoners came into Room 13 and told him to put honey on his eyes to stop the swelling. He smeared it on his eyes and the rest of his face. When Mick came back into their cell, he wasn't the slightest bit sympathetic.

He knew what he was dealing with. He had the money, he had the drugs but didn't want to pay.

– Mick

The next day, Thomas's eyes were blue and his face was swollen. But he would be involved in a further drug drama before walking free. He got a call from an old friend asking if he could buy fifteen grams of smack. Thomas told him to come to a visit in the blue room later that day. He would ask Mick to go and pass over the smack, paying him with a bit for himself. Mick had done it before, taking drugs out in his sandals, and passing them to Thomas's client. But this time, the client didn't want to enter Hotel K. It was guard Pak Giri's day off, so Thomas asked his *tamping* friend, who was a user and dealer, if he knew anyone who could go outside that day and make the delivery. He did.

Thomas gave the fifteen grams to the *tamping*, and the *tamping* passed it to the courier prisoner, who walked out of Hotel K and straight into a trap. Thomas's customer was already in police custody. He'd done a deal with police to set up two or three people for them, so that he could walk free after being caught with drugs himself. The moment the Hotel K courier handed him the smack, he was gone. At the police station, the courier inmate told them he was only the delivery boy for the *tamping*. The *tamping* wasn't immediately taken to the police, but was thrown in cell *tikus*. Thomas had only a few days left in Hotel K, and was desperate to stay out of it. He asked the *tamping* not to mention his name, offering to give him drugs when he was free, and paid him 500,000 rupiah ($70).

Thomas walked free before anyone breathed his name to the police.

CHAPTER 21

NO MORE TOMORROWS

Scott Rush is a 23-year-old death row inmate at Hotel K.

I got a letter the other day, it was just a little Post-it note, and this girl said to me, 'I would rather get killed than be in jail in this place'. Well, sometimes that makes sense to me. Sometimes I think I would rather get shot than have to spend my life in here. Because if I do get life, it's long life, life without remissions, which is here until you're dead. And sometimes I think I would rather get the death penalty than that. That's what makes it easier for me to cope with the death penalty hanging over my head. It's just something to prepare myself for, I guess, mentally. I don't want to go fully crazy before I get executed. I wouldn't want to go out like that.

Do you ever talk to the other three on death row about execution?

No, I don't talk to them about their case whatsoever.

Why?

I think it stresses them out.

– Scott, death row inmate

Being sentenced to many years in Hotel K, with only a faint light glinting at the end of a long, dark tunnel, is grim. But for those inmates living under the shadow of death, spending their empty days in Hotel K, trying to keep going and have some kind of life before they get a bullet through the heart, is soul-destroying.

Scott was sharing a cell in the so-called 'death tower' with another death row inmate, Nigerian man Emmanuel – the same cell that smiling assassin Amrozi was in before he was transferred to Nusakambangan Island and shot dead. Now the same fate loomed for Scott and Emmanuel, and two others in the Bali Nine, Andrew Chan and Myuran Sukumaran, although all were still appealing their sentences. The four rooms in the death tower were filled with all eight men from the Bali Nine syndicate. One day blurred into the next. But somehow, they still got on with life in Hotel K.

I've just got to keep myself prepared for what happens later. I don't believe I should destroy myself, even though everyone mentally destroys themselves every once in a while. I like sport. I prefer to keep myself busy with things with my physical body, it keeps me mentally sane.

– Scott

Sometimes there was only crushing darkness for Scott; periods when he rarely left his cell, preferring to blow up hippos with aliens on his PlayStation. But other times he tried to live in the moment and make the most of the day. During these times, he would often play tennis all day, stopping only when the sun got too hot around midday. He would take a break in his cell, watch DVDs or cable TV and read self-help books.

For most of the Australians, the day was often broken up by a visit in the blue room. Scott's devoted parents came to Bali whenever they could, friends visited regularly and a Balinese friend came once a month to deliver him cash sent from his family.

Scott had checked into Hotel K when he was a teenager. He was nineteen, the second-youngest of the Bali Nine. Life as he knew it finished the Sunday night that he took a taxi to Bali's Ngurah Rai Airport, trying to look like any other tourist set to board a flight to Australia. Under a bright floral shirt and baggy pants, he had just over one kilogram of heroin taped to his legs. Three other Australians, posing as tourists on their way home in almost identical outfits, were also carrying heroin. But they didn't make it to the plane. They were all busted after checking in.

A fifth person, Andrew, then twenty years old, was already sitting comfortably on the plane when police grabbed him. He didn't have any drugs on him but was one of two ringleaders.

Another four, all in their teens and early twenties, were arrested in a hotel room in Kuta. Police found three hundred and fifty grams of heroin in a suitcase, as well as scales, tape, backpacks and mobile phones. None of them had stood a chance. The Australian Federal Police (AFP) had waited for them to leave Australia, then tipped off the Indonesian police, passing on their names, passport details, mobile phone numbers and even black-and-white photos of them, knowingly exposing them to death by firing squad.

An AFP officer had quietly watched 19-year-old Scott check in at Sydney Airport and fly out, despite knowing a crime was going to take place, and despite Scott's father, Lee, having asked the police to help stop his troubled son from leaving the country.

Lee had received a phone call from Flight Centre the day before Scott flew out, asking him to ensure his son called their office as he hadn't yet picked up his ticket from Sydney to Bali. An alarm bell sounded; Lee knew that Scott didn't have any cash and that he was using drugs. He flew into a panic and called a friend, Bob, who was a barrister. 'Look, they're going to use him as a mule,' Bob told Lee, who hadn't yet even heard of the term 'drug mule'.

Lee desperately wanted his son to be prevented from leaving Australia. Bob rang an AFP contact, asking if Scott could be intercepted at Sydney Airport and stopped from boarding the plane. Lee was assured it would happen. That phone call took place at 1.30 am. At 10 am, Lee got a distressed call from Bob, saying, 'Mate, sorry, he couldn't be stopped, he's on his way'. An AFP officer had watched Scott checking in and boarding the flight, but decided not to approach him. Instead, on that same day, after the Nine had left, AFP agent in Bali, Paul Hunniford, passed a letter to the Indonesian police, alerting them to the Bali Nine's trafficking plan.

They had waited until they had all left Australia. The letter gave specific details of a crime not yet committed: who the players were, where they would stay, when they would try to leave, even how they would strap the drugs to their bodies. The AFP had had the group under surveillance in Australia for weeks. Scott had seen a suspicious man watching him buy his ticket at Flight Centre in Sydney – he is now convinced it was an AFP officer. They knew they weren't trafficking drugs into Bali, but were planning to bring them into Australia.

They will be carrying body packs (with white powder) back to Australia with packs on both legs and also with back supports. They have already been given the back supports. The packs will be strapped to their bodies. They will be given money to exchange for local currency to purchase oversized loose shirts and sandals.

– AFP Letter

Scott Rush now says the AFP knew far more than he did at that stage about the trafficking plan.

The letter also named the alleged leader as 20-year-old Andrew, and told them: 'If you suspect Chan and/or the couriers are carrying drugs at the time of their departure, please take whatever action you deem necessary.'

It also instructed the Indonesian police to arrest those at the Melasti Hotel as soon as the airport bust was done. Despite the AFP, when later defending its actions, claiming it wanted to expose the network, find the source and the 'Mr Bigs', the Indonesian police somehow missed the point of sale when the eight kilograms of heroin, worth four million dollars, was handed to the Australians.

The AFP did throw us to the wolves and there's a lot of pressure on them for it, and I don't think they can make up [for] their mistakes. I suppose there's nothing they can do to rewind the past.

– Scott

In a Bali courtroom, all nine Australians were convicted. Initially, seven of them got life, and the two ringleaders, Andrew and Myuran, got the death penalty. They all appealed, and their sentences then varied erratically between life, death and twenty years. The three at the Melasti Hotel had their sentences reduced to twenty years, but when the prosecutors appealed this leniency, they were increased to death. After a final appeal, they were reduced back to life. Andrew and Myuran remained on the death penalty. Scott was the only courier suddenly and inexplicably to be handed a death sentence after appealing. Although the other three couriers carried more drugs, Scott got death, while Renae Lawrence got twenty years and the other two got life.

Don't ask me why. Just sort of happened like that. It's crazy. They haven't even given me reasons why. We all had over five hundred grams, and the law is, if you go over five hundred grams you're eligible for the death penalty. But they kind of just gave it to me.

– Scott

Scott's Nigerian cellmate, Emmanuel, had a similar court experience. He was the first person ever to get the death sentence for drugs in Bali, despite having carried only four hundred grams. Initially, Emmanuel was given a life sentence, but it was upped to death when he appealed.

Emmanuel went nuts. He felt like a victim of everything that was wrong with the justice system and Hotel K. He knew that while he had carried a smaller amount than everyone around him who'd been caught at the airport, they had had cash to buy a lighter sentence. Now he was facing death for drugs, while his captors were blatantly using and selling drugs in front of him.

The hypocrisy of the system turned him into a madman. At nights, he woke angry and crying out like a wounded animal. Some nights he smashed the door, the bars, the bed, everything in sight, with a hammer.

Sometimes I woke at night-time, I feel like I don't want to stay alive. I feel like my body is hot, I feel so stressed. If I had something, like anything to drink, to kill myself, I would.

They put me here because of drugs, but I see they are selling drugs like coffee. They give me death sentence for my drugs, then they bring that same drug and sell in front of me. I watch this and it makes me stressed. I watch the guards sit down and use together with prisoners. They are selling drugs everywhere, no secret, just everywhere drugs here. When it is so corrupt in here, when they are selling drugs everywhere, nobody would be happy here.

Are they all corrupt?

Yes. Many guards have been arrested. Even last year, the chief of security was arrested. Some guards are good, but eighty per cent of them are shit.

– Emmanuel

It was proven that it wasn't just the underling guards who were lured into the Hotel K drug business, when the head of security, the number two boss, Muhammad Sudrajat, was charged with and convicted for drug offences, and sentenced to four years in jail.

Last Saturday the Bali police arrested Muhammad Sudrajat, the Security Head at Kerobokan Prison, after receiving information from ex-prisoners he had been their drug dealer. Sudrajat was set up and busted with 2.45 gram of low-grade heroin in his pocket. As security head, Sudrajat could easily smuggle narcotics into the penitentiary – nobody was suspicious of him.

– *Jakarta Post*, September 2007

Police allege Kerobokan's Head of Security, Muhammad Sudrajat, has been running drugs in and out of the prison since starting work there 14 months ago.

– *NZ Press Association*, 14 September 2007

Mr Sudrajat's lawyer, Muhammad Rifan, said his client was 'surrounded by dealers' and had an amount of 'involvement in the trade', but said he was more a user than a dealer. 'My client admitted he got carried away after getting too close to inmates who were drug addicts,' Mr Rifan told Reuters. 'He became an addict, and became more and more involved.'

– *Today, Singapore*, September 2007

Emmanuel had been in his early twenties when he flew to Bali from Pakistan, with just under four hundred grams of heroin inserted in his anus and in his stomach. He had just cleared Bali immigration when customs officers grabbed him. He was taken straight to a nearby medical centre, given two enemas and fed doses of laxatives until he finally excreted 31 capsules of heroin.

Emmanuel felt sure his Pakistani boss had tipped off the Indonesians. His boss had been angry that he could not carry one kilogram.

They use a machine and push into my anus. I try but I cannot put more … it's too big.

– Emmanuel

With only four hundred grams, the Pakistani boss sent him anyway, as his false Sierra Leone passport and plane ticket were already paid for. So, for the lure of a $2000 cash fee, the young Nigerian flew to Bali and threw away his life.

I hope they are not going to kill me, it shouldn't happen. I'm the first person they give death for drugs here in Bali. But my stuff is the smallest. Many people here … the guy from Mexico had fifteen kilograms, Michael had four kilograms, get life sentence. Juri five kilograms plus, fifteen years; the Bali Nine, some of them already on life or twenty years. Me? I only had four hundred grams. They give me death sentence because of my colour. And because I have no family, no friends and no money.

I'm angry because nobody cares here. But, I believe, one day I am going free. That's what I believe. If I had money in the first place, my case would not be like this. And they hate all foreigners, but they hate black people more.

– Emmanuel

After living on death row for two years, Emmanuel calmed down a bit and started looking after himself. He cut his dreadlocks off. 'If I put water on my head, one litre stuck in my hair. So, make me more stress, so I cut it.' He started working out with weights for an hour a day, spraying himself with Rexona afterwards, and dressing smartly. It helped that he was sharing a cell with Scott, and now also had Scott's lawyer helping him. He didn't feel so isolated and his rage was not so fierce.

Scott bitterly regretted his teenage mistake, and was losing his life day by day. Once, in a fit of anger at himself, he'd scratched his arms with a sharp piece of metal. He'd also shot up heroin a couple of times, chain-smoked, had seen a psychiatrist and taken antidepressants. But the death sentence was always lurking. One of his earlier cellmates had told him he sometimes called out, 'Mum, Mum,' in his sleep. He often dreamed of someone harming his family. Sometimes, he heard the ringing gunshots of his own execution.

The first thing his mother, Christine, had given him after his arrest was their family Bible, and Scott had turned to God for strength. Many nights, he got down on his hands and knees in his cell and asked for forgiveness. He started seeing a Catholic priest at Hotel K's chapel but stopped when the people running it started telling him, 'If you die, you will be going home [to God]'. He didn't like it. They weren't the ones facing death by firing squad. Dying was not going home. 'Who were they to tell me that?'

Scott's parents initially spent five months in Bali, looking after him and trying to find someone they could trust to take money to him from an account they had set up. His parents spent about $340 a month to keep Scott in relative comfort in Hotel K. This was cheap by Hotel K standards. Another Australian was spending $1000 a month on food and payments to guards.

On Scott's twenty-first birthday Lee and Christine flew to Bali with their other two sons, Dean and Cameron, and threw a two-hour party for him in one of the small offices. It was only three months since his sentence had been upped to death, when his mum had walked out of the jail telling waiting reporters that her son was 'scared, absolutely petrified' about his fate.

But they were all making the most of his birthday, with about twelve people celebrating and a chocolate cake. As he took a deep breath to blow out the twenty-one candles, someone joked, 'We know what the wish is, Scott, so just blow'.

When he was handed a framed portrait of his late grandfather, he kissed the image. If he were ever to know how important family was, it was now. And, somehow, for those hours he simply enjoyed being with his loved ones.

'Actually, I feel pretty good. It's good to have my family and friends here. It's amazing to be able to celebrate it and I just feel great today,' Scott told reporters.

Snatching moments of happiness was vital, as the daily grind was so difficult. But if Scott and Emmanuel ever needed reminding that things could get worse, they only had to look out their death tower door. Their cell was luxurious in comparison with cell *tikus,* across the grassy path.

So far since I've been here, two guys have died in solitary cell tikus *from tuberculosis and AIDS. One guy got put in there because he tried to escape from hospital where he was held, that wasn't that long ago, and [the] guy before that just kept getting skinnier and skinnier ... some days he didn't know who he was, and I think they knew he was going to die sooner or later. That's a terrible way to die, I reckon, being put in a little cell like that.*

– Scott

Scott had helped guards carry the body of the prisoner with TB out of cell *tikus*. The second man had been treated in Sanglah Hospital for AIDS and TB, but ran away before they could take him back to Hotel K. He didn't want to die in a jail cell. He was found in a graveyard, taken back, as a very sick and weak man, and thrown into cell *tikus*.

One night, not long afterwards, he died in there. The guards found him mid-morning and pulled his body out onto the grass. His face was covered in vomit and ants. It was unsurprising that the rate of TB was high in Hotel K. The sewage water from cell *tikus* streamed past the small canteen where food was cooked and sold.

If you get sick, they put you in a small room, you stay there until you die so that nobody will see you.

– Emmanuel

The spreading of diseases didn't just come from the bodies pulled out of cell *tikus* or from the sewage water. Some prisoners locked in cell *tikus* without a toilet would throw a plastic bag of shit through the vent and onto the grass outside Scott and Emmanuel's cell. Black Monster – Sonia – was the worst culprit.

When the guards came past to count the prisoners, and Sonia's stinking plastic bag was on the grass, they'd open her cell and make her clean it up. It was a tactic of hers to get out of the cell for a few minutes. Typically, Black Monster put on a bit of a show, throwing water and shit at the guards or at anyone walking past.

This crazy girl, Sonia, threw shit. But not only shit, she put water inside the plastic bag also. It landed in front of my cell on the grass, so everybody can smell it. It makes a lot of problems. She threw shit on guards. And there is nothing they can do. The last time she threw shit at me, and Matthew walking past.

– Emmanuel

Scott and Emmanuel had spent time in cell *tikus* together. They were put in a cell the width and length of two bathtubs, with no toilet. When they needed to relieve themselves, they used a bottle or a plastic bag. For days, they sat leaning against the wall at opposite ends of the concrete cell, with their legs stretched out in front of them. At night they slept close together on the bare concrete.

You have to lie like a dead man.

– Emmanuel

Some days, Scott paid the guards 500,000 rupiah ($65) to get out to a visit. Again, he felt discriminated against because most people paid that fee to be let out permanently.

I got put in cell tikus *with Emmanuel for, like, a month. I got put in there for walking around the jail. Emmanuel got put in there for having a phone. Solitary is terrible. There's no light in there. I got a light bulb to put in there, just to read, and stuff, at night. The worst feeling about cell* tikus *is that they put you in there and you feel like you are completely forgotten.*

That's what it feels like; time goes really, really slowly, especially when you see other people moving around and you get to see them doing what they want to do, and you not being able to walk around and you get envy. And envy is a bad feeling.

– Scott

CHAPTER 22
OPERATION TRANSFER

I couldn't even, in my wildest dream, imagine we were going to fly in a plane that night.

– Ruggiero

It was a morning of utter confusion. At around 4.30 am, Ruggiero was abruptly woken by two guards bursting into his cell. 'What the fuck are you guys doing here?' he barked. 'The boss wants to talk to you,' one of them said. 'Why? It's five in the morning. I'm sleeping.' The guards didn't know why the boss wanted him, but hustled him out of bed. Ruggiero furtively slipped his phone in his underpants as he stood up. He was wearing only short pyjamas and a T-shirt, but there was no time to change. He slid his feet into a pair of sandals as they ushered him out the door. The Brazilian followed the guards down the concrete path that he'd walked literally thousands of times, and was unaware this time would be his last. As he turned the corner to walk into the offices, though, he knew that something big was in the air.

The office atrium was filled with armed police. Standing bleary eyed and half-dressed in the centre were drug lord Arman, Frenchman Michael, Mexican Vincente and two Nigerians. Ruggiero didn't have a clue what was going on and quickly asked the others if they knew. They didn't.

Juri was the next to arrive – in bare feet and wearing only the T-shirt and the shorts he'd slept in, with his dark hair sticking up. He asked the others what was happening and got the same blank response. He asked the guards as they snapped handcuffs on him and started searching his pockets but they didn't know either. It was a covert operation – the police knew that if the guards knew, the prisoners would be informed.

They don't tell us nothing, nothing. Just pick up in the morning and go.
– Juri

Finally, female inmate Nita turned up, looking dishevelled and confused, and wearing only slippers and a nightie. Her hands were already cuffed in front of her, and she, too, asked if anyone knew what was going on. They shrugged. All the way across from Block W, she'd been asking the guards. 'But they just tell me, "No question, no answer".'

Police started moving the eight prisoners out into the car park, which was swarming with police, prison guards and journalists. Photographers snapped pictures of the confused, bedraggled prisoners as they were swept along, gripped on either side by police officers. Ruggiero spotted friendly guard Pak Mus. 'What the fuck's going on, Pak Mus? What's happened?' he asked as he was pulled past. 'Ruggiero, I don't know,' Pak Mus said, looking distressed. 'Are we going to the police station? Are we going to be moved?' 'Ruggiero, I don't know,' he repeated, clearly feeling sorry for the Brazilian.

Juri suspected they were being moved when he heard one police officer asking another, 'Jakarta or Surabaya?' and pointing at the buses. He quickly asked if he could get a bag from his cell. 'No. Cannot, cannot.' But the police officer saw his bare feet and made a concession to his request, sending a *tamping* prisoner to run inside and get his thongs.

I say, 'Can I take my stuff?' They say, 'No. Cannot, cannot'. Not even a toothbrush or a magazine. I say, 'I get asthma. Maybe I get sick. I always have the puffer?' 'Cannot, no'.

– Juri

The prisoners didn't yet know it, but the operation had been planned precisely. Ruggiero, Juri and the two Africans were put onto one minibus, and the other four put onto the second, co-ordinated to match their destinations. Several police with machine guns, and a single guard, climbed onto each bus.

They had one machine gun per prisoner and extra two per bus. So, there were about twelve machine guns, I think.

– Ruggiero

As they drove out of Hotel K's car park, the eight prisoners were unaware that they were leaving the jail for good. Ruggiero was excited; the pre-dawn trip broke the tedium. He didn't know where they were going, but with five prisoners on life sentences and the Hotel K drug lord along for the ride, he knew it wasn't to freedom. He suspected they might be going to police headquarters, for an interrogation about drugs in jail.

Desperately curious, Ruggiero kept trying to get answers from the police. 'What's going on? Where are we going?' 'We don't know,' they kept repeating. 'How come you don't know, man?' he pushed. 'We just don't know'. Ruggiero didn't believe it. 'You guys are joking with me ... you don't know! Are we going for a night tour in Bali?' The bus turned off the potholed roads onto a main highway. Ruggiero kept his eyes glued to the windows, trying to figure out where they were going. When they came to a large roundabout and turned towards the airport, Ruggiero instantly asked, 'Are we going to the airport?' 'We don't know.' But it was clear to Ruggiero that that was exactly where the bus was heading.

He surreptitiously felt in his underpants for his phone and sent a text message to the Brazilian consul – 'We're arriving at the airport. Can you jump on your bike and come? See what you can do.' But it was early and the consul didn't reply. Ruggiero was getting more and more agitated and excited, and turned to Juri. 'Juri, we are going to fly, man, I don't know where to, but we are going to fly.' Juri didn't believe it. 'Are you crazy?' 'We're going to the airport, man,' Ruggiero said, pointing out the window. 'I know this road. We're going to be at the terminal in five, ten minutes.'

Several minutes later, they created a spectacle as the armed police piled out of the buses onto the footpath directly in front of the domestic terminal. Trailing out behind them were the prisoners, with their hands cuffed in front of them. Each prisoner was quickly surrounded by three police officers – two holding their arms and one pointing a machine gun at their back.

Fuck, I'm an extremely heavy criminal ... four grams of hashish – it's a heavy offence. Makes a lot of sense, the money the government spent on protection. I'm a threat to society.

– Ruggiero

Crowds of tourists and local travellers scurried to the sides of the path to let the intimidating group of police and prisoners stride past. They swept towards the glass doors to the domestic terminal. Inside, the prisoners got VIP treatment. There was no waiting, as one by one they were whisked straight through the metal detectors in a tightly choreographed routine in which the police let go of their arms as they approached the machine and grabbed them again on the other side. They were all taken across the busy terminal to a row of plastic chairs, and given bottles of water and brown paper packets of nasi goreng.

The police were friendly but the guys wouldn't tell us where we were going. I went to the toilet. I was relaxed. I wasn't worried about anything, just very curious … extremely. Thank God nobody was sentenced to death, because they would, for sure, think it was going to be the execution because it looked like it.

– Ruggiero

Despite armed police pacing back and forth in front of them, the scruffy, pyjama-clad prisoners looked more vulnerable than menacing. People stood staring. Some curious travellers came up and spoke to them. One young Italian couple walked across to Juri, who was wearing an Italian football T-shirt, asking what was going on.

They asked me, 'Eh, what happened to you? Where are you going?' I say, 'I'm moving. I'm already long time in jail'.

– Juri

They were all reacting differently to the situation. Nita was fretting, Vincente was casual and laughing, and Michael was, still high from an earlier hit of smack. He turned to Ruggiero asking, 'Where are we going, man?' Ruggiero was pumped up, excited to be out in the real world. 'We're going to take a flight, my man. I don't know where to, but take a walk on the wild side,' he said to Michael. 'We always get to fly together, don't we?' he joked.

After almost two hours, it was time to go. Domestic passengers were called first and filled up the front of the plane. Then the eight prisoners and their massive police entourage, minus machine guns, walked down the aisle past the staring faces of the seated passengers. Three empty rows separated the prisoners and the other passengers. Ruggiero, Juri and the two Nigerians sat in the back rows, while the other four sat a couple of rows in front.

An hour later, Vincente, Michael, Nita and Arman got off the plane in the large Muslim city of Surabaya, East Java, which was near their new jails. The other four flew further north to Jakarta.

When we got to Jakarta Airport, police had machine guns again. I felt like the fucking biggest terrorist in the world, walking outside like this, with all the police with their machine guns and everybody watching. I didn't even know where I was, I'd never been to Jakarta in my whole life. It was very hot. It took about one and a half hours to get to the fucking prison. When we got there, it was horrible ... 2000 people, lot of junkies, dirty place. The guards were very hostile at this new jail, Cipinang. Very hostile.

– Ruggiero

Juri and Ruggiero were given T-shirts and uniforms, then taken to the Cipinang security chief's office and told the rules of the jail. As they left to walk across the grounds to their new cell, a guard suddenly kicked Ruggiero hard in the stomach. He buckled over. The guard then turned to attack Juri.

Boom. He punched me three or four times. I still had the prison T-shirt in my hand, so I couldn't try to defend myself. He says to me, 'Here is Jakarta, it's not Bali'. I say ,'Yeah, I know, I don't need to get punched'.

–Juri

Back in Bali, Juri's wife, Ade, turned up for her usual morning visit to Hotel K, handing over the 5000 rupiah fee to get inside. Unusually, the guard refused to take it. She was momentarily confused. The guard looked up from his seat and broke the news that Juri was gone, transferred to another jail, in Jakarta. Ade collapsed. It was devastating news. She'd heard stories about prisoners being viciously bashed as standard procedure on arrival at new prisons. She also knew that Juri's transfer meant that she and his elderly parents would have to abandon the life they'd created in Bali and start all over again in a new city.

Inside Hotel K, the transfer instilled fear in all the westerners. It was a stark warning that everyone was vulnerable to the whims of the Indonesian Government. Anyone could be plucked from their beds in the dead of night. If slinging cash to the guards had given the prisoners some sense of power over their destinies, this transfer undid that.

For the Hotel K guards, the westerners' fears created a new blackmail business. Prisoners splashed around hundreds of dollars to have their names removed from alleged transfer lists. The nastier guards enjoyed taunting the prisoners, 'White monkey, we move you tonight'. Suddenly, prisoners were desperate to stay in Hotel K. It was the devil they knew. With its walls touching paradise, it was a drop-in spot for tourists, and easily accessible for friends and families. And its being filled with westerners meant there was always someone to talk to. Juri and Ruggiero had friends inside Hotel K. They had had their days out, their afternoon drinking parties, their favourite meals delivered from Bali's best restaurants. But those days were now over and they didn't know what lay ahead in the big city jail.

It was like a shock, trauma. It was, like, leave everyone we know. We have friends. I know everyone in there. Kerobokan felt like home after three years. Then move.

– Juri

***

Kerobokan is not really a prison – it's a place to kidnap people and rip them off. It's place for making money. This is why they don't fix anything, why the walls are always falling down, why we have to fix our own toilet or be sick. A place that is about ripping people off is not going to pay for anything.

The whole justice system is simple – it's nothing to do with punishment or rehabilitation. It doesn't matter what evidence you have in court, it's not about the evidence, it's about money. They don't even look at the evidence. That's why someone with 12,000 ecstasy tablets, like Steve from England, gets three years in jail, and some poor local gets four years for one or two tablets. The whole system, from the courts to jail, is to make money. It's not to fight against narcotics. That's just an excuse.

– Mick

***

You feel you're dead when you're breathing in Kerobokan. You're always looking for tomorrow, tomorrow, tomorrow, tomorrow.

– Inmate

EPILOGUE
WHERE ARE THEY NOW?

Thomas

After leaving Hotel K, Thomas was taken to the immigration offices for his third deportation. This time though, the authorities were insisting that he flew back to Europe and not take the short flight to Bangkok. But Thomas had other ideas. Before leaving Hotel K, he'd teed it up with a friend to help him escape from the Denpasar immigration offices. So the moment the police were upstairs playing a game of cards, Thomas sprinted outside, leaped on the back of the waiting motorbike and tore off. The friend took him to a bus stop, and within a day of his release, he was back in Jakarta, living in the shadows and looking over his shoulder.

Within no time, Thomas was dealing again. But his snakes and ladders career would soon take its biggest hit. First he was busted for possession of few grams of heroin and sentenced to eighteen months in Cipinang Jail – his fourth stretch in an Indonesian prison. Then he crashed hard. He was busted dealing more than half a kilo of *shabu* from his cell.

It was a former friend and fellow ex-Hotel K inmate, Atiya, who took him down. Unbeknown to Thomas, Chinese drug dealer Atiya was now working with the police to set people up in return for cash. Out of the blue, he called Thomas in Cipinang Jail, and asked him if he could arrange to get a kilogram of *shabu*. Thomas was reluctant at first, but was soon lured by the smell of cash. He organised a Nepalese boy to bring six hundred and fifty grams of *shabu* into Indonesia through Singapore. But then Thomas made a mistake. He broke his rule of refusing direct contact. Atiya didn't want to use standard procedure of wiring the cash first, and then picking up the drugs from an anonymous hotel room. He wanted to exchange cash for drugs at the same time. As Thomas had known Atiya for years and done deals with him before, he took the bait. He sent his new Indonesian wife to deliver the stash and collect the 40 million rupiah fee ($5300). But a split second after she'd handed over the *shabu*, she was wearing handcuffs.

Thomas had no money to deal. His wife was sentenced to ten years in jail and he got another twelve years on top of the eighteen months he was already serving. During their trials, Thomas and his wife shared a police cell and conceived a child. But in Jakarta, men and women are kept in separate jails, so it will now be years before Thomas sees his wife again. But the Austrian has a new baby son, living with his wife in jail.

Vincente and Clara – the Mexicans

Clara was released from Hotel K after serving five of her seven years. Vincente is currently serving his life sentence in a jail in Java. Their rich Bali-based Chinese drug customer fled Indonesia when things got too hot. He set up a drug business overseas but was busted, and is now being tried, and faces mandatory death if convicted.

Iwan Thalib

Iwan Thalib was moved to Nusakambangan's Super Maximum Security (SMS) Jail to serve the last couple of years of his sentence. He was transferred out of Hotel K by a particularly strict new boss who was trying to eradicate the drug market by getting rid of the bigger dealers. (It didn't work. Drugs are still rife in Hotel K.)

In June 2009, Iwan was released from SMS Nusakambangan prison, after serving only eight years of his sixteen-year sentence. He returned to his family in Bali. Within three or four days, he was back inside Hotel K – as a visitor this time. Iwan and his Dutch wife sat in an office eating lunch with three members of the Bali Nine. The three Australians, formerly on death row, had used Iwan's lawyer to get their death sentences commuted to life and had become friendly with the drug dealer's family. While Iwan was in jail in Java, his wife had regularly visited the Bali Nine in Hotel K, even hosting some of their families in her home near the jail when they flew to Bali from Australia.

Sonia Gonzales Miranda (Black Monster)

Sonia did three stretches in jail in the time it took to write this book. Initially she was in Bangli Prison, about an hour from Hotel K. She saw me visiting someone else, and charged over to say hello in her funky outfit, comprising a blue denim cap, a mini-skirt and tight black top, with a full face of makeup. She relished telling me that she was now famous in Australia after Schapelle's book had mentioned her. She said Australian visitors to Hotel K all knew who she was.

I saw her several times during my visits to Bangli. Even after she was released, I met her there. That day, she was trying to get her daughter back from the family she'd sold her to earlier. But only because she wanted to sell her again. She sat next to me on the visitor's bench in front of the bars, through which we talked to prisoners. She'd set it up, with the help of a prisoner, for the foster mother of her child to come to jail on this morning for a visit. She had a policeman friend waiting outside the door. The air was always charged with Sonia around. She was hiding behind me so the woman wouldn't see her and run off. Sonia's plan was to snatch the child back. As we sat there, Sonia showed me baby photos and talked non-stop about her new sexy boyfriend, showing me photos of a very good-looking European guy. But Sonia's plan failed. The woman didn't come that day. Sonia left disappointed, but still firing with plenty of strategies to get her daughter back.

Before long, Sonia was inevitably back behind bars in Hotel K for thieving. The place had a non-stop revolving door for Sonia. She served a few months, was released, and about six months later was inside yet again, telling people she always liked to be in jail on Independence Day. This was about her nineteenth incarceration.

For many Indonesians jail is not really a jail, it's like a shelter. Sonia, for example, keeps coming back. There are hundreds of repeat offenders. They can't do anything outside but steal.

– Mick

Ruggiero

The thing people don't realise in jail is that every emotion runs much higher; really high, really low, you know. If you're depressed, you get really depressed. If you're happy, you get euphoric for no reason whatsoever – small things – like if I receive an SMS from somebody I haven't heard from for a while, it seems like I won the lottery.

– Ruggiero

After his transfer from Hotel K to Cipinang, Ruggiero spent two weeks locked up in an isolation cell with Juri. The Italian, who'd been shooting up daily in Hotel K, went through painful withdrawals that Ruggiero witnessed up close. He spent hours massaging Juri and trying to help him through it.

We shared the pain.

– Ruggiero

Ruggiero wanted to evolve into a better person in jail, to give some purpose to the otherwise wasted years. He converted to Buddhism, and regularly spent his time praying and meditating in the jail's temples. He applied for parole but failed, his anger at the years of imprisonment fuelled by seeing sadistic killers and psychopaths walking free after only two or three years.

In jail he still drank, smoked, and lost the plot sometimes, trying to forget where he was and the kinds of people surrounding him. In 2011, after almost eight and a half years, he was finally freed and sent home to Rio. Life hasn't been so good, as his years in jail and heavy drinking resulted in liver problems, and he's spent months very sick with stints in hospital.

Juri

Juri's sentence has been reduced from life to fifteen years. He's already served nine of them, and with remissions he could be going home to Italy within a couple of years. His devoted parents were alternating the responsibility of living in Indonesia to care for him, but his father has since passed away from cancer. Juri's Timorese wife, Ade, who he married in Hotel K, lives close to the jail and visits him three times a week, when visits are permitted.

Nita

Nita is still serving the ten-year sentence that she got when she was caught dealing drugs at the immigration housing. She is in a jail in Java. The Filipino wore the prison-issued blue T-shirt and untailored denim pants whenever I visited her, as she has never been able to recover any of her belongings from Hotel K.

Mick

Mick orchestrated a move out of Hotel K because he was losing his grip on sanity. He contrived a story, telling the jail boss he was being threatened by Laskar. For his protection, Mick was put in cell *tikus.* But the guards couldn't do much to protect him long term, so they moved him and his girlfriend Trisna to another prison in Bali. Both still defiantly protest their innocence. To try to manage his fury at his incarceration, Mick does yoga daily and meditates for hours at a time. Like so many westerners serving long sentences, he has tried to find some bigger meaning and point to his incarceration and lost years, and believes it has given him spiritual growth.

My mind changed slowly. Why this was happening to me. My attitude, behaviour, changed 180 degrees. I was a madman chasing the governor. I changed from madman to more enlightened. Now, I think I'm blessed. I couldn't get what I needed outside. It's like a mystery school in here.

– Mick

Mick has served eleven years of his fifteen-year sentence, and expects to be freed within months.

Robert

Robert was released and went back to the UK. He has nothing to do with his child, conceived through the bars in Hotel K.

Arman

Arman is serving out his many sentences in Nusakambangan's Super Maximum Security Jail. His sentence has increased from ten years to nearly thirty since first checking in, and he still has several court cases pending from charges that arose during his time in Hotel Kerobokan.

Schapelle

Schapelle has now spent eight years behind the walls of Hotel K. Many times she's hit rock bottom and lost all hope of ever seeing light at the end of the tunnel. But in 2012 she was given a reprieve – the President granted her clemency, and shaved five years off her 20-year sentence. It means that with remissions, she has now served more than three quarters of her sentence, which makes her eligible to apply for parole. If it's granted she could be out by Christmas 2012, which would mean she is still young enough to regain her life and have the baby she's always dreamed about.

Other westerners, including Ruggiero and Mick, failed in their bids for parole, but Schapelle is in the unique position of having Balinese family who can sponsor her. Her sister Mercedes is married to a Balinese, Wayan, and their three children are Balinese. While locals are regularly granted parole after serving three quarters of their sentence, there is no documented case of a foreigner being released on parole. But Schapelle could live in Kuta with her sister and Balinese family.

Despite reports that a prisoner must admit guilt to be granted clemency, Schapelle has staunchly insisted she is innocent, telling her family that she'd rather die in jail than ever admit to being a drug trafficker.

Saidin

Saidin was released from jail in 2008 after serving a little over six years for the murder and decapitation. He is now living back with his family in Klungkung, earning far less cash than he did when he was top *tamping* in Hotel K.

Michael Blanc

Michael Blanc is living in a prison in Java. In 2009, his sentence was cut from life to twenty years. He has served almost thirteen years already, and with remission could be home in France within two or three years. His devoted mother still lives in Indonesia to care for his needs in jail.

Laskar Bali

The eight Laskar bosses have all been released from Hotel K, none serving any more than a few years for the stabbing murder at the Denpasar Moon karaoke bar. The Laskars are still in full force roaming the bars and clubs of Kuta and Legian. They no longer rule Hotel K, as its bosses are busy outside. Several other gangs have moved into Hotel K, including a Korean crime syndicate. But there are always some Laskars inside.

Bali Nine

The members of the Bali Nine traffickers have been living in Hotel K for nearly eight years. The two 'ringleaders', Andrew and Myuran, are facing a 12-sniper firing squad after losing their final appeals in 2011. With all legal avenues now exhausted, their sole hope of avoiding execution is clemency. Both have filed bids with the Indonesian President. It's a long shot, as he has never before granted clemency for a prisoner on death row for drug convictions. Andrew and Myuran are among 114 prisoners on death row in Indonesia. No one has been shot since 2008.

After winning his final appeal against execution in 2011, Scott Rush now has a brighter future. He is one of six of the Nine serving life, but these sentences can potentially be reduced through clemency bids. This was shown in 2009 when the President cut Frenchman Michael Blanc's life sentence to 20 years.

The only woman in the Nine, Renae Lawrence, has been receiving bi-annual remissions to her 20-year sentence and – as a *tamping* who doesn't mind getting her hands dirty, clearing drains or unblocking septic tanks – she is likely to continue receiving the maximum sentence cuts and could be free in five to seven years. To the others in the Bali Nine, her 20-year sentence is enviable.

All the Australians are living under constant threat of being transferred out of Hotel K to prisons in Java. In early 2012 it looked inevitable after Hotel K prisoners rioted for several days and took control of the prison. All 20 guards on duty fled their posts and were locked out. Inside, prisoners set the jail ablaze, went up into the watch towers, threw Molotov cocktails over the walls, destroyed files, tore doors off cells, burnt mattresses and generally vandalized the entire jail – except Block W which remained locked. It was the second major riot within seven months. After the first night more than 100 riot police stormed the jail and removed three prisoners, but did not regain control of Hotel K. Soldiers and riot police, armed with gas masks, shields and tear gas, sat outside the jail for several days and nights.

Authorities announced all prisoners would be moved out to other jails, and there were reports Hotel K would be closed –

the Kerobokan land is now top real estate. But the situation was settled through phone negotiations; riot police did not storm the jail a second time, and the 60 western prisoners were not moved. The Bali Nine and Schapelle Corby wanted to stay. For now, Hotel K is at least the hellhole they know.

The whole front section, including the boss's office, was burnt to a charcoal shell.

HOTEL KEROBOKAN IN THE NEWS

'Crowding and drugs behind Kerobokan riots' **– Sydney Morning Herald, 5 February 2012**

A stint in Hotel Kerobokan has always been an exercise in surviving in limbo. This week though, the task of survival for the 12 Australian inmates of Bali's largest prison became a lot more high-risk.

Two riots in two days saw the prison burnt and three inmates removed after police shot them with rubber bullets. What followed was a quickly hatched plan by authorities to storm it and forcibly empty it of inmates forever. But so far the Australians, including Schapelle Corby and the Bali Nine, have opted to stay in the prison that's been their home for the better part of 10 years. As they say: better the devil you know.

The riots, which still have the potential to close Kerobokan, erupted on Tuesday night but their cause goes back to events of the previous Sunday, when police arrested three men for the stabbing a fellow inmate.

… The Australians were not involved in the riots that could also be related to overcrowding in a prison designed for 323, but holding 1015.

But some observers believe the riots were well organised by people within the prison linked to the "Laskar Bali" group. Laskar Bali, literally translated as "Bali Army", or "Bali Fighters", has been described as a criminal gang involved in narcotics trafficking and protection rackets.

It's a powerful organisation in Bali and provides much of the security presence at Bali's night clubs … This is a story with some twists left in it yet.

***'Billions of Rupiah more than thought in damages at Bali's Kerobokan Prison'* – Jakarta Globe, 29 February 2012**

Damage caused by days of violent rioting inside Bali's Kerobokan prison was apparently much worse than expected, with officials announcing on Tuesday that it would cost Rp 5 billion ($555,000) to fix.

… More than a thousand prisoners overwhelmed the 20 guards on duty last week, forcing them to flee. The inmates then set fire to prison offices, including the armory.

In a raid some 10 hours later, officers from the police and military used tear gas and rubber bullets to try to quell the uprising. Three prisoners were injured. The riot was triggered by the stabbing of an inmate during a brawl two days earlier. Lax security was blamed for allowing a knife into the facility.

***'Prisoner died after hours of torture by cellmates: Bali police'* – Jakarta Globe, 17 January 2012**

Bali Police are investigating a group of 13 inmates at the notorious Kerobokan Penitentiary over the brutal murder of another inmate there.

Adj. Sr. Comr. Benny Arjanto, the Badung district police chief, said on Tuesday that the 13 men were believed to have assaulted the victim, Edi Suwito, 28, over a 12-hour period on Jan. 11–12.

"The victim was sadistically tortured during this period, in which the perpetrators stubbed out lit cigarettes on his genitals among other things," Benny said, adding that the perpetrators and the victims all shared the same cramped cell at Kerobokan. He said Edi had only been at the prison for a day.

"Among the items that we've seized as evidence include a bamboo pole, a cane, four lighters and a plank of wood,"" Benny said.

***'Violence reflects overcrowding at Kerobokan Prison'* – Jakarta Post, 18 January 2012**

A recent case, in which a prisoner was beaten to death by fellow inmates, reflects the Kerobokan Prison authority's inability to cope with the institution's chronic problems, in particular the problem of overcrowding.

Designed to secure 300 prisoners, the prison now houses more than 1,000, while the total number of security guards is fewer than 100 … Suwito is not the first prisoner to have died in a violent incident inside Kerobokan. In October 2011, another inmate, Muhammad Arif Hamzah, was killed in a clash between two rival gangs of inmates.

***'Kerobokan pot bust opens investigation on prison drug ring'* – Jakarta Globe, 1 July 2012**

The Kerobokan prison in Bali confiscated 1.4 kilograms of marijuana in a raid on Friday, adding to a long list of cases where drugs have been distributed behind prison walls.

***'Kerobokan penitentiary over capacity'* – The Beat, 12 April 2012**

"We want the House to know that Kerobokan is improper, and violates human rights. We want Parliament to allocate the budget for us to build a new prison, or make Kerobokan into two floored building." – Ministry of Justice and Human Rights of Bali officer Taswen Tarib.

***'Money rules in Kerobokan'* – Jakarta Post, 27 February 2012**
A series of interviews with an inmate and a former inmate have revealed that Kerobokan Penitentiary, Bali's largest and most overcrowded prison, is arguably also the country's most comfortable prison, at least for inmates with a lot of cash to spare and share. Illegal levies are a common and accepted fact of life behind the bars of Kerobokan.

An inmate must pay for a list of strange things, such as a Rp 20,000 (US$2.20) monthly fee in the women's block for the right to use the clotheslines, and a Rp 100,000 fee for a guard to bring you 100 grams of drugs. For a Rp 15,000 monthly fee, an inmate can carry around a cellular phone with him 24 hours a day, seven days a week.

… Currently, there are at least five gangs in Kerobokan, four of which are associated with feared local mass organizations at large outside of the prison, and one gang comprises inmates from East Nusa Tenggara. These gangs also run a debt-collecting service for jailed drug dealers. Armed with sharpened eating utensils, their members often trigger violent conflicts inside the prison. "Sometimes, their weapons are seized in security sweeps. But then, it's easy to get them back. Just give the guards some money – they will bring them back," he added.

***'Inmates riot following failed transport of drug convict'* –**
Jakarta Post, 26 June 2011
Hundreds of inmates at Kerobokan prison went on a violent rampage at dawn Saturday following a botched attempt by

National Anti-narcotics Body (BNN) officers to transport a convicted drug dealer.

Inmate A Riadi was a former member of the elite police counterterrorism squad Densus 88 and is currently serving a five-year prison sentence.

The angry inmates attacked the officers and punched and kicked the prison warden and his security chief before vandalizing prison facilities. No fatalities were reported and as of Saturday afternoon the situation inside Bali's largest rehabilitation facility gradually returned to normal following the arrival of a large contingent of fully armed police officers.

'*Bali to have drug rehabilitation center*' – Jakarta Post, 15 April 2011

"We don't have adequate facilities to rehabilitate or treat drug users. It is inhumane to send them to Kerobokan Penitentiary. When they enter the prison they are drug addicts, but when they leave they will be drug users and traffickers," Bali Governor Pastika, explained. It is no secret that prisons and detention centers in Indonesia facilitate lucrative trade in narcotics worth millions of dollars and involve prison officers, inmates and visitors alike.

'*Police to get prison drug raid rights*' – The Bali Times, 1 December 2010

Badung chief of detectives Soma Adnyana said it was clear Kerobokan was a major drug distribution centre both in terms of use inside the prison and as an organisational base by drug-ring bosses serving jail sentences.

ACKNOWLEDGEMENTS

First, thank you to all the prisoners and ex-prisoners who shared their stories with me. For many, it meant opening up old wounds by re-living some very dark, dark moments. For those still living the nightmare of incarceration in Indonesian jails, it was especially difficult at times to live past horrors while regularly enduring new ones.

I would also like to thank those people who were already free, for delving back. While some seemed to struggle with their emotions, others clearly relished telling me their stories, sometimes shaking their heads in disbelief or laughing maniacally at the surreal memories – stories which in Hotel K where everything was so crazed didn't seem so bizarre, but telling them in a normal environment – for the first time – made them seem suddenly wild and shocking – even to the ex-prisoner. In the daily context of the insane world of Hotel K, they had seemed almost normal.

There are four prisoners in particular who I would like to give a very special thanks to: Mick, Ruggiero, Juri and Thomas. All are still doing time, but are incredibly witty, funny and interesting people. Each one of them continually surprised me with just how upbeat they were most of the time, despite the horrific, inhumane conditions they were still enduring. Their positive attitudes were inspiring. They opened up, graphically sharing their life behind bars. Thank you to these four prisoners – I hope you all get plenty of remissions and get out as fast as you can.

Thanks also to a high-ranking guard at Hotel K who helped me to gain access to prisoners, as well as feeding me stories and confirming facts about Hotel Kerobokan.

Thanks to Mercedes Corby for her support and friendship during my time in Bali, for her tips and advice, and for being a great sounding board for stories.

Thanks to Malcolm Holland for his support and encouragement, and for his continual enthusiasm for all the jail stories I endlessly told him for eighteen months. Mal, thanks for being my sanity lifeline while I travelled in and out of jails around Indo!

Thanks to my very good friend and journalist James Foster who, as always, gave me support whenever I needed it.

Thanks to my mum Sue, sisters Louise and Simone, brother-in-law Matthew Cripps and good friend Caroline Frith for reading occasional chapters for me and giving me feedback.

And finally, thanks to Pan Macmillan senior editor Emma Rafferty for her talented and hard work.

And a very big and heartfelt thank you to Pan Macmillan's non-fiction publisher Tom Gilliatt. Without Tom's belief, support and whip cracking, I doubt this book would ever have been written.

Kathryn Bonella
Snowing in Bali

‘Snowing in Bali’

Among Bali’s drug dealers it’s code that the paradise island is full of cocaine.

For the men who run Bali’s drug empires, it’s time to get rich and party hard.

Families, surfers and singles may flock to the holiday islandto relax and play, but among the palm trees and infinity pools lies a seedy underworld of drugs and violence.

Snowing in Bali is the story of the drug trafficking and dealing scene that’s made Bali one of the most important destinations in the global distribution of narcotics.

Kathryn Bonella, bestselling author of ***Hotel Kerobokan***, has been given unprecedented access into the lives of some of the biggest players in Bali’s drug world, both past and present. She charts their rise to incredible wealth and power, and their drug-fuelled lifestyles, filled with orgies, outrageous extravagance and surfing. But running international drug empires in Bali can also be a highly risky business, with terrible consequences for those caught and convicted.

From the highs of multi-million dollar deals to the desperate lows of death row in an Indonesian high-security jail, ***Snowing in Bali*** is an extraordinary, uncensored insight into a hidden world.